Drawing Life Back Into Animation

By the 1980s animated cartoons were seen as an art form in decline. An archaic vestige of the old Hollywood studio system. Yet by the 1990s animation was booming. Blockbuster movies and TV shows, interactive games and special effects extravaganzas all generating billions of dollars. What happened? Did everyone simply wake up one day and decide they liked cartoons again? This is a story of generations and societal change. Artists and moguls. Geniuses and hustlers. Join Tom Sito, a veteran Hollywood animator who was there, as he takes us deep inside the studio corridors to watch the birth of Roger and Jessica, Bart and Lisa, Woody and Buzz, Shrek, Simba, Mario, Lara Croft and Yu-Gi-Oh.

Key Features:

- Part history, part memoir, and written by a top industry insider who witnessed the events as they happened.
- Not focused on one particular studio or label, but a sweeping overview of the animation industry in the 1990s and the societal and technological changes that affected it.
- It is a story of generations. How the artists of Hollywood's Golden Age yielded the baton to the Baby Boom generation, who carried it on into the Millennium.
- It explains how animation, a business once perceived to be outmoded, came back to become central to how we use our modern media.
- This book contains many first-person anecdotes from the backrooms and studio lots where the animation renaissance was created.

Tom Sito is an animator, film historian and professor of animation at the University of Southern California. In 1998, *Animation Magazine* called him "A Key Figure in the Disney Animation Renaissance." His movie credits include *Beauty and the Beast* (1991), *Who Framed Roger Rabbit* (1988), *The Little Mermaid* (1989), *Aladdin* (1992), *The Lion King* (1994), *The Prince of Egypt* (1998) and *Osmosis Jones* and *Shrek* (2001). In addition, his TV series include *The Superfriends* (1978), *He-Man and the Masters of the Universe* (1983) and *She-Ra: Princess of Power* (1985). He is a winner of the June Foray Award (2011) from ASIFA/Hollywood and an Inkpot Award from Comic-Con International (2024). He has lectured on animation around the world and is President Emeritus of The Animation Guild Local #839 Hollywood. He is a member of the Board of Governors of the Motion Picture Academy of Arts & Sciences.

He is the author of several books, including *Drawing the Line: The Untold Story of the Animation Unions from Bosko to Bart Simpson* (University Press of Kentucky, 2006), *Timing For Animation, Third Edition* (Focal Press, 2009), *Moving Innovation: A History of Computer Animation* (MIT Press, 2013) and *Eat, Drink, Animate: An Animators Cookbook* (CRC Press, 2019).

Drawing Life Back Into Animation

A Personal Journey through the Toon Renaissance of the 1990s

Tom Sito

CRC Press
Taylor & Francis Group
Boca Raton London New York

CRC Press is an imprint of the
Taylor & Francis Group, an **informa** business

Designed cover image: Tom Sito

First edition published 2026
by CRC Press
2385 NW Executive Center Drive, Suite 320, Boca Raton FL 33431

and by CRC Press
4 Park Square, Milton Park, Abingdon, Oxon, OX14 4RN

CRC Press is an imprint of Taylor & Francis Group, LLC

ISBN: 978-1-138-50147-8 (hbk)
ISBN: 978-1-138-50145-4 (pbk)
ISBN: 978-1-315-14436-8 (ebk)

DOI: 10.1201/b22394

Typeset in Times
by Apex CoVantage, LLC

To the Animation crew of Disney's *Beauty and the Beast* (1991). As Glen Keane called them, "The best crew we ever had."

Contents

About the Author

Tom Sito is an animator, historian and professor of animation at the University of Southern California. His movie credits include the films *Beauty and the Beast* (1991), *Who Framed Roger Rabbit* (1988), *The Little Mermaid* (1989), *Aladdin* (1992), *The Lion King* (1994), *Osmosis Jones* (2001), *The Prince of Egypt* (2001) and *Shrek* (2001).

He worked on TV series, including *Scooby Doo, The Superfriends, He-Man and the Master of the Universe* and *She-Ra: Princess of Power.*

He was awarded the Inkpot Award from the SDCC (2024), the June Foray Award (2011) for a lifetime of service to the animation community, a Cine Golden Eagle (1988) and a Dusty Award (2016) from the School of Visual Arts for Outstanding Alumni Achievement. Tom served as President of The Animation Guild Local 839 Hollywood (1991–2001), Vice President of the International Animators Society (ASIFA/Hollywood), Member of the Board of Governors of the Motion Picture Academy of Arts & Sciences and was the chair of the Department of Animation and Digital Arts at the University of Southern California. He also belonged to SIGGRAPH, Hollywood Heritage, the Hyperion Historical Alliance and the National Cartoonists Society.

In 1998, *Animation Magazine* called Tom Sito "A key figure in the Disney Animation Renaissance."

His Other Books Include:

- *Drawing the Line: The Untold Story of the Animation Unions from Bosko to Bart Simpson* (University Press of Kentucky, 2006) recommended by the London Review of Books. Recommended in 2006 by the Firestone School of Economics, Princeton University.
- *Moving Innovation: A History of Computer Animation* (MIT Press, 2013), nominated for a Kraszna-Krausz Foundation award for Best Book on the Moving Image. Named one of the Notable Books of 2013 by *Computer Reviews* magazine.
- *Timing for Animation*, Updated Second Edition (Focal Press, London 2009). Updated 40th Anniversary 3rd Edition (Focal Press, 2021).
- *Jews and American Popular Culture*, a three-volume anthology edited by Paul Buhle (Praeger/Greenwood Press, 2006).
- *Walt's People: Talking Disney with the Artists Who Knew Him* Vol. 9, by Didier Ghez (XLibris, 2009) and Vol. 18 (XLibris, 2016).
- *Eat, Drink, Animate: An Animators Cookbook* (CRC Press, 2019) Winner of Best in World by Gourmand Magazine 2020, category: Illustration.
- *On Animation: The Director's Perspective*, Vol 1, 2, Bill Kroyer, Tom Sito, Ron Diamond. (Focal Press, 2019).

Introduction

I think if you had traveled back in time to me as a film student back in 1965, and whispered in my ear what the world of cinema would be like almost 40, 50 years later, the two things that would have surprised me the most would have been the resurgence of animation, and the resurgence of documentaries. Arguably, those are the two most vitally interesting, technologically and artistically adventuresome areas of cinema today.

—Walter Murch (film editor, director, author)

In 1975, one of my first jobs was at a little studio on E.19th St off 5th Ave in New York called TeleTactics. They mostly made educational films for grade school children. But our director, Dan Haskett, only a few years older than me, was determined to make the quality of these films a challenge worthy of our young ambitions. One day a gentle old man came in to talk to us. He did not want a job or want to sell us anything. He just

Chuck Jones Interview

FIGURE 0.1   Chuck Jones and Tom Sito 1998.

(photo by Peter Western)

DOI: 10.1201/b22394-1

heard there was a studio here, and he wanted to talk about animation with other artists. Our studio head was a short-tempered, no-nonsense fellow who saw any time spent not producing as wasted. He thundered at us, "WHAT IS THAT OLD MAN DOING HERE? GET HIM OUT!" The old man was Orestes Calpini. In his time, Orestes was a top animator at the Max Fleischer Studio, who directed the classic 1940s Superman shorts and designed the more dramatic sequences in *Gulliver's Travels* and *Hoppity Goes to Town*. He was a true animation master who asked for nothing more than to share his experience. He was sent away, forgotten and ignored, and a few months later, he died.

When I began my career in animation in 1975, I was entering what was generally considered a dying art form.

The animated characters I grew up on and loved on TV had been done decades before I was ever born. The only reason the films of the 1930s and 1940s filled the TV airwaves of the 1960s was because they were cheap for TV stations to buy and fill the hours between the cereal commercials, which were their true revenue stream. The few new cartoons being made then were of a markedly lower quality.

By 1975, many of the great animation artists of Hollywood's Golden Age were leaving the stage. They had entered the young field in the 1920s and 1930s, had done their best work in the 1940s and 1950s, witnessed the collapse of the great movie studios in the 1960s and began retiring in the 1970s. Walt Disney had died in 1966, Max Fleischer and Paul Terry in 1974, Tex Avery in 1985 and Osamu Tezuka in 1989. By 1975, the famed Looney Tunes Studio, nicknamed Termite Terrace, was but a fading memory. The MGM animated shorts unit closed, and Fleischer Studios was gone. Jay Ward, UPA were no more than a filing cabinet in a copyright attorney's office. Walter Lantz did his last Woody Woodpecker short for theaters in 1973. People gave no thought to the artists and their creations than to the names they stepped over on the Hollywood Blvd Walk of Fame.

In 1975, the only animation work on the U.S. East Coast was commercials, and on the West Coast, Saturday morning kiddie shows. Japanese anime in the US consisted of an occasional little series that ran on TV Sunday mornings against high school basketball and religious programming. There were usually two animated feature films a year in movie theaters: the Walt Disney and one other, like Ralph Bakshi's. In the age of Woodstock and psychedelic rock & roll, the Disney films felt hopelessly corny, lots of "Ooh da lally" Dixieland jazz and barbershop quartet. The kind of stuff my parents liked because they were by and large being created by artists my parents' age. The Walt Disney Company survived on revenue from their amusement parks and the occasional unexpected live-action hit like *The Love Bug*. In 1975, many of the old animation professionals I encountered were bitter. Resigned to the idea that animation's glory days were in the past, never to be seen again.

Yet by the 1990s, animation was a booming business, generating billions of dollars in profit worldwide. Primetime animated shows like *The Simpsons* were considered not merely the most successful series in TV animation, but the most successful show in all of television history. People in faraway places like Ecuador and Kazakhstan knew how to say, "Eat my shorts, man!" Epic live-action hits like *Titanic*, or *The Lord of the Rings*, could not have been made without animated digital effects. Best-selling interactive games like *Donkey Kong, World of Warcraft* and *Tomb Raider* could not exist without animation. Mainstream movie stars, who would not have been caught dead doing a voice in a cartoon before, were suddenly lining up for gigs.

So, what happened? Why this huge seed change in our perception of animation? The time period of this revolution occurred roughly between 1986 and 2003, peaking in 1994–1995 with Walt Disney's *The Lion King*, Pixar's *Toy Story*, Fox's *The Simpsons* and MTV's Liquid Television spawning shows like *Beavis & Butthead* and *Aeon Flux*. Film historians now generally refer to this period as the Great Animation Renaissance.

The Animation Renaissance did not occur just because everyone in the world suddenly woke up one day and decided cartoons were funny again. Huge socioeconomic, generational and aesthetic changes had to occur. New institutions, new players and new ideas about how we consume our media had come into play.

It is a story of generations. The big Baby Boom generation coming of age and moving into the jobs once held by the older World War II, Golden Age animators.

I entered the field of animation at the twilight of the old animation systems and watched the coming of the 2D Renaissance and Digital Revolution, playing a part in these events myself. Starting as an animation assistant on the 1977 musical *The Adventures of Raggedy Ann & Andy*, I drew animation for films like *Who Framed Roger Rabbit, The Little Mermaid, Beauty and the Beast, Aladdin, The Lion King* and *The Prince of Egypt* and *Shrek*. I also worked on TV series like *Scooby Doo, The Superfriends, He-Man and the Masters of the Universe, She-Ra: Princess of Power* and many more.

An old Chinese proverb says, "Many great ideas begin as a hobby." All of the years I was pencil-pushing and flipping paper, I enjoyed reading and writing history. I guess when your full-time job is fantasy, reality is where you go to relax. This side career has enabled me to become the in-house historian of much of the animation scene of my time. I enjoy telling behind-the-scenes stories of my friends, the artists who created some of the world's best beloved cartoon characters.

So, pull up a chair, sharpen your pencil, and let me tell you a story.

TS, 2025

This Business Is Dead

1

On a warm August night in 1990, over 500 people gathered in the imperial ballroom of the Sportsman's Lodge, a venerable old Hollywood hangout in the San Fernando Valley. They were there to celebrate the 100th birthday of Grim Natwick. The career of Myron Henry Natwick (1890–1990), who everyone called Grim, seemed to span the length of the animation history to that time. He began at the Hearst Animation studio in NY in 1918 and later became a senior animator for Max Fleischer. There, he designed the famous flapper, Betty Boop. Legend says when Walt Disney first saw a Betty Boop cartoon, he stood up in the theater and said, "We gotta get that guy!" So Grim headed west and was a lead animator on *Snow White and the Seven Dwarfs*, then returned to Fleischer to animate Princess Glory for *Gulliver's Travels*. Later he created Nelly Bly for UPA's "Rooty Toot Toot". He taught young Chuck Jones principles of animation and numbered several of Disney's Nine Old Men[1] as his personal assistants. He was still animating in his 80s for Richard Williams' London Studio. Animation historian Charles

FIGURE 1.1 Golden Age animators at the 1990 Natwick birthday party.

(Credit Katherine Turner)

DOI: 10.1201/b22394-2

Solomon expressed amazement, "Talking to him (Grim), you forget just how old he is, until he mentions voting for (Woodrow) Wilson!"[2]

That night, the Sportsman's Lodge party was a merry event, with lots of drinking and stories. Walter Lantz, then age 90, joked he wanted Grim to be his pallbearer. Animator Marc Davis, at age 76 and on a cane, said, "I like Grim, because he still calls me sonny." The birthday cake, the size of a door, was provided, at Grim's request, by Martino's Bakery. A Burbank institution that long was a favorite of Walt Disney's.

Beyond the honoring of such a beloved figure, many who attended that night could sense that something larger was happening. Once the word got out that The Animators Society (ASIFA[3]) was hosting a grand celebration for Grim's birthday, all the surviving animators of the Golden Age of Hollywood realized this probably would be their last great blowout, a gathering of the clans of 1930s–1940s studio artists. Frank Thomas, Ollie Johnston, Ward Kimball and Marc Davis of the Nine Old Men were there, along with the other surviving artists of Walt Disney. Mae Questel, the voice of Betty Boop, was there with the surviving veterans of Max Fleischer's Studio. Chuck Jones, Friz Freleng, Arthur Davis, Maurice Noble and the Bob Clampett family came with the veterans of Looney Tunes: June Foray, the voice of Rocky the Flying Squirrel, and Lucille Bliss, the voice of Crusader Rabbit. Other animators were from MGM, UPA, Hubley, Jay Ward and more.

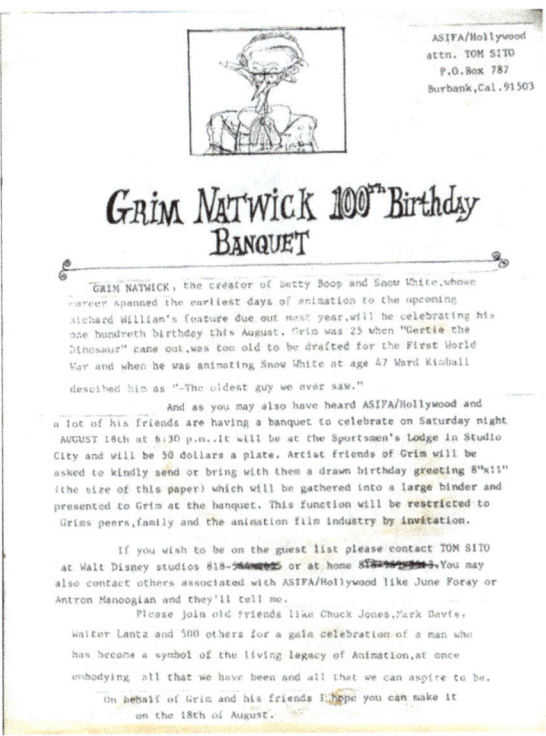

FIGURE 1.2   Grim Natwick birthday party invitation.

(Caricature by Richard Williams.)

FIGURE 1.3   Walter Lantz, Grim Natwick and Mae Questel 1990.
(photo by Katherine Turner courtesy of Bill Turner)

Sitting among these old lions were many of the top names in young Hollywood: John Musker, Ron Clements and Glen Keane, who had just broken out with their smash hit *The Little Mermaid*, John Pomeroy and Gary Goldman from Don Bluth's studio who had created the hit *An American Tail*, Eric Goldberg who created the Genie in *Aladdin,* Matt Groening, David Silverman and Wes Archer who created *The Simpsons*, Bill Kroyer who was a key creative on *TRON* and the director of *FernGully: The Last Rainforest*. Chris Buck who would direct Walt Disney's *Frozen*. Chris Casady who worked on *Star Wars: A New Hope*. Artists who began in the days of silent film mingled with artists who drew on computers.

Everyone there that night sensed the significance of this occasion. You could literally feel you were witnessing the changing of the guard. Old Hollywood was having one last drink together, and Young Hollywood was there to thank them for creating the industry that nurtured us all.

In 1990, the animation industry was going through a great resurgence. The slow decline that the industry seemed to be suffering since the 1950s had finally been shaken off, and a renaissance of interest seemed to be blossoming all around. Everyone felt it was a new era.

Drawing sequential movement was a popular trick in the nineteenth century. Little paper novelties were on sticks and in spinning cans to fool the eye: Zoetropes, praxinoscopes and phenakistiscopes. People began making animated film experiments almost as soon as motion picture equipment was created. In 1906, French artist Emile Cohl hailed animation as a new art form. Avant-garde artists like Jean Cocteau and Max Ernst expressed an early interest in it. But in America, the people who really took to it were the newspaper syndicates. The penny papers were the mass media of the early twentieth century. With hordes of new immigrants filling American cities, many could not read English, but they liked the pictures in comic strips. Characters like Buster Brown, Mutt & Jeff and the Katzenjammer Kids were as popular as Broadway stars. Press barons like William Randolph Hearst and Josef Pulitzer saw sponsoring animated films of their comic strip stars as a way of boosting sales. See your favorite character dance and play! Early synergy. The streamlined simplicity of a cartoon character design made them more suitable to be drawn over and over for the hundreds of drawings required to make a typical animated film.

The first generation of artists and technicians who came into animation was, by and large, the same age. Much like the progenitors of the computer revolution of the 1990s, film and animation in the 1920s were a young person's medium, where the field was wide open to make your fortune. The reason American Hollywood films so quickly outdistanced their rivals in other countries was that Americans industrialized the filmmaking process. While Paris, London, Tokyo, & St Petersburg all had animation studios, they mostly remained a small atelier of a few artists, who made commercials and an occasional short film. In Hollywood, the Big Five: MGM, Warner Bros, Paramount, Universal and Columbia, created assembly lines, producing films in an unending stream: big historical epics, tender love stories, gritty crime dramas and screwball comedies. In addition, each of these films required an accompanying short cartoon featuring a lovable, marketable character. Quite often, the studios' top executives did not even care what was in the cartoon, just so long as they got a completed one from their shorts department every six weeks: Walter Lantz created shorts for Universal, Max Fleischer for Paramount, Ub Iwerks and later UPA for Columbia and Fred Quimby's shorts division for MGM. Walt Disney was unique in that he never let one big studio tether his operation. He financed directly from the Bank of America and released some films through RKO, some through Columbia, some UA and so forth. In 1953, he was doing well enough to distribute under his own label, Buena Vista Pictures.[4]

The owner of Pacific Art & Title, Leon Schlesinger, had aided the Warner Bros. in securing the funds to make their first sound picture hit, *The Jazz Singer*. This initiated the era of "Talkies," replacing silent movies. In gratitude, Warner Bros. granted Schlesinger an exclusive contract to create live-action and animated shorts for WB.

Leon created a new company to create shorts, Leon Schlesinger Looney-Tunes and Merry Melodies. While he was production head, Leon Schlesinger made a point of keeping snooping studio execs off his property. His animators provided him with a dummy storyboard of a Bugs Bunny cartoon they never intended to make. However, Leon was rehearsed in talking about it. He would keep visiting VIPs enthralled in the front conference room, explaining, "This is our next project." And so, leaving the artists alone to create cartoons they thought were funny. Small wonder the first time Chuck Jones ever met the real Warner brothers in 1943, Harry Warner said to him, "I don't know what the hell you guys do, all I know is we make Mickey Mouse?"[5]

At first, animators attempted to draw everything themselves. However, the growing demand for a reliable supply of cartoon shorts proved beyond the abilities of any one person. In 1913, cartoonist John Randolph Bray and his wife/partner Margaret Bray read Frederick Taylor's 1911 book *The Principles of Scientific Management,* which explained the principles behind Henry Ford's assembly line. Instead of one person doing everything, workers given specific job classifications did one task each, as the project moved down the production line. So, the Brays had one artist to write the cartoon, one to animate the key poses and then an assistant and "inbetweeners" provided the additional drawings to flesh out the movement. A layout artist designed the staging, and the background or BG artist painted the setting. An inker traced the drawings onto transparent cellulite sheets or "cels" which were then painted. This way you did not have to paint the background on each frame. The artwork was "checked" by a quality control artist and then photographed onto movie film by a cameraman. Later jobs included a director, storyboard or gagman artist, art director, color stylist and effects animator. A production manager was needed to keep track of where all of the artwork was at any one time. All of these specific jobs became full-time careers for many. In Walt Disney's film *101 Dalmatians,* one animator spent over a year just drawing the spots on the dogs.

Because of the newspaper connection, originally, American animation studios were located in New York City. By the 1920s, animation shed its early press benefactors and moved west with the new independent movie studios to a place called Hollywood, California. Originally, motion pictures competed with theatrical entertainment called vaudeville. A vaudeville theater was a place, where for a flat admission fee, you saw a variety of brief stage acts: a singer, a juggler, a comedian, a sing-along, a magic act and a fashion show. The first movies, and the first animated shorts, were inserted into the lineup of the day's acts. Gradually, as movies grew longer and more popular, theaters began to switch to an all-cinematic format. The movie studios, such as Universal, Biograph, Vitagraph, Ince and Paramount, created package programs resembling the old vaudeville lineup: an action picture, a drama, a short film of a fashion show, a newsreel and an animated cartoon short. By the mid-1930s, show business trade publications were declaring vaudeville to be dead. Since many of the movie studio partners owned chains of theaters nationwide, no one complained except the poorer, itinerant vaudeville acts. They were the first, but certainly not the last, to have their jobs phased out by new technology.

In 1914, when pioneer animator Winsor McCay created Gertie, a living dinosaur endowed with the capricious characteristics of a kitten, personality animation was born. This was not merely moving a funny drawing; this was the first animated performance. A hand-drawn character was acting, just like a flesh-and-blood thespian. At this time, movie studios developed the star system. They saw that audiences flocked to a movie to see a favorite actor or actress more than to what story they were in. "Gable is Back, and Hayworth's Got Him!" In 1919, Felix the Cat became the first true animation star who did not originate from a newspaper comic strip. Popular songs and merchandise were made about him. It was said that Charles Lindbergh had a Felix doll in his plane for good luck when he flew solo across the Atlantic in 1927.

In the late 1920s, a young man from Kansas City named Walt Disney who had moved to Hollywood took this star character idea further. He wanted to create animated characters that were the equal of the top movie stars of the day, like Charlie Chaplin or Mary Pickford. To do that, his animated cartoons had to not just do funny things, they had to behave like real actors do. With recognizable personalities, while other animation studio heads used their profits to buy yachts or chase chorus girls, Walt plowed his profits back into his studio. He paid for his artists to take drawing lessons, acting and dance lessons. He even drove them in his jalopy to "art houses" to see the latest avant-garde film. He created cartoons in color, he set them to classical music and he created a separate department to animate special effects. Walt Disney singlehandedly grasped this infant medium by the scruff of the neck and forced it into his idea of narrative realism, based on the acting animator. His competitors followed suit, and soon Hollywood animation surpassed its rivals around the world in setting the standard of quality.

The beauty of a well-made animated character is when done right, it ceases to be merely paint and paper and becomes a living being. Bart Simpson was not just the design of Matt Groening, or the voice of Nancy Cartwright, or the writing of James L. Brooks, the color styling of Gyorgi Peluce or the animation of David Silverman. All of them together are Bart Simpson. And as a character, you probably know him better than your own brother or sister.

By the 1930s, the motion picture studios had codified a package system of film distribution called "block-booking." When a regional theater ordered a big movie like "Dark Victory," it received a whole afternoon program, the main feature, a "B-Picture," a newsreel, a short subject like a travelogue or fashion show, local ads, maybe a sing-along and a cartoon. Much like the old vaudeville programs, the theaters would not complain because all of the studios did it, and most of the theater chains were owned by the studios anyway. Not many studio executives were concerned about the quality of their cartoons, just so long as their animation unit kept up a steady supply. Once every six weeks, short film producers like Leon Schlesinger and Paul Smith had set an industry standard of 6 minutes for each animated short. Decided on by the budget more than anything else.

The animators of that age polished their skills in a collegial environment of a large movie factory. You drove to work, clocked in, worked, clocked out, then went home to dinner and listened to Fibber McGee & Molly on the radio. Your spouse was usually someone you met at the studio while working on the same productions. Many studios hired the relatives of other artists and executives and later employed their children. People joked that MGM chief Louis B. Mayer put so many of his relatives on the payroll that MGM stood for "Mayer Ganz Mispoche," Yiddish for "Mayer's whole family." Studios held social dances, beach parties, skiing at Big Bear, weekends at dude ranches and golf tournaments. Animators went to nightclubs like the Cocoanut Grove and El Mocambo and rubbed shoulders with celebrities. Animator Jimmy "Shamus" Culhane was once married to the daughter of Chico Marx of the Marx Brothers. Animator Ben Washam mentioned once being in a bar across the street from Warner Bros, where Humphrey Bogart walked in with a parrot on his shoulder and bought everyone there a round of drinks to celebrate renewing his contract with the studio. Walt Disney toured VIPs around his studio like H.G. Wells, Sergei Eisenstein, Orson Welles and Frank Lloyd Wright.

All through the twentieth century, while the rest of the world blew itself up in endless wars and strife, far away in the sunny, never-never land of Los Angeles, the life was good. The weather was mild, the studios made millions, and there was always another film to work on and another crew to jump to. Beyond animating on a top studio project, there were many smaller studios doing industrial and educational films. Some animators might spend their whole career in one place, doing one character. It all seemed like the kind of life that would never change.

But change did come. The beginning of the end began in 1938; independent producers filed a federal suit against the major movie studios, alleging practices in violation of the Sherman Antitrust Act of 1890. The case, titled "*Petitioners vs. Paramount Pictures Inc, et al.*"[6] took several years to wind through the courts, delayed by World War II, and finally wound up at the Supreme Court in Washington. On May 3, 1948, the high court ruled 7–1 that the motion picture industry was indeed guilty of monopolistic practices. They ordered the studios to sell off their chains of regional theaters and end block booking.

Once the regional theaters were free to choose their own programming, they opted to drop the newsreel and short subjects in favor of more showings of the main feature film. This brought in more paying customers and more money. The public was getting their news and shorts anyway, thanks to a new technology that coincidentally began to assert itself in 1948, television. In 1941, there were only 7,000 TV sets in all of America. Ten years later, there were 15 million and rising. For the new postwar middle class, moving out to the new suburbs and raising kids meant that going to the movie theater was a more complicated operation. As TV shows grew in variety and popularity, people opted to stay home. Where before people went to a movie several times a week, now it has become less frequent, maybe twice a month. The old movie moguls called television "the enemy" and tried to win back the public's attention with wide screen, full color, 3D spectacles. But the story of Hollywood in the 1950s was of one long, agonizing retreat. Even high-quality classics like *Treasure of Sierra Madre* and *Key Largo* could not stem the dwindling Box Office. In 1946, 78 million Americans a week went to a movie theater. By 1971, even with an increased population, that number was down to 15 million a week.[7] Columnist Peter Bart wrote, "The movie industry was more on its ass than any time in its history. Wiped off the face of the earth."[8] Most of the major dream factories were looking for corporate buyouts to save themselves. Once independently financed, they have now become just another name in a large corporation's investment portfolio. Warner Bros became Warner Media, then TimeWarner, then AOLTimeWarner, then Warner Discovery. Universal became MCA Universal, then a division of Seagram's, the whiskey distiller. In 1967, young director George Lucas said, "Hollywood feels like an industrial town where the mill has closed."[9]

Animated short cartoons, once the bread and butter mainstay of animation studios, became less and less in demand. Despite some of the most memorable cartoon shorts being done in this time period: *What's Opera Doc?, Broomstick Bunny and The Two Mousketeers,* the orders for new shorts became less and less. Walt Disney complained, "You can't make money in shorts anymore. You have to sell them in bunches, like bananas."[10] By 1970, shorts had all but disappeared from movie houses.

As the big studios retreated, they outsourced studio services to save money, like costumes, props, vehicles and animation. One by one, the animation units began to close. MGM closed its unit in 1957. Paramount, which was once Fleischer, was acquired by CBS television and closed in 1969. Terrytoons died around the same time. UPA producer Steve Bosustow sold his studio to businessman Henry Saperstein in 1960, and he converted it to all low-budget TV production. In 1972, Saperstein sold off the remainder of UPA Studios and retired. Its most popular character, Mr. Magoo, now only appeared in TV commercials selling GE light bulbs.

By then, the old studio moguls, who began in the silent era, were also dead and gone. Darryl F. Zanuck of Twentieth Century Fox and Jack Warner of Warner Bros were the last of that generation to retire in 1972.

The greying animation artists and tech people looked toward the new decade of the 1970s with anxiety. The 1940s and 1950s were about optimism and prosperity. The 1970s pop culture was steeped in disillusionment and cynicism. America was mired in an endless war in Southeast Asia. Psychedelic drugs, the Manson Family, Watergate corruption, the Generation Gap, the Counterculture and its conservative backlash made going to the movies feel like a political statement. What would animation's role be in all this? Shrinking job prospects, fewer new projects and no one to succeed them.

Could this be the end of the animation business?

NOTES

1 In 1949, Walt Disney dubbed nine of his key animators as his Nine Old Men. He borrowed the term from President Franklin Roosevelt, who invented the term for his Supreme Court.
2 Charles Solomon to the author, 1990.
3 ASIFA stands for Association Internationale d' Film Animation. An international nonprofit organization founded in 1960 by animators John Hubley, Norman McLaren and several others as a way to promote cultural understanding through the medium of animated film. ASIFA Hollywood for many years was their largest chapter.
4 Buena Vista Pictures was named after the street the Walt Disney studio lot was located.
5 And Friz Freleng responded, "Yes we do." Friz saw no reason to stir up trouble.
6 Paramount Studios stood in as representative of top Hollywood Studios, called the Big Five. Paramount, Warner Bros. MGM, Universal and Columbia. Walt Disney was then considered a junior player.
7 Peter Byskind, *Easy Riders and Raging Bulls*, pg 20.
8 Quoted by Byskind, *Easy Riders and Raging Bulls*, pg 20.
9 Quoted by Byskind, *Easy Riders and Raging Bulls*, pg 20.
10 Quoted in *Drawing the Line,* Sito, pg 215.

The Rise and Fall of Saturday Morning

1959–2002

2

In 1939, when World War II broke out, many men and women held off marriage and starting families for the next 6 years. As Humphrey Bogart said to Ingrid Bergman in the 1942 film *Casablanca*, "it doesn't take much to see that the problems of three little people don't amount to a hill of beans in this crazy world." As soon as the war was over in 1945, millions of people took off their uniforms and went back to their private lives, which included zealously generating lots of children. The exponential rise in the postwar birthrate was known as The Baby Boom. After 1945, the postwar primary school classrooms went from 16 students to 35 students each, and teachers told the latecomers to go steal chairs from other classrooms.

This generation grew up in front of the family TV set, watching reruns of Golden Age movies and cartoons. They zealously collected comic books and read the Sunday funnies comic strips. They developed a taste for quality animation and filmmaking, and as they came of an age to enter the jobs market, many burned with a desire to also create great films, much like their idols did in the 1930s. However, when they did come to Hollywood, they saw not an industry rising, but an industry in decline.

Many old studios were gone, the past masters retired and those few remaining were bitter. Not every Golden Age artist retired rich from Disney stock options. Maurice Noble, the unquestioned master art director of the Looney Tunes, got nothing more from Warner Bros but his straight weekly salary. In his retirement, he lived off his Cartoonists Union pension, Social Security and selling an occasional lithograph.

The Supreme Court's Paramount Decision of 1948, which broke the monopoly of the Hollywood studio system, coincided with two other big changes in the media landscape. Television and the Baby Boom: Coping with both of these spawned an institution known as Saturday Morning Kidvid.

Since its invention in the 1920s, the development of television had been held back by the global political climate of the 1930s and 1940s. There were early attempts at

DOI: 10.1201/b22394-3

FIGURE 2.1 Children watching *Tom Terrific*.

(collection of the author)

entertainment programming sporadically in Britain, America and Germany. The Germans televised the entire Berlin Olympic Games of 1936. However, very few people then had the means to watch them. Deutsches Rundfunk set up ten storefront television parlors where people could gather to watch. When World War II was declared on September 3, 1939, the fledgling BBC television service shut down for the duration. They did not want the broadcast signal to be used as a beacon to guide the Luftwaffe bombers toward London.[1] They interrupted a Mickey Mouse cartoon, *Mickey's Gala Premier*, to broadcast Prime Minister Neville Chamberlain's declaration of war. Seven years later, on June 7, 1946, with the war over, BBC television started back up by the announcement, "Good Afternoon everybody. How are you? . . . Well now, where were we?" and resumed *Mickey's Gala Premier*.[2]

It took several years for the general public to get over the wartime privations like rationing, move out to the growing new suburbs and embrace consumerism. By the 1950s, there were millions of television sets being sold. The major radio broadcasters,

Columbia Broadcasting System (CBS), National Broadcasting (NBC) and the Blue Network or American Broadcasting Network (ABC)[3] began a competitive race to see who could expand into television the fastest. While some countries like England charged people a subscription fee to watch television, American TV followed the earlier example of radio: free programing financed by selling commercial advertising. As it was in network radio, at first advertisers paid for an entire program: The Lux Liquid Hour, etc. Then network executive Pat Weaver came up with the idea of selling blocks of commercial airtime to advertisers in 30-second slots, several during each show. By the 1950s, the home TV viewer had the choice of the three network channels, three local stations, and one public access educational station, usually on the usually on the public TV frequency band. Stations could only broadcast for 8–12 hours a day and then shut down. After midnight, you saw a brief news recap, then a weather report or prayer and then the National Anthem. Your TV screen then went to grey snow (static) until 6:00 AM the next day. Alongside the big national networks, local stations like KTLA Los Angeles in 1948 began regional TV programming, filling time between local events and news with old black and white movies and shorts, bought in bulk from declining movie studios.

Animated cartoons were always part of the development of television. In the 1920s, the first image English inventor John Logie Baird chose to broadcast was of a Felix the Cat doll on a record turntable. The simple black and white shapes were more easily seen on the weak televisor signal. In the 1950s, when the early television station affiliates were looking to film their schedules with entertainment programming, original animated shows were as yet too expensive for them. Most content then was recycled from the old movie studio libraries. Except for Walt Disney, who retained tight control of all his studio's output, the movie studios regarded their old short films as little more than yesterday's newspaper. They were happy to make a little extra money getting all those film cans out of their storage. Also because of contract deals with The Screen Actors Guild (SAG), short films pre-1950 did not have to pay residuals out to the talent. As a result, many children of my generation grew up adoring black and white 1930s era comedians who were long dead before we were born: Laurel and Hardy, The Marx Brothers, the Three Stooges, as well as Betty Boop, Popeye and the Looney Tunes. I recall one local station played a program called "Farmer Alfalfa," which consisted of several Terrytoon silent short cartoons run together with Brahms Hungarian Rhapsody played over it in a continuous loop. Even as a child, I noticed they were out of sync.

The massive influx of children born between 1945 and 1962,[4] known collectively today as The Baby Boom, needed food, toys and distraction. That is where television came in. No matter how cranky or fidgety the child, turn on the TV and the tot stopped screaming, and stared at the screen. It was like having a pause button for your kid. This was especially useful on a Saturday morning, when working parents craved a few extra hours of shuteye, while their little rug rats were up at dawn. Statistics going back to the radio years showed that the peak tune-in hours for children were between 10 AM and noon on Saturday mornings and 4 PM to 6 PM weekdays. When the children began to go to school, kids programming reduced during the week. All of the focus went to the weekend programming. Since Sunday still retained an echo of old Victorian propriety, discouraging entertainment shows on the Sabbath, the focus centered on Saturday. Because all of the coverage of the major sporting events were in the afternoon, the emphasis narrowed further to the 4 hours of Saturday morning between 8:00AM and 12:00 PM. Sponsors selling child-related items like toys and breakfast cereal saw that they had a huge, guaranteed viewing audience in place for those 4 hours. Many of these old live-action and animated shorts were introduced by live local show hosts: Bozo the Clown, Buffalo Bob, Officer Joe Bolton, Sandy Becker, Shari Lewis, Tom Hatten, Chuck McCann, Claude Kirschner and Clowny, Ray Heatherton the Merry Mailman, Sonny Fox and Wonderama, Captain Kangaroo. Between the Popeye cartoons and Three Stooges shorts, these televised baby-sitters improvised banter, sang songs and pitched products to amuse children. In 1957, the Howdy Doody Show introduced the character *Gumby*. These were made with stop-motion claymation by the artist Art Klokey. Around the same time, the Captain Kangaroo Show premiered the character *Tom Terrific*. This show was done by Terrytoons, but by then, the old founder Paul Terry had retired, and the show was really the brainchild of UPA animator Gene Deitch.

The problem with good quality character animation was that it took time and was relatively expensive. The Golden Age of Hollywood animation was accomplished with Depression Era wages. But everyone was doing badly, so an animator's wage then was considered pretty good compared to others. Yet by the 1950s, the rising middle-class standard of living and unionization were pushing up wages and budgets with them. By the late 1950s, an average 6-minute Looney Tunes or Tom & Jerry cost $35,000, each. Max Fleischer's Superman shorts had cost over $45,000 each. Television producers were offering only $9,000 for a comparable amount of screen time. Some early Ruff & Reddy shorts were done for $2,700.

The earliest attempts at animation like Andrew Anderson and Jay Ward's *Crusader Rabbit* (1948) were little more than a storyboard with narration. Yet the stories were engaging and new, and the show had a long run in reruns on many NBC regional stations. Ward and writer Bill Scott teamed up to create a show in 1959 called *Rocky and Bullwinkle*. They put all their creative muscle into clever writing and soundtracks. The studio tried to save money by having all the artwork done in Mexico City. Although Ward was disappointed with the final look of some of the animation, the TV audience did not seem to mind. They just liked the humor. The big TV networks then were taking their cues more and more from their sponsors like Sunoco and Oldsmobile. They in turn listened to their Madison Ave advertising execs who insisted that the new animated shows be geared squarely at children. Jay Ward and Bill Scott clashed repeatedly with the network censors, trying to slip more adult humor in. For instance, in one episode, bad guy spy Boris Badenov made a gun that shoots Goof Gas. It was a gas that turned people stupid. Boris and Natasha slipped into the U.S. Congress, determined to spray them all as an act of sabotage. But after listening to the congressmen's debate, they leave. Natasha asks, "Boris, aren't you going to shoot them with Goof Gas?" Boris sighs," Natasha, did you hear them? That IS Goof Gas." Veteran Warner Bros director Bob Clampett also ran into this same roadblock when trying to create his *Beany and Cecil Show*.

In 1959, Clark Haas and Cambria Productions tried an adventure series called *Clutch Cargo*. It featured a strange technique called SynchroVox that matted real-time human mouths inside of animated characters. The image of the character's head remained motionless, while the human mouth floated around on the face. It was an action show that barely moved. Even to a 6-year-old, the show looked odd.

By the mid nineteen forties, Walt Disney saw that the days of theatrical shorts were numbered. He had been discussing the possibilities of television since 1940, when it was still very much in the experimental phase. Despite industry-wide pressure to boycott the upstart new medium, Walt Disney premiered his Disneyland television show on ABC in 1954. It was only on Sunday nights and consisted of content primarily to showcase his new theme park Disneyland. He set up veteran animator Ward Kimball with a team of young animators to produce animation exclusively for the television show. They did some notable shows like The *Truth About Mother Goose, The Plausible Impossible* and created the popular character Ludwig von Drake. Yet, it was not on a regular basis, and the programs were interspersed with their recycled old theatrical cartoons, as well as low-budget live action. Walt Disney scored such an enormous success with the live-action Davey Crockett and Zorro series that the live-action shows eclipsed much of the animated output. After Walt Disney's death in 1966 and the completion of Walt Disney World in Orlando in 1970, the Wonderful World of Disney TV show settled into a quaint banality of endless reruns. The show ended in 1990.

Into this arena entered William Hanna and Joe Barbera. After a hugely successful 17-year run creating the Tom & Jerry series of shorts for MGM, winning seven Academy Awards, in 1957, the studio unceremoniously laid them off and closed their shorts division.[5] Bill and Joe had seen the writing on the wall and had already begun planning to start their own company. As early as 1951, they anonymously freelance animated some promotional spots for the hit TV show *I Love Lucy*. A while later, when talking with their retiring producer, Fred Quimby, Fred advised them, "You fellows really want to see how to handle TV?" You should take a good look at those TV promos for I Love Lucy. "THAT'S the way this TV stuff should be done!"[6] Initially, Hanna-Barbera planned to launch yet one more theatrical short series, *Ruff & Reddy*. But after seeing waning interest from the dwindling number of movie distributors, they decided to turn their idea into a television show. Likewise, 10 years later, Looney Tunes director Friz Freleng partnered with Warner's producer David DePatie to rescue the remains of the sinking Warner Bros animation ship to form DePatie-Freleng. Bob Clampett and Chuck Jones and their teams had already left to form their own companies. The DePatie-Freleng group first did some theatrical shorts but soon segued to television: *The Pink Panther* and the *Ant and the Aardvark*.

The problem was that the type of animation they were good at was pantomime comedy. Tom and Jerry never spoke. It was all physical action. Many 1930s animators were inspired by Charlie Chaplin, Harold Lloyd and Buster Keaton, who were all silent comedians. And good physical comedy in animation was very elaborate, time-consuming and expensive. In the 1945 musical *Anchors Aweigh*, Jerry did a classic dance number with dancer Gene Kelly. MGM animation inkers actually had to painstakingly ink and paint Jerry's upside-down reflection frame by frame, to match Gene Kelly's reflection on the shiny linoleum floor. To match Kelly's live action, all of the animation had to be "on ones," no shortcuts. Every single frame had to be hand-drawn, hand-inked and hand-painted: 24 drawings for every second on screen, filmed in beautiful, if expensive, Technicolor. No such elegant attention to detail was possible in the "faster, cheaper" new world of television.

FIGURE 2.2   Bill Hanna and Joe Barbera.

(collection of the TAG 839 Archives, CSUN)

So Bill Hanna and Joe Barbera developed their system known as limited animation. Simplified designs, simplified staging, fewer colors, better suited for the poor resolution of early television. Simplified actions, reusable scenes of walks and runs and close-up dialogue with standardized mouth shapes, the A-D system: A was the closed mouth, and D was the wide open. Reusable background sets like the "bicycle pan," the same window and tree moving endlessly behind a running character. Like Jay Ward's *Rocky and Bullwinkle* and Bob Clampett's puppet show *Time for Beanie*, Hanna-Barbera focused on strong scripting and voice talent to carry the entertainment rather than slapstick action. Joe said, "the basis of these television cartoons would have to be story, not a chase, and the story would require dialogue."[7] Veteran animation writers like Michael Maltese and Cal Howard came to work for them. They assembled a strong, versatile team of voice actors, Daws Butler, Don Messick, Jean Vander Pyl, Alan Reed and Mel Blanc. Also, their MGM veteran animators understood just where to cut corners and still make the visuals interesting. They spent extra effort and money on the title sequences, a snappy, singable song, usually by Hoyt Curtin, knowing it would be seen over and over for every episode. The *Ruff and Reddy Show* was their first try with this system, but the concept really came into its own with the *Huckleberry Hound Show* (1958). This success was soon followed by hit series after hit series, such as *Yogi Bear, The Flintstones, the Jetsons, Johnny Quest, Top Cat, Scooby Doo, the Banana Splits, Jabberjaws* and many more.

Many of these shows' initial run were on primetime TV, but they soon migrated to Saturday mornings, where the new shows could be alternated with reruns of old

FIGURE 2.3 Early *Yogi Bear* storyboard.

(collection of the author)

ones. Hanna-Barbera became the kings of TV animation. At their peak (1979), they had 12 series in production at one time, made commercials, feature films and employed over 1,200 employees. Other studios like Filmation, DePatie-Freleng and Ruby-Spears offered competition but could not seriously outdo Hanna-Barbera's output. As the output of the network grew, they soon pushed to the side the smaller regional kiddie show hosts showing old libraries of 1930s–1940s films. By the 1970s, Saturday Morning was all of the network game, and Hanna-Barbera owned fully half of it. Their shows ran internationally as well. Joe Barbera liked to say that there was not 1 hour in 24 when an H-B cartoon was not running somewhere on earth.

In those times as theatrical projects dried up and movie studios shed their animation units, many animators could get steady jobs on the Saturday morning shows. It became their bread and butter, a training ground for some and their retirement home for others. For many legendary animators, Bill Tytla, Tex Avery, Friz Freleng, Retta Scott, Laverne Harding, Dave Tendlar and Ken Muse, did their final work was on Saturday morning shows.

Hanna-Barbera developed close relationships with top network executives like Fred Silverman (called The Man with the Golden Gut) and created new shows with their input. They in turn granted them exclusivity, shutting out other rivals. Saturday Morning TV production worked on a system called The Season. Bill and Joe would

FIGURE 2.4   Hanna-Barbera animation crew.

(1979 courtesy of the Animation Guild Archives)

develop and pitch new shows in February and March. The networks would greenlight the ones they liked for production in April–May. Then the talent would work on creating the shows in an assembly line. As the first shows are premiering in September, the final shows are being completed. While Bill Hanna worked on completing the shows, Joe worked on developing pitches for new shows. The last are episodes usually done by November. Then by next spring, the whole system would start again. Jay Ward director Bill Hurtz lamented, "They (Hanna & Barbera) move animation around like real estate. It is all very competent. Very professional."

Animator Homer Jonas was asked by his son if he considered what he was doing "making art"? Homer smiled, "Nah, I'm selling cereal."[8] All of the big networks cared about was that they had hours of children's entertainment to fill out the time from 8:00 AM to noon every Saturday Morning. When maverick outside producers attempted to sell concepts to the networks, the network execs would just point to H&B. That is who we do business with.[9] This system seemed like it would go on forever, year after year and season after season.

So, what finally happened? Several things.

One issue that came up regularly with creating cartoon content for children was government regulation. As we saw previously, the cartoon shorts of the Golden Age were not done primarily for children, but for a general audience. Parents' groups pressured studio censors to ensure animators were not corrupting children's morals. Betty Boop, in particular, was a target for groups like the Catholic League of Decency. After the Hays Commission enforced the Motion Picture Production Code in 1936, Betty became more and more respectable, her hemline became longer and longer, and she became less and less interesting. Until by 1939, she was gone. However, during the 1950s, the kid TV shows were not regulated as zealously yet. As a result, young kids saw lots of pre-code cartoons, shorts with black and Mexican racial stereotypes and wartime propaganda shorts with blatantly racist portrayals of the then Japanese enemy. The live TV hosts filled the time between the films and commercials with their own ideas of humor. Most of it was benign, but some bits skirted the limits of propriety. One show's crew hired a stripper to dance nude just out of the camera field to try to distract the on-air host. It seemed like no adults were paying attention. The most notorious incident was on New Year's Day 1965, host Soupy Sales asked his kid audience to go into mommy's purse while she was asleep, take out all of those green pieces of paper, and mail them to Soupy Sales, c/o the studio. All that week, Soupy received thousands of dollars in small envelopes. The resultant outcry from parents kicked Soupy off the air. He later said, "I think my agent is still wandering down Chandler Blvd, moaning, "I dunno! I thought it was funny!!"

In 1961, Newton Minnow[10] was set up as the chair of the Federal Communications Commission (FCC). The FCC had been around since 1934, but it was not until now that it seriously began to examine the area of unregulated children's television. One thing they zeroed in on was how it was increasingly hard for kids to tell the difference between cartoons for entertainment and cartoons advertising products. A host like Sandy Becker or Sonny Fox would play charades with the live in-studio audience of kids, then walk over to a table and make a pitch for Cocoa Marsh chocolate syrup. They ended the practice of TV hosts selling products in the body of the show. In 1966, there was a show called *Linus the Lionhearted*, where all of the cartoon characters were also featured on boxes of Post Alpha-Bits cereal. The rules the FCC passed said a trademark entertainment character cannot be used to sell a consumer product. Likewise, a product cannot be turned into an entertainment show. Tony the Tiger and Toucan Sam could not get their own shows. The government funded more educational TV like the Children's Television Workshop, which did Sesame Street and Via Allegre. But for many, that was not enough. The 1980s right-wing Moral Majority movements saw the rise of grassroots consumer pressure groups like Action for Children's Television led by Peggy Charen (1928–2015). She took up her crusade in the 1960s, when she was rearing two young daughters in a Boston suburb and was frustrated by what she saw on television for them, rampant advertising for toys and sugary cereals and, as she once put it, "wall-to-wall monster cartoons." Senator Ed Markey said, Ms. Charren was "the principal defender of children's television in America" and "a conscience sitting on the shoulder of every commercial broadcaster."[11] They demanded more stringent regulation of children's broadcasting.

The revival of the syndication system in the 1980s ate into the hegemony of seeing cartoons only on Saturday Morning. Independent TV stations were growing, and in the late 70s, the FCC set out guidelines for their content. They decreed that a significant portion of the morning and afternoon programming be set aside for children's programming. Then in 1983, President Ronald Reagan's business-friendly administration removed the prohibition on merchandising content for children. This set off a boom in original children's programming, all based on toys. *Strawberry Shortcake* and *Herself the Elf* were the first examples of children's programming and toy marketing planned as one whole campaign. Then came the big campaigns of Filmation's *He-Man and the Masters of the Universe, She-Ra: Princess of Power,* then Marvel's *G.I. Joe* and *JEM.* These shows ran five days a week on local station affiliates and did not need to adhere to the TV season. Instead of creating 12 episodes a season, syndication wanted 65 shows a season. One annoyed independent director told me, "I used to go to the children's book section of the library for inspiration. Now I have to go to Toys R Us."[12]

Starting also in the 80s, cable TV providers began to eat into the network's dominance. Cartoon Network, MTV and Viacom's Nickelodeon network offered children cartoons not just on Saturdays, but whenever they wanted. In the 1990s, the resurgent Walt Disney and Warner Bros. Studios offered 24-hour content on their own stations. Disney Channel, Kids WB, Nicktoons. The resurgence of primetime animation with shows like *The Simpsons* and *Southpark* also gave kids more choices. When Ted Turner bought Hanna-Barbera in 1991, he shifted HB's enormous library away from Saturday morning and into Turner's new cable channel, Cartoon Network.

Hanna-Barbera had developed an elaborate system of outsourcing animation work overseas to countries where the labor costs were a fraction of doing them domestically, particularly in Japan, China and Korea. As the taste for exotic titles like *Power Rangers, Digimon* and *Yugi-Oh* supplanted interest in local shows, some Asian content producers saw they could deal directly with the American networks without needing Bill and Joe as intermediaries.

When kids were offered more opportunities to see cartoons on demand on 24-hour channels, cassettes, DVDs or downloads, the need for Saturday morning cartoons began to wane. The Baby Boomer generation was not cranking out children as zealously as their parents had. That meant lesser viewers for kids TV. Then increased consumer group pressure on the FCC caused increased federal regulations on children's television. The Communications Acts of 1990 and 1996 placed further restrictions on children's content that many cable stations did not have to follow. Influenced by consumer pressure groups like ACT, they mandated significant portions of the children's programing day be given to "E/I" educational and information programing. Ultimately, the retreating networks found with all of these increasing market alternatives and regulations, Saturday morning was simply not as lucrative as it once was. It became simpler and cheaper to run low-budget local programming, like high school sports and magazine-format shows emulating *The Today Show,* except for kids. NBC ended its Saturday morning lineup on September 12, 1992, going to a "kids' magazine" live-action format. CBS in 1997. ABC canceled its remaining Saturday shows in 2002. On September 27, 2014, the last traditional Saturday morning network cartoon block, *Vortexx* on the CW network, ended and was replaced by the magazine show *One Magnificent Morning.*

By then, Hanna, Barbera and the artists of their generation were gone. Bill died in 2001 at the age of 89 years, and Joe at age 96 in 2006. Their company, which they had sold to Taft Enterprises, and later to Ted Turner, was ultimately merged into Warner Bros. WB initially intended to completely phase out their brand name from the

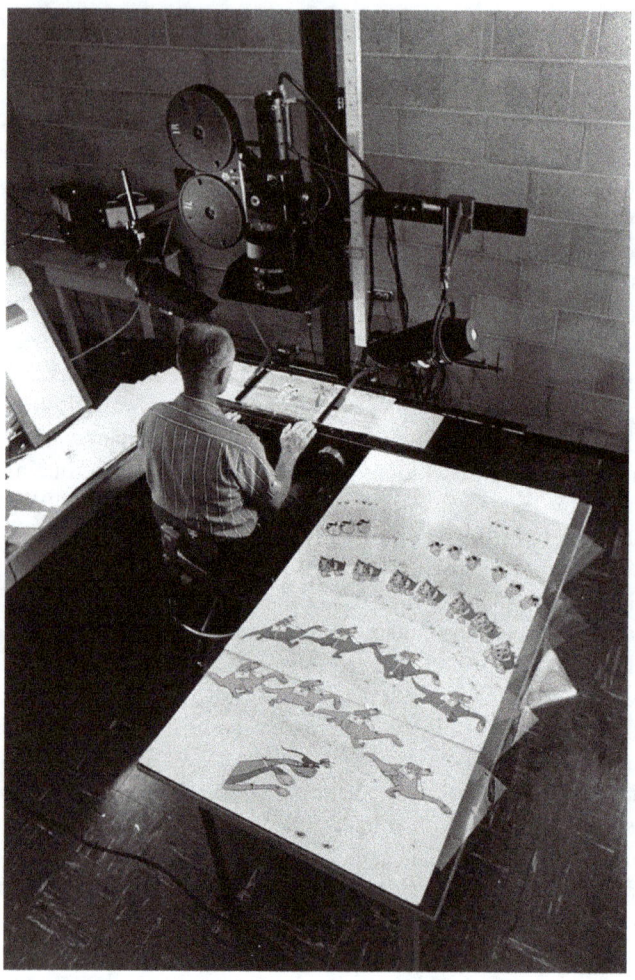

FIGURE 2.5   Animation Camera.

(HB 1979 courtesy of the Animation Guild Archives)

shows, but for the popular backlash over fan base loyalty for old TV reruns on Cartoon Network. The satire program created by Mike Lazzo, *Space Ghost Coast to Coast*, and J.J. Sedelmeir's *The Ambiguously Gay Duo* on SNL, created an unexpected craze for the old 1960s-style characters. It appealed to middle-aged nostalgic boomers. *Space Ghost Coast to Coast* began in 1994 and ran for 11 seasons, twice as long as the original show it was based on.

Despite it all, children still do go to school Monday through Friday, still wake up ahead of their parents on Saturday Mornings, still eat cereal, and still want to be entertained. There are periodic attempts to revive a Saturday Morning animation block. NBC tried it in 2012, etc. But kids have much more options. Games on their phones, streaming services 24 hours. We probably will never see that huge block of Saturday Morning viewers that their parents enjoyed back in the 1960s and 1970s.

NOTES

1 In 1941, Japanese bombers locked in on the radio signals broadcast from Honolulu to guide them to their targets at Pearl Harbor.
2 Museum of Broadcasting, Southbank Centre, London.
3 There was one more network, the Dumont Network, but by 1956, it had failed.
4 Scholars still debate when the Baby Boom officially ended. Somewhere between 1962 and 1967.
5 MGM kept the copyright to Tom & Jerry. Shortly after firing Hanna-Barbera, MGM realized its mistake and tried new series of shorts, first with Chuck Jones and then with Gene Deitch operating out of Prague, Czechoslovakia.
6 Joe Barbera recollection "My Life in Toons."
7 Joe Barbera recollection "My Life in Toons."
8 Jeff Jonas to the author, 2020.
9 Lena Tabori to the author, 1982.
10 Newton Minnow became famous for once describing TV as "a vast wasteland." The TV sitcom Gilligan's Island named their ship the S.S. Minnow in his honor.
11 From the NY Times Obituary of Peggy Charen by Bruce Weber, Jan. 22, 2015.
12 Michael Sporn to the author, 1984.

What Would Walt Do?

3

I just felt creatively the company was not going anywhere interesting. It was very stifling.
—Roy E. Disney

In the late 1960s, as one after another of the great animation studios were closing or transitioning to TV, what was happening at the biggest of them all? The Magic Kingdom of Walt Disney?

When Walt Disney died in December 1966, he had left his company in relatively good shape. While other major Hollywood studios had to yield their independence and become

FIGURE 3.1 Walt Disney death 1966.

(courtesy Doheny Library USC)

DOI: 10.1201/b22394-4

subsidiaries of larger multinational corporations, The Walt Disney Company stood its ground. The market for theatrical shorts had died, and animated features were not burning up the Box Office as they once had. Yet Walt's diversifying into live-action movies, merchandising, theme parks and real estate more than made up the difference. Walt Disney had leapt into television production in when most Hollywood studios were boycotting this new medium. A virtuoso at synergy, Walt watched television provide a ready-made audience to entice customers to his movies, theme parks and buy his name-brand merchandise. Walt Disney had begun to move into live-action film production beginning with *Treasure Island (1950)*. He found that they were not as high risk as the animated features were. If done frugally, you could knock out a feature in a few months, while animated features took years. Instead of big Box Office movie stars, Walt chose talent on their way up (Haley Mills, Guy Williams, Fess Parker, Kurt Russell) or older stars on their way down (Fred MacMurray, Buddy Ebsen, Linda Darnell). His *Davy Crockett* TV show exploded into a national craze and made millions. Little kids across America clamored to buy their own imitation coonskin caps. *Zorro* with Guy Williams caused an equal sensation. Live-action movies like *The Parent Trap, The Absent Minded Professor* and *The Shaggy Dog* brought in huge returns. The first Best Picture Academy Award nomination ever for a Walt Disney feature film was for the live-action musical *Mary Poppins* (1964).[1]

Walt Disney cultivated a unique culture and a name brand of all things Disney, in a way no other studio did. They called it, "The Franchise." That when you reach for a facial tissue, your mind thinks Kleenex. When you want a photocopy, you think Xerox. And when you want safe, quality, family-friendly entertainment, you think Walt Disney. Walt even made himself into a brand-name character. Not many people beyond the Sunset Strip cared what Jack Warner or Louis B. Mayer looked like. But here, on TV, every week was smiling Uncle Walt, fatherly, clean-cut, like a secular Santa Claus. He came into our homes every Sunday night and regaled us with stories about his movies and parks. He personally maintained a clean family image and made sure his publicity department squelched any photos of him with a cigarette or a cocktail in his hand. This was not that hard because despite being a well-known figure in the Hollywood film community for decades, no personal scandals ever surfaced about him. No chippies on the side or bookies to pay hush money to. While other well-known autodidacts of his generation like Charlie Chaplin and Orson Welles developed elitist tastes, Walt Disney still liked cold Hormel's chili out of a can. As he projected a wholesome domestic image, he expected his people to also. When Art Babbitt was a young animator, he was known as a rake who liked to chase skirts. One time, Walt suddenly stopped Art in the hallway and strongly urged him to calm down, find a nice girl and get married. Another time, Walt fired an artist for swearing too much during a story pitch meeting.[2]

In the 1960s, as middle-class America grew exhausted with assassinations, ghetto riots, Vietnam, youth rebellion and psychedelic drugs, people kept coming back to Disney as a comfortable refuge from reality. In his final years, Walt Disney leaned more toward the conservative side of the burgeoning culture wars. Richard Nixon and Ronald Reagan were family friends. No hippies, no drugs, no social criticism. Just small-town America and apple pie. Comedians Cheech & Chong were denied admission to Disneyland just because of their reputations.[3] When Andy Warhol painted a portrait of Mickey Mouse in 1981, he was not commenting on the character. He was commenting on the cultural icon it had become.

When Walt Disney died of lung cancer in 1966, it left an obvious gap at the top. At first Walt's older brother Roy O. Disney delayed his own retirement (he was age 73) and faithfully continued his brothers plans to complete Walt Disney World in Florida, EPCOT, and other projects. Roy died only a few years later in 1971. The chairmanship first went to executive and former cameraman Card Walker, in collaboration with Don Tatum and producer Ron Miller. Ron had played semi-pro football but had married Walt's daughter, Diane.

In 1949, Walt had named nine key character animators as his Nine Old Men:[4] Wolfgang Reitherman, Les Clark, Frank Thomas, Oliver Johnston, Milt Kahl, Marc Davis, John Lounesbury, Eric Larson and Ward Kimball. Since Wolfgang, "Woolie" was the film director of the bunch,[5] he emerged as the de-facto leader of the team and so of the entire animation division. As Walt's full attention drifted away from theatrical animation, he increasingly relied upon his Nine Old Men to maintain the quality of their animated films. Ollie Johnston recalled, "When Walt died, we got together and voted to leave things as they are."[6] These animators knew what they were doing and were at the top of their game. Woolie changed very few of the team leaders. The company mantra became steady as she goes.

FIGURE 3.2 Wolfgang "Woolie" Reitherman.

(courtesy of TAG 839 Archives)

The classic problem with any institution built by a controlling genius is that their management tend to become populated with subordinates who are better at taking orders than generating new ideas. Approving characters, plots costumes, rides, for 43 years Walt Disney the man had the final word on everything. He was talking about the possibilities of television 15 years before they even had a TV show. He had been planning to endow an art school 13 years before the first shovel full of dirt was moved to build CalArts. At his death in 1966, Walt had green-lit (approved) every movie project up to calendar year 1981. What other person could replace such a mind? Many of the middle-management types who rose in importance under Walt seemed to rate their military service, i.e., their ability to follow orders, above anything else. Now that the guiding light was gone, the underlings were all left staring at one another wondering what to do next? For many years, Disney execs would openly say in meetings, "What would Walt do?"

Walt Disney had planned the company's progress through the next decade, but eventually society moved beyond even his far-sighted view. The dynamic cultural currents that were transforming American society in the 1960s–1970s had little effect on the Disney ethos. The trends that made the 1970s such a culturally explosive decade— Acid Rock music to Soul to Funk to Disco to Punk. *Shaft, The Godfather and Superfly* to *Star Wars*, had little impact on The Mouse House. While Hollywood enjoyed an age of *auteur* film directors like Peter Bogdanovich, Sidney Lumet, George Roy Hill, Martin Scorsese and Francis Ford Coppola, Disney just had Woolie Reitherman. Years after Woodstock, they still thought their audience would prefer homogenized Dixieland jazz and barbershop quartets. Culturally, they began to behave like the kingdom of The Sleeping Beauty.

Walt Disney was known for taking big gambles for big results. Without him, the Disney management became increasingly averse to take any risks. As the era of the Sixties moved into the Seventies, popular tastes changed. The endless grind of the Vietnam War and the revelations of the Watergate Scandal made the public more cynical; people were not as interested in *Revenge of the Boatniks* and *Herbie Goes Bananas*. An industry joke at the time was "Some people work at Disney and some people work in film." Film production began to cut back. Young animator Tad Stones remembered climbing to the top of the catwalk in an empty sound stage and dropping super balls to see how high they would bounce. There was no fear of being caught because there was nothing in production there.[7] There was an old story that the studio turned down the chance to make *Star Wars (IV A New Hope)* when it was offered to them. People at the time did remark that *Star Wars* and *Close Encounters of the Third Kind* were the type of movies Disney used to make high quality family films like *Twenty Thousand Leagues Under the Sea* and *Treasure Island*. Disney's *Wonderful World of Color* TV show played more reruns and fewer new shows. The animation unit reliably turned out a feature film every few years for their reliable core audience of Disney faithful. And that was that. Marc Davis once laughed,[8] "We used to work until 11:00, go have a martini at lunch, then play golf." The real income earners were the parks, and the occasional live-action hit like *The Love Bug*. By the 1980s, even the Disney merchandising monolith was being out-paced by the newer characters in Charles Schulz's comic strip *Peanuts* and the Muppets on *Sesame Street*. Disney licensees complained that children had not seen Mickey, Donald or Goofy in a film for years.

The company was facing the same generation gap that was bedeviling the rest of Hollywood. In 1940, on *Pinocchio*, the average age of a Disney animator was 26. In 1970, that average age was 60. The youngest of the Nine Old Men was 55. Some animators like Les Clark began in silent film. Don Bluth recalled John Lounsbery saying to him, "The other Old Men and me, we're holding strong for now. But we won't be around forever."[9] Yet while studios like Paramount, Warner Bros and Universal advanced a new generation of filmmakers to assume creative control, the Walt Disney Studio power structure remained cemented in place. The company promoted from within, and those who did move up did so by learning not to stick their necks out. The original thinkers like Bill Peet, Mary Blair, Bill Tytla, Jack Kinney and Ward Kimball by now had all left or been marginalized.[10] The generation of animators who created masterpieces like *Bambi* and *Pinocchio* were retiring. Because the Disney studio encouraged its artists to stay in place and not move around like the rest of the Hollywood creative talent pool, the problem was even more acute. Many young animators who came in soon realized that with all of the senior artists remaining in place there was no route for advancement. Assistant animators who had been waiting 20 years for their chance to move up were still waiting. The TV animation studios like Hanna-Barbera had more opportunities and paid better. So, they quit. Between 1958 and 1975, the Walt Disney animation division had added only 20 new hires.

"It was obvious that we needed young talent." Don Hahn recalled, "It was really driven by Ron Miller. He came to the conclusion that if we don't do something, we're all going to retire, and animation will retire with us."[11] But animation is a pretty specific skill that needed to be cultivated. You cannot just put an ad in the paper and bring in a few new people to fill seats. The few schools that taught animation did so as an elective of their film departments. Young animator Ron Clements had arrived in Hollywood from Sioux City, Iowa to look for work. Browsing a magazine stand on Hollywood Blvd, an article in Filmmaker's Newsletter caught his eye. "Walt Disney Animation Looking for New Talent." Not every master artist can be a good teacher. Milt Kahl was a great animator who was bad at articulating how he did what he did. "Awww . . . just f**king draw!"[12] Of the Nine Old Men, Eric Larsen seemed the most enthusiastic about working with young people and developing their skills.[13] Eric was sent on a tour of universities around North America to recruit potential new talent. The studio also sponsored creating a course program at the new California Institute of the Arts that focused on classic character animation. Their existing animation program, led by UPA veteran Jules Engel, was more focused on more avant-garde experimental forms of filmmaking, as was the style of the time in arts education. Classic character animation like Snow White was seen as outdated, like teaching rock & roll musicians to play the harpsichord.

The Nine Old Men with several key department heads and producers formed an Executive Review Board to screen candidates. An applicant would be entered into a trial program where they would be given a desk and 3 months to animate a simple scene. Marc Davis wrote out the curriculum for the program. Up to this time, the upper ranks of animation production had been exclusively white and male with a few notable exceptions like Mary Blair and Tyrus Wong. Ron Miller stressed that now the new candidates had to include women and minorities.

FIGURE 3.3 The Small One crew. L-R John Pomeroy, Don Bluth, John Musker, Brad Bird, Jerry Rees, Heidi Guedel, Linda Miller, Emily Jiuliano, Greg Vanzo, Gary Goldman, Chuck Harvey and Bill Hajee.

(courtesy of Charles Harvey)

The first group of trainees included many who would become leaders in the industry: Dale Baer, Brad Bird, Tim Burton, Henry Selick, Nancy Beiman, Jerry Rees, Rebecca Rees, John Musker, Ron Husband, Bill Kroyer, Heidi Guedel, Sue Nelson (later Kroyer), Louis Tate, Randy Cartwright, Linda Miller, John Pomeroy, Dan Haskett, Darrell Van Citters, Phil Nibbelink, Bruce Morris, David Block, Emily Jiuliano, Phil Young, Donald Townes, Hendell Butoy, Daryl Rooney, Bill Frake and Chuck Harvey.

Don Bluth was an animator who had first joined the staff in 1956 as an inbetweener, then rose through the ranks. He was caught in the staff downsizing after *Sleeping Beauty* and spent the 1960s doing TV animation, theater, and his Mormon missionary obligation. He returned to the studio in 1971 with the new youth emphasis, and his draftsmanship and leadership skills began to attract the attention of the old men. Woolie Reitherman decided to groom Don Bluth to take over when he retired.

Don Bluth like many of the young generation wanted to move away from "safe" ideas and recapture the dynamic, dramatic ideas, some would say darker European style of Disney animation in the later 1930s–1940s. Scenes like Bambi's mother getting shot or Malificent summoning "All the powers of hell" to transform into a scary dragon would be unthinkable in the films they were doing now. Even Frank Thomas admitted what they were doing was much lighter and cutesy than before. Mel Shaw and Ken Andersen were pushing to do a story from books by Lloyd Alexander called *Chronicles of Prydain.* They announced it in the press as *The Black Cauldron.* That it would be a return to the dramatic, gothic storytelling of *Snow White* and *Sleeping Beauty.* But the project bogged down in "development hell." Too many cooks, too many directions, too many ideas. No Walt to set a clear course. It kept getting delayed and deadlines pushed into the next decade.[14]

Historian Ferdinand Lott, in his analysis of the decline of ancient Greco-Roman art, described part of the problem being the "stultifying effect of masterpieces." Clients did not want new works but copies of the old. The animation artists who remained at the Disney studio similarly felt the greatest works of their studio had ever done had already been done. That no one could ever hope to create animation today that might rival *Bambi, Pinocchio* or *Sleeping Beauty.* Young animator Dan Haskett on *The Fox and the Hound* recalled that he would approach his handling of the dog character Copper by studying the movement of real dogs. But his supervisor dumped on his desk a thick stack of dog studies drawn by Marc Davis 20 years before for *101 Dalmatians* and told to just stick to those.[15]

After *Sleeping Beauty* (1958), there had been a big layoff of animation personnel. The staff downsized from 400 to just 120. Artists who had been there since Bambi were suddenly out on the street. For the remaining team, the emphasis was to be economical. Corporate management continually pressured Woolie Reitherman to keep his budgets down, with no discernable loss in Disney quality. Effects animator Ted Kierscey recalled in every production meeting at one-point Woolie would always repeat "We gotta get this done cheaply."[16] Switching from hand-inked cels to xeroxed drawings saved a bit. Don Bluth recalled every time we went on a break, he noticed some managerial-type looking at him and then eyeing his watch. The remaining Nine Old Men, Frank Thomas, Ollie Johnston, Milt Kahl and Eric Larson knew how to produce quality work easily and quickly. But as they began to slow down with age, Woolie turned to repurposing old animation to make up the difference. Animation fans today delight in pouring through 1970s movies like *Robin Hood* to spot the recycled scenes from *Snow White* and *Sword in the Stone.* Many joked about "The Mowgli Stick-Kicking Scene" The young boy trudges off frustrated, eyes downward and kicks a random stick in his way. It popped up again and again in films like *The Small One* and *The Black Cauldron.* When Woolie asked Don Bluth to redraw a scene of Snow-White dancing into Maid Marian dancing, Milt Kahl exploded in rage. Not at Woolie, at Don as if it was his idea. The poor guy was just following orders.

By the time, the studio began work on *The Rescuers* in 1975, it was decided that this project would be the one where the old guard and the young pups would work the closest together. Woolie offered co-directorship to Don Bluth. But Don felt it was too soon for him to take on such a large project. He declined in favor of first directing a short *The Small One.* *The Rescuers* would be directed by Woolie, John Lounsbury and Art Stevens. It was veteran animator Milt Kahl's last movie. He created a masterful performance of Madame Medusa, and his henchman Mr. Snoops. The trainees would work under the old guard until they were ready to spread their wings and go for themselves. Glen Keane recalled being given a scene to animate of one of Medusa's alligators playing a pipe organ to force Bernard the mouse out into the open where he could eat him. When he brought his completed scene to Oliver Johnston to approve, Ollie snapped,

"What? That's not how an alligator plays a pipe organ!"[17] But despite much trial and error, the young crew slowly began to master their craft.

Between the youngsters and the old guard, there was a middle group of Disney vets.

A cadre of veteran-assistant animators who like army drill sergeants were relied to keep the younger artists on track. People like Dale Oliver, Stan Green, Bud Hester, Tom Ferriter and more. These artists had longed to reach the upper ranks. They were told if they played along and behaved, then one day they might get their chance. But after a while, they realized the ranks of The Nine Old Men would not be refilled with replacements after the originals left. Once they were gone, that was it. And the new influx of youngsters they were pushing up were already moving into the supervisory jobs. So, many left bitter. Older artists like Mel Shaw and Ken Anderson pitched projects they had hoped to direct themselves one day. Then they heard the new big project called *The Black Cauldron* was to be directed by a new kid out of CalArts named John Musker! After some backroom politicking, John suddenly had to share the directorship with old vets Art Stevens and Ted Berman (both started at Disney in 1940). And then editor Richard Rich. Soon John Musker was off *Cauldron* and on to something called *Basil of Baker Street*.

By the production of *The Fox and the Hound (1982)*, Woolie Reitherman finally reached the end of the road. During production, he pitched an idea for two whooping cranes voiced by popular nightclub entertainer Charro and Phil Harris, the voice of Baloo in *The Jungle Book*. They would sing the song, "Scooby-Doobie, Doobie-Doo, Let your Body Go." The song added nothing to the plot. The main characters just heard a commotion, parted some reeds and there they were dancing. Woolie even brought Charro and Harris in to film live-action reference, which mostly consisted of the shapely Latin singer gyrating in a sweaty pink leotard. Ultimately everyone from Ron Miller on down said it was a terrible idea, and it was dropped. Woolie walked back to his office, plopped dejectedly into his chair and said to Art Stevens, "You know Art, maybe this IS a young person's medium."[18] Wolfgang Reitherman stepped away from *Fox and Hound* into developing one more unrealized property *"Catfish Bend,"* then retired.[19]

Don Bluth had attracted a number of the young trainees around him who felt the way he did. But not everyone was on board. The example of leadership left by Walt Disney was difficult to emulate. Up to now, in every creative disagreement, Walt's decision was law. When Walt was gone, Woolie's decisions were equally respected because of his awesome reputation. But when Don Bluth now insisted on the same kind of obedience to his decisions, friction began to appear. It is one thing to take orders from a white-haired legend who worked on *Pinocchio* and *Bambi*. Quite another to take the same orders from someone who a moment ago was sitting next to you. Most creative studios have office politics. Why did he get the promotion and not me? Why did she get that plum assignment when I could do it better? With a studio of creative artists, the disagreements are even more acute because it involved questions of taste. Don Bluth became so obsessed with his perceived role as the new Walt; he even grew a small mustache and wore vintage golf sweaters. While some thought he was being charming, others thought it odd.

When working on *The Small One*, Don kept asking his team to rely more on live-action reference. Many of the young animators initially felt that relying on live action for their character work cheapened their quality. After all, Bill Tytla did not use live action to animate Stromboli in Pinocchio, or Preston Blair to animate his sexy dancer "Red" in the Tex Avery cartoons.[20] To reinforce his point, Don screened for the crew examples from previous Disney classics. At one point, he ran the scene from *Sleeping Beauty* when Prince Phillip fought his way out of Malificents' castle. When Philip suddenly turns to confront a cohort of piggish animal warriors rushing down stairs to attack him, animator Brad Bird called out "Look out! Cartoons!" And the room erupted in laughter. Witnesses said Don did not think this was funny, which made it all the more.[21]

The group of animators that clashed with Don Bluth most often seemed to all be centered in one room. Bill Kroyer, Brad Bird, John Musker, Dan Haskett and Henry Selick. They were dubbed, "The Rat's Nest," because legend has it one day Don came into their room and accused them all of being just that. The animators embraced the title and called themselves The Rats Nest thereafter.

On the plus side, Don Bluth gave equal assignments to the women animation trainees when the old men were still grumbling. Lorna Cook recalled master animator Milt Kahl saying to her, "I don't like to train girls. Because pretty soon you meet a fella, get married, have kids and drop out of the business. And I've wasted my time."[22] Another old veteran drew boos from a college audience when he said women do not make good animators. Don took them seriously and gave them equal responsibility.

Don Bluth desired to go further than the training program and create new movies from scratch. Over lunch with Gary Goldman and John Pomeroy he complained, "The whole approach of the Nine Old Men is teaching technique. The way I see it, when the Nine are gone, the art of animation is gone. Do either of you know how to structure a movie to capture an audience's attention? I sure don't."[23]

The three decided to work on their own short project after work in Don's garage. Something they could cut their teeth on. Titled *Banjo the Woodpile Cat*. Many friends from the studio joined them. The project was worked on in spurts over 4 years. It proved to be the place where Don's core team bonded as a unit. People around Hollywood who knew them called them The Bluthies. When directing the short *The Small One*, some artists felt Don was playing favorites by giving the best scene assignments to his *Banjo* animators. All sides lamented the toxic work environment in the studio.

In early 1979, Don Bluth was showing his *Banjo, the Woodpile Cat* around town as a work-in-progress, hoping to get funds to complete it. He met with a consortium of former Walt Disney investors called Aurora Productions. They suggested that beyond Banjo, they would back Don in the formation of his own studio.

On his birthday, Thursday, September 13, 1979, Don Bluth, Gary Goldman and John Pomeroy resigned from the studio to go start their own company. The following day more resignations kept coming, until in all about a third of the studios young animation staff left to join Don's new company. Ron Miller and the old guard were shocked. They felt all of these young people who they invested so much time and effort to train had just stabbed them in the back. They had provided them with every opportunity, even enforcing a mandatory retirement at 65 to push out the few stubborn old timers who would not take the hint. And they did this. They blamed it all on Don Bluth. Ron

Miller called the remaining crew together for a pep talk. He began with, "Now that the cancer has been excised."[24]

The bad feelings remained for a long time. Ten years later in 1987 when planning *Who Framed Roger Rabbit*, director Richard Williams noticed Disney executives were still openly discussing how they could "Get Don Bluth!"[25]

The studio ended the 1970s by releasing *The Black Hole* (Dec. 21, 1979), an embarrassingly bad attempt to capitalize on the current Star Wars mania for science fiction. It had a beautifully designed spaceship designed by Peter Ellenshaw that looked like a throwback to the glory days of *Twenty Thousand Leagues Under the Sea*. But it had a weak story and the Maximilian Schell badguy Dr. Hans Reinhardt came off like a pale imitation of James Mason's Captain Nemo. It had kooky robot sidekicks that looked like R2D2 but with big silly cartoon eyes and the hillbilly voice of Slim Pickens. It was supposed to hover, but in many shots, you could easily see the strings holding it up. This from a studio that used to count its visual effects movies in Academy Awards.

In 1980, Card Walker stepped away from his CEO responsibilities and Ron Miller took over the chairmanship. Trying to infuse younger ideas into upper management, he promoted a 29-year-old named Tom Wilhite up from the publicity department to be VP of production. Wilhite immediately set to work promoting new ideas such as a computer-animation project called *TRON*, and a young animator with a taste for the macabre named Tim Burton.

Steven Lisberger was a filmmaker who had an animation studio in the Boston area. He developed a fully animated project to coincide with the Olympic Games called *Animalympics*. A number of young Disney-trained animators worked on it like Bill Kroyer, Brad Bird, Dan Haskett and Jerry Rees. The animation was very good, but the film became the unexpected victim of international politics. In a last gasp of the Cold War, when the Soviet Union invaded Afghanistan in 1979, U.S. President Jimmy Carter retaliated in part by boycotting the Summer Games in Moscow. This included NBC dropping all ancillary programming like *Animalympics*. During this time, Lisberger became intrigued with the burgeoning field of computer graphics. He played the video game Pong and saw how the arcade game craze was catching fire across the country. He conceived of a movie about a brilliant programmer who gets zapped into a video game, where he needs to fight life and death contests to destroy the DCM master. On a trip to the Palo-Alto facility Xerox PARC, he met scientist Alan Kay, one of the originators of the first laptop computers. Kay advised Lisberger to try to do all of the computer graphic scenes using real computer graphics. Up to then, there was very little digital animation in mainstreams movies. Steve Lisberger's producer Bill Kushner took the project to Walt Disney, where Tom Wilhite thought it was just the kind of project the studio needed to retake the lead in animated film.

There was only 15 minutes of actual CGI in the entire movie. Many parts were made to look like computer graphics. Actors wore tights with phosphorescent tape up and down their bodies to look like vector outlines. There were no good digital paint systems yet, so the images the computer created were printed out on animation paper and painted and photographed just like traditional cartoon animation was.

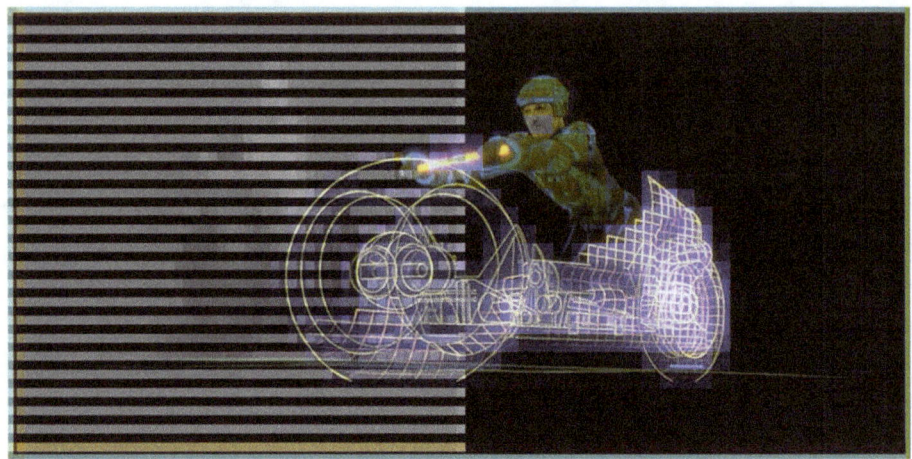

FIGURE 3.4 *TRON*.

Animation by John Van Vliet. Courtesy of Walt Disney Productions.

TRON was originally slated for a Christmas 1982 release. But when Ron Miller learned that Don Bluth and his rebel band were going to put out their first movie, *The Secret of NIMH* that 4th of July, he moved up Tron's release date to counter them. This put Tron now against some of the biggest Box Office movies of the year. Blockbusters like *E.T. The Extra-Terrestrial, Star Trek 2 The Wrath of Khan,* John Carpenter's *The Thing, Conan the Barbarian, Poltergeist* and *Blade Runner. TRON* got generally good reviews, but shortly before it opened a Wall Street stock analyst saw a sneak preview at the Motion Picture Academy and began advising his clients to sell their Disney stock. This bad word-of-mouth got out, and it also hurt the film. *TRON's* opening weekend did $4.8 million in Box Office, while *Wrath of Khan* did $14.5 million. It ultimately made money, but not before the studio took a $17 million write off on it.

Then the live action *Something Wicked This Way Comes*, an attempt at a darker scary movie written by Ray Bradbury came out and bombed as well. Up to this point, Tom Wilhite was feeling confident enough in this new direction to encourage a test of digital graphics combined with 2D character animation based on Maurice Sendak's book *Where the Wild Things Are.* Young animator Glen Keane did the character animation, John Lasseter did the computer work. They did not quite have the rights to the book yet, but they reasoned they could use this test to convince Sendak. Pre-production had also begun on the *Brave Little Toaster*, directed by Jerry Rees.

As if there were not enough problems, in 1982, the studio was crippled by a union strike. The Motion Picture Screen Cartoonists Local #839[26] struck all of Hollywood to demand a protectionist clause go in their basic contract to guarantee animation work would not be outsourced to countries where the costs were cheaper. Walt Disney Studio at the time did not and had no plans to outsource any animation, but the union felt for the strike to be effective it had to shut down all productions in town. The union president Morris "Moe" Gollub and Business Agent Bud Hester were former Disney artists.

For several weeks, production was stalled while artists walked picket lines like their forebears did in 1941.

Finally, the more conservative elements won out. Tom Wilhite left the studio to do his own projects. Bill Kroyer, Jerry and Rebecca Rees and the other enthusiasts for CGI left as well. John Lasseter and Tim Burton were fired for wasting the company's money. Soon afterward, Lasseter ran into a fellow named Ed Catmull and was hired by the Lucasfilm Graphics Group, that would soon change its name to Pixar. The NY-based computer company MAGI/Synthevision that had helped make Tron had relocated to Hollywood in anticipation of more projects with the Mouse House. They were cut loose and wound up breaking up. Chris Wedge and Gene Troubetskoy took the survivors back to the Hudson valley and set up a new company called Blue Sky. Jerry Rees and Tom Wilhite took *The Brave Little Toaster* project with them and completed it in hand-drawn animation partly done in Taiwan. The endless *Black Cauldron* project's release was pushed back yet again so *Fox and Hound* could go first.

Many more young animators walked out from frustration. Dan Haskett, Glen Keane, Chuck Harvey and more. They wound up in unusual productions like *The Chipmunk Adventure* and *Starchasers the Legend of Orin in 3D*, and more. Chicago film critic Roger Ebert wrote, "the market is looking for a turnaround in management after years during which Walt Disney's magic touch was lost in a series of dreary children's movies aimed at an audience that no longer exists."[27]

By 1984, everyone still remaining at Walt Disney realized something had to change.

NOTES

1 The studio had a basketful of Oscars for animated shorts. *Snow White and the Seven Dwarfs* was awarded a special Oscar in 1938. *Beauty and the Beast* earned a Best Picture nomination in 1991. The Best Animated Feature category was created in 2001.

2 Jack Kinney, *Walt Disney and Other Assorted Characters*.

3 Jimmy Cheech and Tommy Chong were famous for their drug-culture jokes and movies like *Up in Smoke*. Ironically, in 1987, Cheech was hired by the studio to do a voice on Oliver & Company.

4 Walt borrowed a phrase Franklin Roosevelt used in 1937 when the conservative Supreme Court struck down key components of his economic program "The New Deal." He said, "Nine Old Men must not hold back the progress of the American people."

5 Disney had several animation directors, Clyde Geronimi, Dave Hand, Wilfred Jackson, Ham Luske and Charles Nichols. All had retired or otherwise moved on by the 1970s.

6 Ollie Johnston quoted by Didier Ghez in *The Hidden Art of Disney's Early Renaissance*, pg 12.

7 Tad Stones to the author, June 2022.

8 Marc Davis to the author, 1990.

9 Don Bluth, *Somewhere Out There*, pg 156.

10 Ward Kimball had grown frustrated by the rigidifying creative culture at the studio. From the TV unit, he moved over to Imagineering. In 1968, he animated by himself an independent short called *Escalation*, a political satire mocking President Lyndon Johnson and his Vietnam War policy. In 1973, Ward officially retired.

11 Mindy Johnson, *Ink & Paint*, pg 312.
12 Chuck Harvey to the author, 1978.
13 Marc Davis was also a good teacher and had taught drawing classes at Chouinard. But by the 1970s, he had moved from animation over to Imagineering, designing for the parks things like *The Pirates of the Caribbean*.
14 Development Hell is not a new concept. Many stories like *Frozen* languished for years before full production began in earnest.
15 Dan Haskett to the author, 1978.
16 Ted Kierscey to the author, 2021.
17 Glen Keane to the author, 1988.
18 Steve Hulett to the author, 1992.
19 Woolie Reitherman died in a car accident in 1985.
20 Bill Tytla did use some life action footage of Bela Lugosi and Wilfred Jackson posing to create his Chernobog devil in the Night On Bald Mountain sequence in Fantasia.
21 Dan Haskett to the author, 1978.
22 Lorna Cook to the author, 1997.
23 Don Bluth, *Somewhere Out There*.
24 Dorse Lanpher to the author, 1987.
25 Richard Williams to the author, 1988.
26 In 2001, they became The Animation Guild, Local 839 Hollywood.
27 Roger Ebert, Interview with Tom Wilhite, RogerEbert.com 2012.

13 Soho Square

<big>**4**</big>

In the 1970s, as the Hollywood film industry collapsed in on itself and young animators looked around for good projects to work on, a unique alternative emerged. London.

Americans fancy themselves the originators of animation,[1] but since its birth animation was always being done around the world. In France, Italy, Japan, China, Argentina and Eastern Europe, domestic studios made comics, features and TV programs in the local languages. Characters like Asterix, Lucky Luke, Peach Boy, Monkey King and Mr. Rossi were just as popular locally as Mickey Mouse or Bugs Bunny.

When the filmmaking and animation industries began, the British Empire was at its peak, and London was the great commercial and financial center of the world. But the World Wars caused Britain to suffer the same economic problems as many of the other industrial post-colonial powers had. And the enormous output of the Hollywood studios overwhelmed their domestic product. The lure of Hollywood also drew away key European talent to help create their films. "Americans love accents" as writer Quentin Crisp observed. And the British enjoyed the sunshine and the lack of rationing of consumer goods.

After 1945, many nations coming out of World War II enacted strict limits on imports in order to help local businesses recover. This included film. Britain put a 300% tariff on American films shown in England. As a result, Britain, France and

FIGURE 4.1 Richard William's still from Tony Richardson's *The Charge of the Light Brigade* 1968.

DOI: 10.1201/b22394-5

Italy enjoyed a golden age of domestic filmmaking without having to compete with the Hollywood imports. The great Ealing comedies, Cinecitta', Cinema Verite' and more. Americans, in turn, went to Europe to film because with the exchange rate, their dollars went much further, the cultural inspiration, and to escape the Hollywood Blacklist back home. Hollywood stars like Charlie Chaplin, Orson Welles, Ava Gardner, Tyrone Power, Olivia DeHavilland, John Huston and more relocated their primary residences to Europe.

England in particular appealed to Americans for its cultural and linguistic affinity. Even with the British Empire in decline, London was still a major economic and cultural center for much of Europe. Britain's most famous animation studios then was Halas & Batchelor, formed by Hungarian immigrant John Halas and his artist-wife Joy Batchelor in 1940. Their most famous work was the animated adaptation of George Orwell's novel *Animal Farm* in 1954. In 1957, they did the UK's first TV commercial, for Murray Mints.[2] In 1946, former Walt Disney director Dave Hand went to England and, for J. Arthur Rank, established Gaumont British Animation at Moor Hall. They produced the *Animaland* and *Musical Paintbox* cartoon series. Australian-born animator Bob Godfrey left Gaumont to set up his own place. Canadian George Dunning set up his studio TVC in July 1957. By the late 1960s, London had a flowering of pop culture, exporting her rock & roll, Beatle haircuts and the Carnaby Street look. In 1967, George Dunning directed the animated feature *The Yellow Submarine*, designed by Czech artist Heinz Edelmann, and featuring the music of the then most popular rock & roll band in the world, The Beatles. The lads themselves were only minimally involved with the project. They were happy that this film satisfied the last of their three-picture contract with American studio United Artists, without making any further demands on their time. Their voices were supplied by impersonators. After the Beatles saw the movie, they decided that they liked it and filmed a little live-action epilogue. *The Yellow Submarine*'s revolutionary artistic style, evocative of the mania for psychedelic posters and pop art, the Carnaby Street Style, swept the world. Although in some cities like Singapore, when the locals realized the film was a cartoon and not the real Beatles, they rioted.

When television was introduced into the British home, England quickly developed a robust business generating content for young children. The government-funded BBC had a show on the radio for 10 years called *The Children's Hour*. When they moved into TV in 1946, it debuted as *For the Children*.[3] While American studios just dumped their old libraries of 1930s–1940s era short cartoons on TV stations, England excelled at creating new programs aimed at developing young minds. *The Clangers, The Magic Roundabout, Thomas the Tank Engine,* later *Danger Mouse* and *Peppa Pig*.

Theatrical filmmaking and children's television for domestic consumption were good, but what really paid the bills then was advertising. London as an economic power center also extended to her huge advertising industry. Postwar nativist regulations insisted that consumer products be packaged and advertised at home. So if an American company wanted to sell corn flakes in Europe, they needed to commission one commercial for Portugal, one commercial for Switzerland and so forth. Even the Czechs and Slovaks of Czechoslovakia insisted on separate commercials. Most countries like West Germany, Portugal and Denmark could not afford to sustain a home-grown advertising industry. There simply was not enough demand. So a Portuguese importer of American corn flakes would contract a British studio to create their commercials. Until the Maastricht Treaty threw down all protectionist laws in the European Union, the British advertising industry boomed. Doing commercial spots for much of Europe. The robust work environment pulled in talented international animators to fill the desks of these studios. Oscar Grillo from Argentina, Uli Meyer and Harold Seiperman from Germany, Nicolette Van Gendt and Rob Stevenhagen from Holland, Borge Ring from Denmark, Richard Purdum and Eric Goldberg from America, Richard Chang and Helen Koo from Hong Kong and Ken Duncan, Roger Chiasson, and Phil Valentine from Canada, all augmented the ranks of British animators.

The nerve center of the British film and animation industries was the West End London theatre district called Soho. J Arthur Rank and Bob Godfrey's studio were on Wardour Street. George Dunning opened TVC on Dean St., Klacto on Great Marlborough St and so forth. While many Londoners lived on fish & chips off a wagon, Soho was the place you could find exotic cuisine like Malaysian and Hungarian. Like Times Square in New York, the low-rent parts of Soho had an unsavory reputation for "adult" entertainment. Eric Goldberg recalled, "Down each street you would find a peep show, an adult bookstore, then an animation studio." Open doorways posted a small card that read "Big Busty Model One Flight Up." Many animators were doing commercials, then all knew each other and moved around from studio to studio. The studios were close enough to one another that a custom on Friday nights was Pub Night. Friday afternoon, the studios would all ring each other up and decide on one pub to rendezvous. After 6:00 PM, the entire animation business would all meet up for a beer after work. It became a cherished custom. No matter how tight the project deadline, everyone could still spare some time to hop down to the pub for a pint.

The studios then were very influenced by the 1960s graphic style of design developed by the American studio United Productions of America (UPA). Its clean, simple graphic designs read well on early television screens and appealed to many cultures. It was a reasonable alternative to the Walt Disney, Looney Tunes classic animation styles.

Into this world came Richard Williams (1933–2019). He was born in the quiet Toronto suburb of Scarborough. At the age of 5, his parents took him to see *Snow White and the Seven Dwarfs*. Even at that early age, he understood the film was made with drawings. His mother, after all, was an illustrator, so he was brought up around conté crayons, gesso, and Arthur Rackham illustrated books. He began drawing furiously. Those who knew him knew he did everything "furiously." Dick seemed to be made of energy.

At the age of 15, he went on a 5-day bus trip to Hollywood. He took the Walt Disney Studios tour three times and was ejected once for breaking away from the group to try to go talk to the animators. This chance to watch these master artists at work had a great effect on him. He formed a lifelong friendship with the legendary animator Milt Kahl. Milt became a mentor to him. Later in his teens, Richard Williams discovered other master artists like Rembrandt, Titian and Ingres. He tried to be a serious painter and lived for a time in Ibiza, Spain, studying the great masters. However, after a time, he grew disillusioned with painting. "I couldn't stand the idea of doing paintings for rich industrialists' wives and that whole art world was just repulsive as a way of life."

FIGURE 4.2   Richard Williams.

At that time, the art world was dominated by the philosophy of abstract expressionists like Jackson Pollock, Frank Stella and Mark Rothko. The artistic elites looked down their noses at people doing representational realism as outdated and kitsch. Williams returned to his first love, animation. "My paintings were aching to move, anyway."

Richard Williams began working for animator George Dunning at Graphics Associates. When Dunning accepted an offer from UPA to set up a London office, Dick followed him across the Atlantic. When UPA closed its British operation, Dunning set up the company TVC, and Williams went over to Bob Godfrey. He described his first years living in London as a starving artist, "living on peanut butter, fish & chips and milk." At first, full of the arrogance of youth, he was disdainful of wasting his talents on commercial spots for soap and tea. The veteran director Clive Donner put him in his place, "He said listen smarty, you think you are so hot? You just try and draw something that will convince millions of people to buy something. It's not as easy as it looks."[4] Dick did hunker down and learn the craft. First with George Dunning, then with Bob Godfrey. He also drew a lot of freelance illustrations for magazines.

Dick became so good at animating commercial spots, he soon broke away and set up his own company. He announced himself by virtue of a little short he animated in his spare time, *The Little* Island, that won a BAFTA in 1958, the British equivalent of the Academy Award. Richard Williams Animation, RWA, set up shop in a charming seventeenth-century row house at 13 Soho Square. Giacomo Casanova, the famous Italian writer and lover, had lived nearby during his London years.

Dick said back then part of the charm of British commercials was that they were not the "hard sell, bang you over the head" variety of American advertising. "The British advertising executives then were by and large, younger son graduates of Oxford and Cambridge, who studied philosophy and ancient languages. Then their influential daddies got them those jobs. Knowing little and caring less, they would say to us (in upper-class British accent) "Oh, just do something funny." Then they would go to their club for a whisky and soda and leave us alone. "It was wonderful."[5] In a style similar to Monty Python, Dick began to mix his love of classical art with his advertising design. For a diaper commercial, he animated a group of baroque cherubs in a ceiling fresco by Tiepolo discussing the merits of a particular nappie (i.e., diaper). When he did a spot for men's cologne that emphasized male sex appeal, he animated a Frank Frazetta-style barbarian on a mountaintop, battling the lightning. He made a spot about "Old Sailors" brand sherry to look like nineteenth-century scrimshaw carving, accompanied by a concertina.

Dick developed a system of cascading dissolves. Putting a three–four frame camera fades in between the individual in-between animation drawings. This allowed animation drawn with complex cross-hatching and other heavy rendering techniques to move smoothly and not strobe or flicker. Today, this can be gone digitally with digital motion blur, but in the pre-digital years, it was a painstaking process for the camera operator. "I never yet made a project that was easy for the cameraman." He also developed a system of drawing directly on acetate cels with special grease pencils. This eliminated the extra steps of inking and/or xerography, and it gave the spot a more illustration-like look. Dick built a team of top-notch animators and illustrators around him, including Roy Naisbitt, Roland Wilson, Russell Hall, Richard Purdum, Tony White, Barbara McCormack, Oscar Grillo, Shelley Page and more.

They enjoyed the variety each new spot demanded, becoming an artistic chameleon. While other studios stuck with a set, in-house graphic style, Richard William Animation delighted in giving the client a chance to do anything. "People may say I am a flake. That my animation is cold. But one thing I know. I can draw in any f**king style you can throw at me. Disney, MGM, UPA." Art Babbitt said of Dick, "He's a dreamer. He has more to learn as far as animation is concerned, but God, he can draw like a bastard!"

Like Walt Disney a generation ago, Richard Williams found that by ploughing his profits back into his studio, he was upping the quality of his work. He demanded better and better quality in his spots, even beyond what the clients initially intended. These projects earned him design and commercial awards that he lined up in the anteroom of his studio. He called those awards his "armor." Soon rival studios, including some founded by RWA alumni, began to compete in Dick's philosophy of high-quality design and execution. Dragon Studios, Klacto, Passion Pictures, Richard Purdum Animation and Hibbert/Ralph. Back in New York advertising, production managers were dumbing down scenes, pulling drawings out and shooting them on "4s." "Don't give the client more than he asked for. He'll come to expect it." New York studios competed by underbidding each other. At the same time, London blossomed in an age of beautiful, high-quality animation.

Creating print adverts for movies, and then animation, it only follows that Richard Williams would make the jump to doing title sequences for movies, many of which were co-productions between London and Hollywood. English movie directors like Clive Donner, Ridley and Tony Scott had come out of advertising. Animated title sequences from art directors like Saul Bass (*Vertigo, Spartacus*) were quite the fashion then. His friend Clive Donner had moved on to directing movies and asked Dick to create animated opening titles for his comedy *What's New Pussycat? (1965)*. It was a riotous comedy with Peter O'Toole, written by Woody Allen with Tom Jones singing a new hit song by Burt Bacharach. Dick later described *What's New Pussycat* as "a mad, loupy movie. But it was a big hit, and it made a lot of money."[6] He followed it up with *Casino Royale* (1967) and soon made a big splash doing clever designs and titles. For Richard Lester's "A Funny Thing Happened on the Way to The Forum," he animated ancient Roman wall paintings. For Tony Richardson's *The Charge of the Light Brigade,* he brought to life the propaganda cartoons of the Victorian era, as seen in magazines like Punch. For *The Pink Panther Returns* (1975), he had 77-year-old Bugs Bunny veteran animator Ken Harris animate a masterful solo of the Pink Panther doing a soft-shoe dance.

The high-profile success of these title sequences brought Richard Williams into direct contact with major Hollywood Studios. Added to this, Dick had an old friend from his Toronto school days who also became an animator named Carl Bell. While Dick moved to London, Carl went to LA and became an animator for Bob Clampett and later Chuck Jones. Carl worked on projects like *Beanie and Cecil* and *The Grinch Who Stole Xmas.* Carl introduced Chuck and Dick together, and a deep friendship ensued, like he had with Milt Kahl. Chuck used his influence with ABC (he was then head of children's broadcasting) network to engage Dick to create a version of Charles Dickens' *A Christmas Carol* as a holiday special. The film used the top interpreters of the characters, then like Alastair Sim and Michael Hordern. Dick's young son Alex provided the voice of Tiny Tim. Dick and his staff used all their skills to bring to life the original Victorian illustrations done in the 1840s by John Leech. *A Christmas Carol* was so successful, it was released theatrically and won an Academy Award for Best Animated Short (1972).

At this point, Dick Williams did something extraordinary. He closed his studio down for a month and paid for his crew to take animation lessons from several Golden Age master animators he flew out from Hollywood. Art Babbitt, Ken Harris and Grim Natwick. He even invited animators from rival studios to come and participate. His financial guru Carl Gover said the whole stunt nearly bankrupted them. But it worked. Up to then, most British studios looked inward in their employee development, much like the homegrown studio cultures of France and Japan. In the live-action projects, Dick saw that London already had an umbilical reaching out to Hollywood. Stanley Kubrick and Richard Lester had shifted their base of operations to England; there were always a number of Hollywood projects being filmed in town. George Lucas and Steven Spielberg seemed to prefer filming at British Pinewood and Elstree Studios instead of Burbank. Why not extend to Hollywood animation as well?

A thing Dick had learned from his mother and his study of the old masters of painting was that "we stand on the shoulders of giants." Rather than reinventing the wheel each time, we can go further when we work out from the experience all done before us. The master animators of the Hollywood Golden age indeed wanted to pass on all of the tricks and techniques they learned, but in the 1960s, they found that nobody really wanted them. It was an age of motion graphics rather than pure personality animation. The kind of beautiful character performance that graced the great Disney, MGM, and Warner Bros. cartoons was then seen as anachronisms, out of touch with modern tastes

FIGURE 4.3   Richard Williams's crew including the old masters in front of their offices at 13 Soho Square.

and much too costly to ever be profitable. It took 16 years for Dick Williams to prove that a high-quality cartoon could make serious profits.

Richard Williams Animation became a sanctuary for the study of classic character animation. Like the medieval monasteries of old, which spent decades preserving and transcribing the collected knowledge of ancient Greece and Rome, 13 Soho Square became a repository for the study of personality animation. The animator is an actor with a pencil. With this wisdom, Richard Williams began to formulate a plan to do the ultimate film. His magnum opus. Based on a medieval Persian fairytale, *the Nasrudin*, he titled it *The Thief and the Cobbler*.[7] He wanted to do it in the style of Persian miniature painting. Layout designer Roy Naisbett created some remarkable designs of the Sultan's palace. Paintings larger than a dinner table. Famous actors like Vincent Price, Peter Lorre and Sir Anthony Quayle did voice work. As Dick's dreams for the Thief grew more grandiose, he said he wanted to make "The War and Peace of Animation!" "The greatest animated feature ever made!"

One thing Dick Williams was never good at was the more predatory aspects of modern business. The arguments between artists and the businessmen who hired them are as old as the Renaissance. Dick's idea of the ideal producer was someone who signed a blank check and left the room. Commercials were one thing, but theatrical features were a high-stakes gamble. In live action, big studios could afford little prestige films, so long as they made the occasional blockbuster. But animated features had no such luxury. They had to be huge hits to be profitable. Back then, Walt Disney seemed to be the only place that made features with significant profits. And most of that was due to their marketing and merchandising directed at their loyal core audience.

In 1975, Richard Williams agreed to help create an animated musical based on the Raggedy Ann stories of Johnny Gruelle. Produced by Bobbs & Merrill Publishing, a division of the ITT corporation, which wanted to branch out into entertainment. Originally conceived as a stage show, the fantasy elements of the story lent itself to be animated for the big screen. They acquired top Broadway producers Richard Horner and Lester Osterman and the music written by Joe Raposo, who created all of the music for Sesame Street. To not be too distracted from his main project, initially Dick planned to oversee the project, while it would be directed by Abe Levitow.[8] It was to be animated part in Los Angeles, and part in New York. Old Disney/Fleischer veteran Shamus Culhane had worked as production manager to design a modest 2.5-million-dollar budget. When Levitow unexpectedly died at age 52, Dick took over directing the film. With his trademark enthusiasm, Dick began pushing the designs and upping the quality, breaking with Shamus who soon quit the project. Dick rounded up the finest Hollywood animators outside of Disney. Tissa David, Art Babbitt, Hal Ambro, Emery Hawkins, Grim Natwick, Charlie Downs and John Kimball. He also used this opportunity, as he had in London, to recruit a new generation of young artists to work and learn under the old master. Dick's own daughter Claire played the role of Marcella in the live-action scenes.

However, soon Raggedy Ann's structural weaknesses began to show. Although there were some beautiful pieces of solo animation in the film, particularly Tissa David's "Ragdolly," and Art Babbitt's "Camel Song," there was no real villain or conflict in the show. Merely some kooky characters who get in the way. It played best to very little children, not a big demographic that buys movie tickets. It never really shed its theater roots. Characters would simply stop the plot to sing a big song and then carry on with what they were doing. Joe Raposo had written 16 songs for the film. By contrast, Walt Disney's *Pinocchio* had four. When Dick attempted to cut some songs, the producers overrode his decision. The overly complex designs, drawn on wide screen Panavision cels and paper, stretched the limits of his animators. He clashed with the local NY trade unions over overtime. The NY animation local enforced a 35-hour workweek. Anything beyond was time and a half. When the producers forbade Dick to create animated opening credits, he angrily shut his office door and designed and animated them himself. "I made my name in animated credits. I'll be damned if I'm not going to have them on my first movie!"[9] The budget mushroomed to twice the original estimate from $ 2.5 million to almost $7 million. The producers finally decided to replace Richard Williams with fellow Anglo-Canadian director Gerald Potterton to complete the project. There were many areas where a trained eye could see the cheats and budget cutting. *Raggedy Ann & Andy, A Musical Adventure* opened in April 1977 to tepid reviews and weak Box Office.

One day, during his battles with the producers, Dick came into "The Taffy Pit," where a team of us assistant animators were working on Emery Hawkins' Greedy monster sequence. Because our office was at the far end of our NY office building, Dick would come there to safely vent. "I'm not getting anything out of this!" He grumbled. "The only ones who will come out of all of this with something is YOU! You are getting the best animation education outside of Disneys." And indeed, we knew we were. Many of that young crew went on to long, successful careers in animation. For many years, Dick would not even talk about his experience directing Raggedy Ann and would leave it off his official biography.

Dick went back to England and resumed his work on the *Cobbler and the Thief.* He shut down the New York operation, but he kept his satellite studio in Hollywood to do American commercials. The LA studio on Hollywood Blvd. near Western was originally Quartet Productions, a commercial house owned by Art Babbitt and retiring Tex Avery animator Michael Lah. When I went out to LA and worked for Dick on a spot. I experienced his commercial pattern. With six weeks to create a commercial, Dick would spend most of the time playing his jazz cornet (his other great passion) and eating Vietnamese food. Then the last week, he would emerge from his office looking green, having done several all-nighters to finish. Then, all the rest of us worked equally hard to complete things. Richard Williams never worked people harder than himself. But he worked himself VERY hard. So we all strove to match his energy.

In 1972, a novel by Richard Adams about the lives of rabbits in the wild titled *Watership Down* became an international best seller. Because the story involved realistic animals speaking, any film version had to be animated. Entrepreneur Martin Rosen, who produced the popular British hit *Women in Love (1968),* acquired the rights to the story. He set up an animation studio called Nepenthe, with funding from a consortium of British banks. He hired Oscar-winning animation director John Hubley to direct, but they clashed over the design and tone of the film. Hubley quit after completing a 10-minute intro. Martin Rosen decided to produce, write and direct the film himself. To complete the animation, he relied heavily on Arthur Humberstone (1912–1999), a venerable animator from the J. Arthur Rank days who had previously worked on John Halas' *Animal Farm* and *The Yellow Submarine.* Together they completed *Watership Down* in 1978. It was a great international success, despite its unflinching look at animals dying violently. One critic said it "arguably traumatized an entire generation." Releasing the film just before Easter did not help things. Their next film was Richard Adam's follow-up book, *The Plague Dogs* (1982).[10] This was also an uncomfortable look at animals used in an experimental laboratory. It did well although American audiences did not quite know what to make of its graphic violence. Many of that generation were still used to the idea that animated cartoons were only for children.

Another Hollywood director who liked working in London was Steven Spielberg. He had shot the big ending of *Close Encounters of the Third Kind* there among other films. His friend Jeffrey Katzenberg at Walt Disney had made him aware of a novel they had optioned a few years back by a man named Gary Wolf called *Who Censored Roger Rabbit?* It was an homage to old Raymond Chandler-style film noir, except it was about a detective investigating a murder involving a cartoon character. In this alternative world, animated characters lived and worked alongside humans. Steven Spielberg had a good relationship with Warner Bros since helping them revive their animation division with *Tiny Toons Adventures.* He also worked with Don Bluth and produced his hits *An American Tail* and *The Land Before Time.*[11] Steven agreed to exec produce the film and gave the director's reigns to Robert Zemeckis. Bob Z had just scored big hits with *Romancing the Stone* and *Back to the Future*. There had been an original director attached to the project in LA named Darrell Van Citters. But Darrell and Zemeckis clashed over the project's creative direction, so Disney management removed Darrell and his team from the project.

Roger Rabbit was a joint production between Spielberg's Amblin Entertainment and Walt Disney. In looking for where to create the animation, the Disney people wanted it done on their lot, the Amblin people preferred the Paramount lot, and effects house ILM said they could do it up in Marin County. The compromise was London. For Hollywood power people, London was like Switzerland. Everyone was neutral there. But what about the animation director? Producer Robert Watts showed Steven and Zemeckis a 10-minute teaser promo of *Cobbler and the Thief* that Dick was sending around to try and attract investors. Watts said, "Richard was the guy they wanted from the moment they saw the reel. It had to be Richard or nothing."[12]

Richard Williams formed an animation unit in Camden Town made up of an international crew, half Disney animators and half his own people. He still kept a nominal crew working on The Thief. The team turned in some masterful work, and when *Who Framed Roger Rabbit?* came out, it was the hit of 1988. It was tops at the Box Office and earned Dick two of the film's three Oscars. A sequel was never made because the rights issue impeded an agreed-upon production, and both Bob Zemeckis and Richard Williams wanted to move on to the other projects.

Dick's arrangement with Amblin and Disney was not that they would fund the Thief, only that they would agree to "look" at it. Spielberg looked at it and said that he did not understand it. Jeffrey Katzenberg looked at it and concluded that "it was too weird to ever do well commercially." But Warner Bros had caught the animated blockbuster bug and made a deal with Dick to fund completing the Thief in 5 years for $50 million US.

Steven Spielberg had separated from Don Bluth. He now reorganized the rest of the Roger crew not going with Dick and set up Amblimation in the London suburb of Acton. His directors were two lead Roger Rabbit animators, Simon Wells and Phil Nibbelink. Their first film *American Tale 2: Fieval Goes West* was a moderate success. But their next project, A Comedy of Dinosaurs in Modern Cities, *We're Back, A Dinosaur's Story (1993)*, failed even though it rode on the coattails of Spielberg's *Jurassic Park*. Still more movie animation poured into London. Sequences of Disney's The Goofy Movie, and Disney tried another Williams veteran animator, Richard Purdum, on an early draft of *Beauty and the Beast*. The London visual effects scene was doing very well also. Houses like Mainframe and The Framestore scored major successes with hits like *The Matrix*, etc.

The problem with all of this feature work is its effect on commercial spots. Doing feature length cartoons are a long-term commitment. When you take your team off to animate feature films, you blow off your regular advertising clients, who then go elsewhere. When you are done, they do not usually come back. This is the reason the Bruno Bozzetto Studio in Italy never did a follow-up to their international hit *Allegro Non Troppo (1976)*. They just got in too much commercial work as a result.

At the end of the contracted 5-year period, Richard Williams was still not done with his masterpiece. So the completion bond company contracted with Warner Bros seized the film from Dick on May 19, 1992. There were only 15 minutes of work left to do. They brought the art to Los Angeles, where it was finished off by a TV company in the San Fernando Valley named Fred Calvert Inc. A section was also subcontracted to Don Bluth's studio in Dublin. Old actor Jonathan Winters was brought into improv dialogue over much of the Thief's pantomime. In this truncated form, Warner released it under the name *Arabian Knight*. It did poorly and went quickly to home video. Dick Williams later said to me. "Well, contrary to many of my friends' best wishes, I am NOT suicidal." Dick Williams closed his London studio and moved with his family to an island on the west coast of Canada for a few years. When he emerged, he had written a how-to book on the animation technique "The Animators Survival Guide" and devised a lecture course of instruction that he took around the world. He also completed his own short film "Prologue," which was nominated for an Academy Award in the states and a BAFTA in Britain. Richard Williams died of cancer in 2019 at age 86. He still felt he had a lot left to do.

The waning of the high period of London Animation began with the 12 nations of the European Common Market in February 1992 signing the Treaty of European Union, more commonly called the Maastricht Treaty. The Maastricht Treaty created the European Union, with a single currency, the Euro. In the years since, the 12-nation European Union grew to 27 countries. Most notably, Great Britain refused to junk the English Pound for the Euro, and in 2020 voted to leave the EU altogether.

But what hurt Soho most was with Maastricht, all of those advertising barriers across Europe were thrown down. The aforementioned example of a company importing American corn flakes could now run the same TV spot in all 27 counties. "This dropped the demand for new TV spots by 4/5ths," said Klacto Studio co-director Ted Rockley.[13] This struck at the same time as the new demand for computer-animated spots was surpassing hand-drawn work. Studios that could not or would not make the change were soon left behind. In addition, other nations like Canada and Australia were upping their game to subcontract Hollywood work. Even non-English speaking countries like France and Spain were doing Hollywood films. For instance, Illumination's *Despicable Me* movie franchise (2010–2024) was animated in Montreal, Paris and Budapest, with recording in London and postproduction in Los Angeles. *The Lego Movie* (2014) was animated primarily in Sydney, Australia.

By then, a number of Hollywood studios had some and gone, and a number of films done. *The Goof Troop Movie* for Disney. Freddy as F.R.O. 7. After the film *Balto (1995)* about the sled dog of the Iditarod Alaska race, Steven Spielberg shut down the Amblimation facility in Acton and moved the crew back to California, where they formed the nucleus of the new DreamWorks SKG animation studio. After 2001, Peter Jackson's effects house Weta[14] became a powerhouse to equal ILM and Mainframe thanks to their *Lord of the Rings* movies.

London continues today as a vital center of animation and visual effects. But not as in the glory days of Soho Square.

NOTES

1 Animation pioneers Eadweard Muybridge and James Stuart Blackton were both born in England.
2 Initially, British television worked on a subscription system. You paid a fee to watch the BBC. In 1957, the first channel funded by commercial advertising began. ITV.
3 On Sunday June 9, 1946, *For the Children* premiered with several shows including a magician, Hogarths Puppet Circus and Muffin the Mule.
4 Richard Williams recollection to the author, Hollywood, 1978.
5 Richard Williams recollection to the author, Hollywood, 1978.
6 Quoted in *Adventures in Animation*, by Richard Williams and Imogen Sutton.
7 The project had several names over the years. *The Thief and the Cobbler, Cobbler and the Thief, The Amazing Nasruddin, The Thief Who Never Gave Up. Once . . . .* And more._
8 Abe Levitow (1922–1975) had a long career at Disney, UPA and Chuck Jones Prod. In 1964, he directed the successful *Mr. Magoo's Christmas Carol*, as well as *Gay Purr-ee* and *The Phantom Tollbooth*.
9 Richard Williams to the author, New York, 1977.
10 In 2000, after a long court case, Rosen lost the rights to *Watership Down* and *Plague Dogs* back to the Richard Adams estate.
11 Both films were animated in Dublin, where the tax situation encouraged artists to move there.
12 Ross Anderson, *Pulling a Rabbit Out of a Hat*, pg 40.
13 Ted Rockley to the author, London, 1992.
14 People assume Weta stands for Wellington Entertainment Technologies Association. But it does not. A Weta is a big cricket the size of a baseball that is native to New Zealand.

Japan

5

I can't believe companies distribute my movies in America. They're baffling in Japan!
—Hayao Miyazaki

In the last quarter of the twentieth century, many of the animators of my generation felt driven to try to recreate the glory days of golden age Disney and Warner Bros. But a number of others derived their inspiration from a new directio few of our parents' generation would have considered: Japan.

Japan has had a tradition of drawing and printmaking that reaches back centuries. The prints of artists like Hokusai, Utamaro and Hiroshige were prized by artists like Monet and Daumier. Scholars theorize that the predilection of the Japanese toward picture storytelling stems from the pictographic nature of their calligraphy. Osamu Tezuka said, "I don't consider them pictures. I think of them as a type of hieroglyphics . . . in reality I am not drawing, I am writing a story with a unique type of symbol."[1] The great Russian film director Sergei Eisenstein saw a link between the ideogram and the inherently cinematic nature of Japanese culture. The process of combining several pictographs to express complex thoughts was a form of montage much like the storytelling in movies today.[2] The oldest surviving example of the Japanese drawing anthropomorphized animal characters go back as 1140, the *Chojugiga, Animal Scrolls,* by Bishop Toba. These were being drawn at the same time that West Europeans were fighting the Crusades. The oldest Japanese animation, the *Katsudo Shashin*, dates back to 1907, contemporary with Emile Cohl and Winsor McCay. Like many industrialized nations, the Japanese were avid fans of cinema. The first animated feature by Mitsuyo Seo, *Momotaro's Sacred Sea Warriors* (1943), was staged more like a live-action war movie than a typical Hollywood cartoon. Early films were subsidized by the military to present a strong pro-nationalist message. In Kenzo Masaoka's *The Spider and the Tulip* (1943), a spider tries to lure a little ladybug into his web to devour her. The spider is dressed as an Al Jolson blackfaced minstrel representing the seductive charm of American jazz culture, while the little ladybug is an innocent Japanese child. In the *Momotaro* ("Peach Boy") films, we see them defeating obvious caricatures of Popeye and Bluto.[3]

By 1945, the politics of World War II encouraged most Americans to dismiss Japanese culture as backward, barbaric and cruel. The Pearl Harbor surprise attack, the depredations inflicted on Chinese cities, and more fanatical aspects of the Japanese Warrior Code, Bushido, outraged many Americans. The war in Europe was seen as a crusade against Hitler and his Nazi regime. After all, how could the people who gave us Beethoven, Einstein and plastics be so cruel? It must be purely politics. While the war

DOI: 10.1201/b22394-6

in the Pacific was portrayed more racist in nature. Despite the contributions of Japanese Americans to the war effort, U.S. propaganda encouraged us to think the whole of Japanese society was out to kill us. The complete victory of 1945 seemed to justify Americans' feelings of cultural superiority.

As the Japanese under occupation cleared away the rubble and began to rebuild, one segment that flourished was newspaper comic strips and comic books called **manga**. While most average Japanese could not afford a theater ticket or a radio, print was an easy source of distraction from the hardships of life during reconstruction. As the western powers built up Japanese industry and manufacturing to become a bulwark of capitalism against the communist nations like China, North Korea, and The Soviet Union, the rapidly urbanizing Japanese workforce enjoyed reading their manga stories while commuting to and from work.

The Toei Company (TMS)[4] began in 1949 as a movie/TV studio. They started an animation division in 1956 and avoiding older artists who worked on wartime propaganda, they concentrated on hiring and training new talent from schools. Animators called it Toei University because they trained so many future animators. In 1958, they released their first full-color animated feature film, *Panda and the Magic Snake*, directed by Yabushita Taiji. It was based on an old fairy tale from the Chinese Song Dynasty, but the look owed a lot to Walt Disney's *Snow White and the Seven Dwarfs*. A strong female lead surrounded by cute, funny little characters. It was released in the USA in 1961 but did not do very well. Still, it inspired young student Hayao Miyazaki to get into animation.

The first important Japanese animator was Osamu Tezuka (1928–1989). He has been called the Japanese Walt Disney and The Great God of Manga. In 1941, at the age of 16, he saw the Chinese animated feature *Princess Iron Fan* by Wai Laiming.[5] This inspired him to become a cartoonist and animator. He began drawing manga comic stories in 1947, starting with *New Treasure Island, Kimba the White Lion, Phoenix, Princess Knight* and *Tetsuan Atom*, which became *Astro Boy* in the West. Osamu Tezuka was greatly influenced by Walt Disney cartoons. He claimed to have watched *Bambi* more than 80 times! He said films like *Bambi* are what gave him the inspiration to give his characters such large eyes. He mixed his love of Walt Disney with the traditional iconography of the Kabuki and Noh theater to create a uniquely Japanese style of animation.

In 1960, Osamu Tezuka went to Toei Studio's animation division to storyboard and direct *Saiyuki, A Journey to the West*. He clashed with a number of creative and production types there and wound up eventually leaving the project. It was completed by Yabushita Taiji and Daisaku Shirakawa, although Tezuka contractually received the director credit. Released in the West as *Alakazam the Great* (1960), it was the first animated feature to feature Tezuka's simplified graphic design style for characters and movement that we recognize today as classic Japanese Anime.

Osamu Tezuka now set up his own studio, Mushi Productions, and produced a number of popular shows for television. In 1963, he developed his *Astro Boy* as a TV series and made a deal with the American network NBC to show it in the USA. He followed that with *Kimba the White Lion* and several more series. Other studios and animators inspired by Tezuka's work created their own series, and the 1960s anime industry boomed.[6]

American animation producers wondered if they might utilize this highly skilled yet relatively cheap labor force in Japan, Taiwan and Korea. Animation artists in Japan

FIGURE 5.1   *Alakazam the Great* (1960).

were paid ¼ of what their counterparts in Hollywood were paid. The Japanese system of farming out work to be paid by the foot instead of hourly made it even cheaper. In the 1960s, American studios like Jay Ward had experimented with getting their TV shows animated in Mexico and in Canada. Hanna-Barbera worked out a relationship with TMS among others to complete their shows. These contacts continued into the 1990s when Japan's own successful economy made their cartoons too expensive, so studios moved their work to places like Vietnam and India.

At the same time, artists like Takao Saito (1936–2021) disliked manga and anime's simplified designs and same old fairy tales and wanted to go into darker, more adult subjects. Saito disliked being called a Manga artist. He and his type called their style Gekika or Theatrical Images. His big hit was *Golgo 13*, published in 1968.

On June 15, 1985, Studio Ghibli was founded, headed by the directors Hayao Miyazaki, Isao Takahata and producer Toshio Suzuki. The studio was founded after the success of the 1984 film *Nausicaä of the Valley of the Wind*, written and directed by Miyazaki for Topcraft and distributed by the Toei Company. The name Ghibli was coined by Hayao Miyazaki. Miyazaki was the son of an aircraft designer and had grown up around airplanes. The name was in reference to the Caproni Ca.309 Ghibli airplane. The Italian noun "ghibli" is based on the Arabic name for the sirocco or Mediterranean wind. He said the Ghibli studio would "blow a new wind through the anime industry."[7]

Even though Japanese animation was very popular at home and in neighboring Asian countries in the 1960s, it struggled to gain a foothold in the North American market. American media networks felt the Japanese series were too "culturally specific" and too exotic to attract a mainstream American audience. The Japanese style of animating mouths was a bit too off-putting for Americans accustomed to animation like Mickey Mouse and Bugs Bunny. Japanese lipsync was always limited because the show was going to be redubbed from Japanese to Mandarin, Cantonese, Korean and Malay. Rather than large TV networks like NBC, Japanese programs like *Astro Boy, Gigantor,*

FIGURE 5.2 Studio Ghibli founders, Hayao Miyazaki, Toshio Suzuki and Isao Takahata. Courtesy of Yasuki Hamano.

8th Man and Speed Racer were shown on smaller unaffiliated TV stations on off-peak times like Sunday mornings. Even though Japanese anime always had its niche audience of die-hard fans (called in Japanese *otaku*), mainstream American society was not that interested. To be fair, the French, Italian and German animation industries also had difficulty breaking into the American market.

That began to change in the 1980s. As mainstream society pluralized, Americans of different colors and cultural backgrounds looked for heroes and role models different from the white Christian icons they had been force-fed for so long. The strong moral code and societal discipline of Japanese society provided an alternative to many. And many got to know Japanese culture through the new technology of video games.

The first interactive game SpaceWar! was created by MIT graduate students in 1962. It required a massive mainframe computer just to operate. So, it remained mostly a novel distraction for scientists after hours. In 1972, Ralph Baer invented the first console game, the Magnavox Odyssey, and out in Sunnyvale California, Nolan Bushnell and his engineer Alan Alcorn invented Pong. The fame of these games spread across the world, and naturally, the huge Japanese electronics industry wanted in on the action. The Nintendo Company had formed in 1849 to make hand-painted playing cards. In the 1950s, the company moved into electronics, making pachinko games. Sort of a slot-machine game you played at specific stores, pachinko parlors. When they saw the mania for Pong, Nintendo and their competitors began creating games of their own. Their first big hit was *Donkey Kong*. Nintendo avoided the great video-game crash of 1983 by gambling on the emerging market of home computers while Anglo-American companies stuck with video arcades. Engineer Gunpei Yokoi invented a video game player you could carry in your pocket. He called it a Game Boy. He loaded several games on it like the Russian stacking blocks game Tetris.[8] Soon on many city trains and buses, commuters had Game

Boys instead of reading the morning newspaper. When smartphone technology came in 2007, Nintendo games moved easily onto that format. When before American companies felt Japanese titles were too exotic for mainstream Americans, by the 1990s, they were all enjoying *Pokémon, Digimon, Sonic the Hedgehog and Dragon Ball Z.*

On July 16, 1988, the same summer as *Who Framed Roger Rabbit* and Don Bluth's *The Land Before Time*, Katsuhiro Otomo's film *Akira* premiered in Tokyo. It opened

FIGURE 5.3 *Akira* (1988).

in America a year later. It was the first Japanese Anime film to go beyond the domestic and niche otaku fan base and appeal to a wide global audience. This was followed by Miyazaki's *Princess Mononoke, The Castle of Cagliostro* and Mamoru Oshii's *Ghost in the Shell*. Isao Takahata even reached back to World War II memories of Hiroshima for his poignant *Grave of the Fireflies*. This was when people collected movies at home on VHS video cassettes. I recall seeing in my local Blockbuster Video Store one lone copy of Akira. Pretty soon, more titles filled the shelf. By the following year, there was an entire wall of titles under the label Anime.

In 2003, Miyazaki's *Spirited Away* won the Academy Award for Best Animated Feature. Defeating *Lilo and Stitch, Ice Age, Treasure Planet and Spirit Stallion of the Cimarron.*

The film was unapologetically Japanese. A film filled with enigmatic spirits, sprites and creatures unique to Japanese mythology. But world audiences loved it anyway.

Miyazaki said. "I can't believe companies distribute my movies in America. They're baffling in Japan! I'm well aware there are spots . . . where I'm going to lose the audience . . . Well, it's magic. I don't provide unnecessary explanations. If you want that, you're not going to like my movie. That's just the way it is."

FIGURE 5.4 Animators' graffiti on the walls of a coffee shop near Studio I.G. Tokyo. (collection of the author)

But we did come to like it. Since then, an entire generation has been raised on anime and games on their smartphones. By 2025, it seems more young people know who Hayao Miyazaki is than know who Chuck Jones was.

NOTES

1 Frederik Schodt, *Manga! Manga! The World of Japanese Comics*, pg 25.
2 Frederik Schodt, *Manga! Manga! The World of Japanese Comics*, pg 25.
3 American cartoon studios did equally negative caricatures of Japanese people in *Bugs Bunny Nips the Nips* and *Tokyo Jokyo*.
4 Later renamed Tokyo Movie Shinsha or TMS.
5 Although animation in China got an earlier start with *Princess Iron Fan*, the Chinese animation industry was not allowed to develop due to the political climate. Civil Wars, the Warlord Period and The Japanese invasion held back the development of a domestic animation industry until after the Cultural Revolution of the 1970s.
6 When Osamu Tezuka was dying of cancer in 1989, his last words were to a nurse, "Go away! I'm trying to work."
7 Hayao Miyazaki, *Starting Point*, 1979–1996
8 Tetris was created by Soviet engineer Alexi Pajitnov in 1984.

Education
The Struggle to Pass the Torch

6

Walt is dead. You missed it.

—Ward Kimball to students

Winston Churchill once observed, "Art without tradition is like sheep without a shepherd." Animation, like any art form, needs to regenerate periodically with new generations of artists in order to keep growing and evolving into the future. Part of that generational growth requires training neophytes in the traditions of what came before, in order to build upon the collective memory in order to create new works. Like the old maxim goes, "We can see far when we stand on the shoulders of giants." Thus, Michelangelo learned fresco painting while apprenticed under Domenico Ghirlandaio, NC Wyeth learned painting from Howard Pyle and Glen Keane learned animation under Ollie Johnston. As with all new media, it took a generation or so before a regular curriculum of education could be established for the training of new animators.

Animation began as a trick film novelty, and as it became associated with newspaper cartoons, it attracted scores of young cartoonists. Some of these artists studied in serious drawing schools like the Art Student's League of NY or the Art Institute of Chicago. Grim Natwick took advantage of the post-Great War strength of the U.S. dollar to study drawing at the École des Beaux-Arts in Paris. Some had no training at all, just some talent at drawing funny characters. Beyond the singular genius of a Winsor McCay, most animators in the Silent Era acquired just enough technique to get paid, and that was it. Walt Disney first learned animation from a book he found in the public library.[1] Animators like Otto Mesmer and Earl Hurd streamlined the print cartoon designs to make them easier to draw repeatedly for animation. Peanut-shaped bodies and three fingers with a thumb on each hand. Most rendering techniques like crosshatching or stipple were dropped as impractical. Then as far as the animation-timing technique goes, you picked up what you could on the job as you went along. By the end of the Silent Era, many staff animators discouraged innovation among their peers. Do just enough to get paid. That is why so much animation from that time looked the

DOI: 10.1201/b22394-7

FIGURE 6.1   Eric Larson going over Andreas Deja's work.

(courtesy of Hans Bacher)

same. The quaint "rubber-hose" style. Professional animators referred to their business as, "The Racket." Small wonder in 1934, when old Winsor McCay was honored with a banquet by the industry, he did so much to build, and he dismissed them all by saying, "I gave you boys an art form and you turned it into a business. A trade! Too bad."[2]

By the early 1930s, Walt Disney's Mickey Mouse shorts had moved him to the forefront of his competitors. Walt wanted to improve the overall quality of his films. Especially if he intended to eventually do feature films. To gage the challenge to come in 1934, he made *The Goddess of Spring*, a Silly Symphony attempting to draw realistic human beings. It was terrible and proved to Walt that if he ever wanted to create a successful film with believable human characters, his artists needed to up their game. Walt heard his young animators Art Babbitt and Bill Tytla had on their own been paying to hire a model for weekly life drawing sessions at their house after work. Walt brought these life drawing classes into the studio and engaged a professional life drawing teacher, Donald Graham, to teach his team. Graham was affiliated with LA's local drawing school, the Chouinard Art Institute. Walt Disney liked the results he was getting with Don so much that he soon had him looking at portfolios and sent him on a nationwide talent hunt for new artists. Disney formed a working relationship with Nellie Chouinard and the Chouinard Institute, exchanging faculty and facilities. Walt had decided it would be easier to train some young people from school to be animators

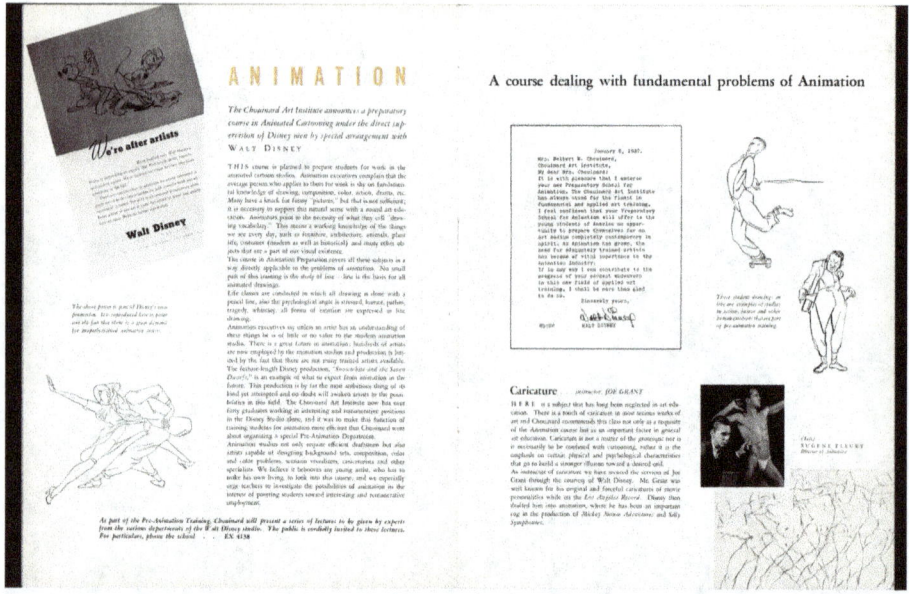

FIGURE 6.2   Brochure for Chouinard's Disney classes 1937.

rather than rely on the old pros to make the effort to improve. The way he explained it to Fleischer vet Shamus Culhane, *"We've just hired three or four fellows out of New York, and most of them are bringing a lot of goddamn poor working habits from doing cheap pictures. I've decided to take in more kids right out of school and train them my way. It's a lot easier than trying to retrain somebody who's used to doing crap."*[3] Walt Disney sponsored several of his animators like Marc Davis and Joe Grant to teach their own classes at Chouinard in 1937. This can be considered the earliest animation courses to be taught in a school. Many artists who came out of that school were grateful for the start it gave them. Animation director Bob Kurtz said, *"If there is a Heaven, I hope they have a Chouinard there."*[4]

At this time in mainstream academia, there were no college-level animated film courses yet, because animation and moviemaking in general were looked down on as vulgar, low-class entertainment. "The Flickers." When Dick Huemer told his Bronx mother he intended to draw cartoons for a living, she exclaimed, "Grown men! From THIS you are making a living?" At Max Fleischer Studio, animator Bill Buckner held training courses for young artists like Jacob Kupferberg, who would one day leave animation for comic books and become Jack Kirby.[5]

In 1928, the University of Southern California (USC) started the first university-level program in motion pictures, "Introduction to Photoplay," with the sponsorship of some top movie stars like Douglas Fairbanks and Mary Pickford. The first chair of the USC film department, Dr. Boris Morkovin, had a PhD in psychology and sociology from the University of Prague. He had no practical experience with filmmaking, but this was at a time when most academic classes were more focused on theory than practice. Prof. Morkovin's background provided a platform for him to develop the science of demographics.[6] He was impressed by the quality of Mickey Mouse cartoons, and in 1932, he included them in his own lectures on cinema humor. The first true animation instruction on a university level. High-school dropout Walt Disney was flattered by the praise from such a high-falootin' Russian professor. Disney story artist Homer Brightman recalled," *Walt (Disney) was really impressed with people who had a college education, because he didn't. He took a fancy to certain people and promoted them, though they might not know anything about the work."*[7] Walt Disney actually put Boris Morkovin on his payroll for a time to lecture his team on humor the way Don Graham was then teaching drawing. Unfortunately, much of Dr. M's high academic style of lecturing went over the heads of most of the animators. Shamus Culhane recalled, "We didn't understand anything he said."[8]

Beyond Don Graham and Boris Morkovin, Walt brought in guests like Frank Lloyd Wright, Charlie Chaplin, H.G. Wells, Sergei Eisenstein and more to meet his artists and talk about their technique. He would drive his team in his own jalopy to an "art house" movie theater on Fairfax to see the latest experimental and avant-garde films like Luis Bunuel's *Un Chien Andalou* and the Dreyer's *The Passion of Joan of Arc.*[9]

Walt Disney's competing with pure quality to improve his cartoons caused the other studios to try to match him, and by the late 1930s, all of the studios were pumping out markedly better-quality films than before. It was the Golden Age of Animation. Much of this training came to an end with World War II. But some of it was renewed after the war but severely limited due to the lean postwar times. By then, most of that generation of animators' mature technique was set. Drawing courses would now be followed less rigorously, more about polish than retraining. The animation union conducted night classes. Young artists relied on correspondence schools like The Famous Artists School begun in 1948, who conducted drawing and painting courses through the mail.[10] As the 1950s wore on and the big studio units shrank or were phased out, the industry relied more and more on a core of professional animators who moved from studio to studio. For example, Bill Littlejohn, who started in 1933 in New York, went on to animate for MGM, Walter Lantz, Warner Bros, UPA, Storyboard Prod., Jay Ward, Bill Melendez Prod, Film Roman and Heavy Metal: the Movie.

In 1969, young animator Mark Kausler moved out to LA from Kansas City, precisely like Walt Disney had done 47 years earlier, to follow his dream to be an animation cartoonist. He went straight to the Chouinard Institute to learn from the master artists as they had in the past. But once there, he discovered Chouinard was run down and going out of business. Don Graham had long since retired. Walt Disney had died, and his brother Roy was overseeing completion of a project he had been planning for a decade. A new college north of the LA County line that combined the resources of Chouinard and the LA Conservatory of Music called The California Institute of the Arts.

By the early 1970s, when the Greatest Generation retired, who would replace them? At an international animation festival in Montreal in 1967, Shamus Culhane, now an elder statesman, echoed his generation's despair when he rhetorically asked, "Twenty years from now, who will you hire?"

By then, Shamus was teaching animation at The School of Visual Arts in New York. Silas Rhodes and Burne Hogarth began it in 1947 as the Cartoonists and Illustrators School and changed its name to Visual Arts to broaden its curricula to include courses in film, video and sculpture. It boasted teachers like Harvey Kurtzman, Will Eisner, Milton Glaser and Howard Beckerman. The New York Public School system then boasted an impressive system of vocational oriented high schools like The High School of Performing Arts, Music & Art, Art & Design and The Fashion Institute of Technology. When I went to Art and Design, I was able to take courses in cartooning and animation as early as the 10th grade. Upon graduating in 1973, I looked around for a college that taught animation. There was not much. There was CalArts in LA, and UCLA had started a workshop under former Bill Tytla and assistant Bill Schull, soon to be succeeded by his protégé Dan McLaughlin. My animator friends Eric Goldberg and David Silverman attended Pratt Institute.

Sheridan College in Ontario was created in 1968. It had an animation program that turned out many fine artists, even though the demand for animators domestically was quite limited beyond the National Film Board (NFB). And the NFB preferred hiring international high-profile filmmakers. When working at many studios outside of Canada, it was not unusual to see many Canadian artists on staff.

When I got to Hollywood in the late 1970s, much of professional animation was still being taught master-to-apprentice in small groups. The animation union MPSC #839 held regular night classes taught by professionals. At Hanna-Barbera, new recruits took Harry Love's class. Harry Love (1911–1997) was a career animator who worked at many of the major studios. At HB, he trained many young talents in the art of TV animation production until his own retirement in 1989. Disney animator Art Babbitt (1907–1992) taught regularly at HB, the union and other schools like USC. Even at Richard Williams' London Studio (see Chapter 4), Dicks notes from Art's lectures were copied and xeroxed endlessly by their proteges. The Babbit Notes were the mostly widely read unpublished animation book of all time. Interestingly, Art Babbitt was never invited to CalArts. The Disney family, who were its primary backers, retained Walt's animus toward Art because of his leadership of the great Disney Strike in 1941.[11]

While at Hanna-Barbera in 1978 a friend told me, "Have you heard of Benny's Class?" It was an open secret that the first Tuesday of the month Chuck Jones animation star Ben Washam (1915–1984) gave lessons at his home in Laurel Canyon. At the appointed time, Ben would hold court in his garage, regaling all us youngsters with stories of his career while demonstrating for us the finer points of classic Hollywood character animation. He tutoring was so good, I once asked him why he did not charge or do this in a college? He explained that "animation has been good to me, and I want to give something back."

When The California Institute of the Arts was created, the initial idea was not to train future studio cartoon animators, but to develop conceptual artists and filmmakers. CalArts' first president Robert Corrigan came over from NYU Tisch School of the Arts and Provost Herbert Blau from Lincoln Center's repertory company. The school quickly gained a reputation for wild experimentation. The world of art in the broader sense was then dominated by Abstract Expressionism and Pop Art. Nonlinear, nonobjective work.

FIGURE 6.3   CalArts Course Announcement with Michael Scroggins 1972.

Rothko, Pollock and Warhol. Universities adopted the Black Mountain College form of open curricula over rigid rule lessons. Teaching realism was seen as kitsch and old-fashioned. The director of the Animation Program, Jules Engel, was a well-known art director at the studios like UPA. He was also an iconoclast who stressed experimentation. Underwater music concerts, mushroom hunting expeditions and overlooking lots of skinny dipping in the dorm swimming pool.

On the more serious side, when artists first began to experiment with computers to create art and music, CalArts embraced the emerging technologies. Courses were offered and taught by experimental animators Vibeke Sorensen and John Whitney. Faculty like Jules Engel, Christine Panushka and Michael Scroggins sat to learn the new tools. After a lesson, Jules rubbed his hands together and would say *"Now, how can we do things differently? I'm just interested in making mistakes, because that's where you find the limits."*[12]

Down in Burbank, the Disney animation department, which until now had not taken training seriously, suddenly realized they needed to do more than just letting some old geezer use their lunch hour to regale young pups "How we did it in the old days." They needed to train new talent before their studio turned into a senior citizen's center. So, in 1975, they moved their nascent training program up to CalArts and dubbed it The Disney Program, later Character Animation. It functioned as a separate but equal department to the Experimental Division. The faculty were all studio veterans like Elmer Plummer, Thorton "Tee" Hee, and Bill Moore. Turns out not every great animator could teach. Disney legend Ward Kimball (Jiminy Cricket) told the assembled young talent, "Walt's dead. You missed it."

That first 1975 Disney Program Class became famous as the incubator of much of the key talent of the Toon Renaissance. Tim Burton, Brad Bird, Mike Giaimo, John Lasseter, John Musker, Jerry Rees, Mike Peraza and Henry Selick. Their classroom A113 became a beloved inside joke (easter egg) in movies. Since Brad Bird slipped it into his *Family Dog* episode of Steven Spielberg's *Amazing Stories*, it has since appeared over and over in American films and TV series.

As these artists moved into leadership positions, they tended to hire talent from CalArts since they already knew and trusted their training. By the 1980s, it was said that you could not hope to get hired at Disney or Pixar without first going to CalArts.[13]

In the 1960s, the "trendy elective" at universities was psychology. In the 1970s' it was film theory. By the 1990s with the animation renaissance in full swing, many colleges got serious about animation studies. The Vancouver Film School, Savannah College of Design, Ringling College in Florida and NYU Tisch School of the Arts under Oscar-winning filmmaker John Canemaker, all set up degree programs. With the evolution of interactive games, many schools have developed game platform education.

USC film school had run animation courses since the 1930s as electives of the cinema production department. Teachers like Art Babbitt, Bill Melendez (*A Charlie Brown Christmas*), Gene Coe and Les Novros (*2001: A Space Odyssey*). One of the young film student George Lucas' first films was animation, moving photos under a down-shooter camera (*Look at Life*, 1965). In 1994, USC finally established an MFA degree in animation taught by Dr. Richard Weinberg and Disney animator Tom Sito. Since 2009, USC's interactive games division was many years considered a leader in the industry.

With animation processes become central to the development of digital media and games, such growth will only continue and spread into the future.

WALT DISNEY PRODUCTIONS

500 SO. BUENA VISTA ST. • BURBANK, CALIFORNIA 91521
(213) 845-3141 • CABLE ADDRESS: DISNEY

June 13, 1975

Miss Nancy Beiman
124 Mohawk Drive
Cranford, New Jersey 07016

Dear Miss Beiman:

In view of your still being only seventeen years old and the fact that you
have evidenced an interest in further education which we surely think wise,
I took the liberty of showing your work to Mr. Jack Hannah who will head a
new classical or character animation school at the California Institute of
the Arts at nearby Valencia, California. Jack is interested in having you
in his beginning group, and I understand he will be talking to you on the
telephone soon.

Perhaps it would be well for me to tell you that this new school at CalArts
is funded independantly from the rest of the school. It is being established
at the urging of our studio animation people, and it will specialize in our
kind of animation as opposed to the graphic animation CalArts has produced
in the past.

It is anticipated that this first class will be composed of under twenty
students. The curriculum while aimed at fundamental art will result in a
B.F.A. degree with a major in classical animation. The graduate should be
ready to enter many art fields even if he should never work in animation.
The faculty is being very carefully selected and it is our intention at the
studio to assist Mr. Hannah in any way we can - tours, lectures, personal
contact or whatever proves most helpful. We are interested in quality, not
quantity, and in today's world of education, this interest is not always
evident.

I hope that things work out for you to attend this new CalArts school, but
regardless, we are interested in your development and hope you stay in touch
with us. We do have a talent development program in the Animation Department, but we prefer you to have a little more formal education and age before
discussing it with you. However, I will enclose a brochure you may find
interesting.

I intend to hold your portfolio for a few days in case Mr. Hannah desires
to show it to others, and I will write you again when it is returned.

Sincerely,

Don A. Duckwall
Animation Production Manager

DAD/pl
Encl.-1

FIGURE 6.4 Nancy Beiman Letter 1975.

(Courtesy of Nancy Beiman)

FIGURE 6.5   The CalArts Disney Program students with instructor Elmer Plummer 1976. Jerry Rees, Harry Sabin, Michael Cedeno, Nancy Beiman, Brad Bird, Doug Ikler and John Musker.

(Courtesy CalArts Archive)

NOTES

1   The book was *Animated Cartoons - How They Are Made, Their Origin and Development* by Edwin Lutz, 1920.
2   Shamus Culhane in conversation with the author, 1979, Jack Ozark to the author, 1984.
3   Shamus Culhane, *Talking Animals and Other People*, pg 110.
4   Bob Kurtz to the author.
5   Jack Kirby became a top artist at Marvel Comics, defining characters like The Fantastic Four, Thor and the Hulk.
6   Daniel Starch and George Gallup pioneered consumer market research in the 1920s. Hollywood studios then had a system of showing rough cuts of films to selected test audiences to gage their reactions. Stan Laurel had a stagehand with a stopwatch time how long an audience laughed at a joke. Boris Morkovin was the first to hand out questionnaire cards and evaluate the results scientifically.
7   Homer Brightman, *Life in the Mouse House*, pg 69.
8   Shamus Culhane, *Talking Animals and Other People*, pg 110.
9   Marc Davis to the author, 1991.
10   The Famous Artists School most well-known instructor was painter Norman Rockwell.
11   In 1991, shortly before his death, Art Babbitt and Roy E. Disney buried the hatchet.
12   Vibeke Sorensen quoted in Sito, *Moving Innovation, a History of Computer Animation*, pg 70.
13   This was not unique. George Lucas tended to hire people from his alma mater USC and so forth.

Moguls, Mavericks and Movie Brats

7

Do I own this, too?
> —Ted Turner in an art supply store across the street from Hanna-Barbera Studio

After the old studio merry-go-round broke down, and its remnants swallowed up by large corporations, the 1970s and 1980s saw the emergence of a new kind of power brokers in Hollywood. The Movie Mogul and The Movie Brats. Movie Moguls were private businessmen buying their way into show business. As a practice, this was nothing new. In the early years of Hollywood banker Joseph Kennedy, theater owner Joseph Schenk, newspaper baron William Randolph Hearst, and aircraft tycoon Howard Hughes were among those daring young capitalists who wanted to produce movies, date beautiful movie queens and be seen at all the right nightclubs. In the 1980s, the new generation of business tycoons did not just want to invest in a particular film project; they gobbled up whole studios, cutting them up or schmooshing them together like children's playdough. Sumner Redstone, Ted Turner and Akio Morita. While Sumner Redstone of Viacom and Akio Morita of Sony stayed away from direct meddling in their animation productions, Ted Turner enjoyed playing Walt Disney.

Ted Turner's career began when he inherited his father's outdoor billboard company, Turner Outdoor Advertising after his dad committed suicide in 1963. In 1970, he bought an Atlanta TV station and started Turner Broadcasting. In 1980, he started Cable News Network, CNN, in Atlanta. It advanced a radical idea of 24-hour news programming. "You give us twenty minutes, we'll give you the world." This was successful because it addressed the need for modern businesspeople who traveled around the world and wanted to hear timely news in American English. The Lingua-Franca of modern business. CNN news established a reputation for integrity with Ted acting like a new Bill Paley or David Sarnoff.[1] Ted also indulged his love of old Hollywood movies by buying up neglected film archives and sought to build new audiences for old black and white movies by using digital technologies to colorize them. He was called "Raider of the Lost Archive." At first, his colorizing of Bing Crosby's *Going My Way* (1944) and some Laurel & Hardy short comedies were welcomed. But when he announced he would colorize Citizen Kane (1941), he was denounced by filmmakers like Martin Scorsese and Woody Allen.[2] Orson Welles on his deathbed said, "Keep Ted Turner and his crayons away from my movies!"[3] Ultimately, Ted got the message and instead used

DOI: 10.1201/b22394-8

his resources to digitally preserve many classic films for the future. He began the TV channels TNT (Turner Network Television), AMC American Classic Movies, and TCM Turner Classic Movies. Then he went into independent production of his own films with Turner Broadcasting System (TBS). This was his production company based out of his base in Atlanta, Georgia, wanting to make old Dixie into a new Hollywood. Part of his strategy was to also include animation.

Ted Turner began in 1990 by creating an animated TV program with a strong environmental message entitled *Captain Planet and the Planeteers*. It ran first at TBS, later in the waning days of the Saturday Morning lineup, *Captain Planet* ran on CBS. The show got strong ratings and was very popular. At this time, other than Walt Disney Studios' policy of owning every print of their animated films, most old Hollywood studios treated their shorts like old junk. Fleischer (Paramount), Universal, MGM and Warner Bros' Looney Tunes were dumped unceremoniously on small distributors and local TV stations. Ted Turner now bought up all of these shorts. He collected up and reunited all of the old Looney Tunes and MGM shorts together for the first time in 30 years. He also made sure that they were cleaned up and digitally restored. Ted Turner did not accumulate all of these old cartoons and old cartoonists solely out of disinterested preservation. He had a bigger idea in mind. Ted hired Betty Cohen from Nickelodeon and asked her to create a channel to handle all his animation properties. In 1991, Ted Turner bought Hanna-Barbera Studios from parent Taft Enterprises.[4] Bill Hanna, Joseph Barbera and senior staff like Iwao Takamoto continued on as staff. By then, Bill and Joe were in their 80s and unable to run things day-to-day. So, Ted Turner gave the helm of HB to producer Fred Seibert.

Walt Disney had launched a cable station to show their stuff in the 1980s. In 1987, Swiss firm L'Oreal Nestle engineered a takeover of the studio Filmation because it wanted its film library for the 24-hour European network SkyTV. Ted's Cartoon Network was launched on October 1, 1992 and was an immediate success. An entire new generation of kids fell in love with the old cartoons and the newer shows that the re-energized HB was creating like *Power Puff Girls*. *Teen Titans Go*, and *Adventure Time*. Later, when Turner merged with Warner Bros, some WB execs wanted to phase out the Hanna-Barbera masthead on the shows. They were convinced not to by the Cartoon Network people. They argued that all of the new young viewers have now come to love and trust the HB brand name as their favorite cartoons.

Ted Turner also tried to get in on the success of animated features in 1993 by having Hanna-Barbera create a feature with an environmental theme called *Once Upon a Forrest*. Directed by Charlie Grosvenor. In 1991, he formed a unit separate from HB called Turner Feature Animation. They produced films like *The Pagemaster, Flash and Dash*, and *Cats Don't Dance*. *Cats Don't Dance (1997)* was produced by David Kirschner (*An American Tail*), directed by Mark Dindal (*Emperor's New Groove*), art direction by Brian McEntee (*Beauty and the Beast*) and music by Randy Newman (*Toy Story*). *Cat's Don't Dance* was a witty send-up of classic MGM musicals, with the classic MGM star Gene Kelly as dance consultant in what became his last work. *Pagemaster* and *Cats Don't Dance* were moderately successful but not the kind of blockbusters like *The Lion King, An American Tail* and *Beauty and the Beast* were.

61st year   Wednesday, October 23, 1991   75¢ *(California)* $1.25 *(Elsewhere)*

Turner ready to wrap H-B deal

AFM crowd still counting on boost from latecomers

• Related stories on page 7.

By ROBERT MARICH

Though hall traffic was light, the American Film Market registered solid, although not spectacular business in its second day Tuesday, with many distributors expecting business to pick up later this week.

A wave of movie execs is expected to wash ashore later this week at AFM in Santa Monica from MIFED, the competing market in Milan. The migration is expected to boost the second half of the AFM, which runs until Sunday.

So far at AFM, which is being held at the Loews Santa Monica Hotel, activity seems to be building.

— continued on page 2

Japanese find MIFED lacking

• Related stories on page 6.

By JAMES ULMER

MILAN, Italy — Poor business and low expectations have given a twist to the outlook for Japanese buyers at this year's MIFED: While they've come out in force this time around, next year they may have to be forced to come out.

"I doubt whether it was worthwhile for us even to have come over

— continued on page 6

Griffith sisters set to make 'Eyes'

By GREG PTACEK

Melanie Griffith is set to star in "The Eyes of the World," along with her sister Tracy Griffith, who wrote the script for Taurus Entertainment.

Scheduled to begin production next summer for release in late fall 1992, the feature film marks the first

— continued on page 2

But $300 million buyout still leaves Kirschner role unclear

By STEVE BRENNAN

A $300 million deal by cable mogul Ted Turner to buy Hanna-Barbera will become final by the end of the week with an announcement as soon as Friday, according to sources.

Completion of the deal, which has been subject to a preliminary agreement since early September (HR 9/3), reportedly follows a move under which a major bulk of animated product reverts from distributor Worldvision back to the Hanna-Barbera library. The completion will leave the door open to Turner's plans for a global kids cable channel (HR 9/27).

The deal with Worldvision involves a straight cash payment as well as the Quinn Martin library, with ownership of such evergreens as "The Streets of San Francisco," "The F.B.I." and "Barnaby Jones" going to Worldvision. Hanna-Barbera currently owns the library, which is distributed by Worldvision.

— continued on page 2

Baseball CBS' hit Series; 'Jackie' NBC's first lady

By LISA de MORAES

CBS hit a grand slam with four top-10 postseason baseball games the week of Oct. 14-20, scoring a first-place 15.3 rating/25 share overall, according to A.C. Nielsen Co. figures out Tuesday.

NBC was second at 13.3/22 — its best weekly numbers of the five-week-old season — thanks to a Jackie Onassis miniseries and the return of "Matlock." ABC ranked third with a 12.1/20. And FBC pulled in a 7.9/13 for the week — the only network competing against CBS' Major League Baseball coverage that managed to gain in weekly averages vs. the previous week.

Sunday's Game 2 of the Atlanta Braves-Minnesota Twins World Series was the most-watched show of the week, scoring a 21.7/34. That rating was flat compared with Game 2 last year (21.8/37).

Next in the baseball lineup was

— continued on page 22

ShowEast opens; attendance and spirits are strong

By DORIS TOUMARKINE

ATLANTIC CITY, N.J. — Only hours into Tuesday's opening day of ShowEast's annual convention and trade show at Trump's Taj Mahal, the number of registrants was up 15% over last year to a record of nearly 1,300, and the mood, in spite of boxoffice doldrums, was upbeat.

"With the summer we've had, you can only feel hopeful and think something will happen," an exhibitor said.

Confirming what the attendance

— continued on page 16

Russell president Multimedia Prods.

Neil Russell has been officially named president of Multimedia Entertainment's newest division, Multimedia Television Prods., formerly Carolco Television Prods.

Multimedia Entertainment acquired Carolco Television Prods. in September, renaming the division

— continued on page 16

British Institute rings alarm over film prod'n woes

By EDWIN RIDDELL

LONDON — The British Film Institute has called for urgent government action to tackle the crisis in the industry.

At a press conference Tuesday, the BFI revealed the results of three damning new surveys into the state of U.K. film, which, despite record cinema attendance levels, is starved of production cash.

In a hard-hitting statement, BFI director Wilf Stevenson said: "Annual investment in British films plummeted by over $223 million during the final years of the 1980s."

Last year, Stevenson said, saw the

— continued on page 2

Orion's Platt may join Swedlin in her new Uni company

By ANDREA KING

Orion Pictures president of production Marc Platt is reportedly in talks to partner with former CAA agent-turned-producer Rosalie Swedlin in her newly formed company at Universal Pictures, insiders confirmed.

Platt was out of the country on vacation and unavailable for comment. Swedlin declined comment.

One source said that while Platt still has a year and a half to two years left to go on his contract at Orion, he

— continued on page 17

Inside

Telco report drawing fire	3
"Brooklyn Bridge" moved	3
PPV bell tolls for Tyson	4

FIGURE 7.1   Announcement of Ted Turner buying Hanna-Barbera.

(Courtesy Doheny Archives, USC)

On October 10, 1996, Ted Turner attempted one more big throw of the dice by merging all his media companies into Warner Bros, then called AOL Time Warner.[5] He did this in hopes of becoming a major player at Warner Bros. But the powers there were not interested in letting him be the bull in their china shop. Once they had taken control of his channels like CNN, TCM, Cartoon Network, and WCW, they maneuvered him to the back of the room. He also lost billions in the Dot.Com crash of AOL. Ted Turner left the board of directors in 2006. He was invited back in 2009 in an advisory status but declined because of ill health from advanced age.

Along with the movie moguls, a new generation of film directors seized the means of production. *The Movie Brats.* Francis Ford Coppola, George Lucas, Steven Spielberg, Warren Beatty, Robert Altman, Martin Scorsese, etc. A generation raised on movies, reared in film schools and sound stages. With a nostalgic love of old-style moviemaking, inspired by the 60s European New Wave concept of the auteur film director. The director as the sole artist, armed with the newest technology. Not studio employees who clocked in like John Ford and Howard Hawks, but auteur filmmakers, who chose their own projects, chose the studios and grew their success themselves.

Fueled with the success of their monster hits like *Jaws, The Godfather* and *Star Wars,* George Lucas and Francis Ford Coppola's high-profile relocation to San Francisco started a new wave of interest in filmmaking in the Bay Area. Before that, even movies set in San Francisco like *The Thin Man* and *Vertigo* were actually filmed on Hollywood soundstages. Lucas and Coppola also used their financial clout to encourage auteur filmmaking. Helping Akira Kurosawa get funding to complete *Kagemusha* and financing film historian Kevin Brownlow's restoration of the 1925 Abel Gance silent epic *Napoleon.* In 1980, they held a well-publicized weekend conference on emerging digital media, nicknamed The Interface Conference. Between outdoor barbecue and Humboldt County pot, they declared that amazing heresies like one day celluloid film itself would be obsolete because everything would be on a computer.

But for most of the Movie Brats, their interest in producing animation was minimal because up until that time, animation was still not yet considered serious filmmaking. The monster profits of animated films were still 10 years in the future. Animated features then were known to take a long time to make and were too low yielding in profit to be ever worth the trouble. Walt Disney had been the exception because he had his parks and brand-loyal fan base.

Among these auteur directors, two exceptions were George Lucas and Steven Spielberg. Unabashed film buffs, these shy boys grew up in the movie theaters of the late 1940s and 1950s. Where they escaped the dreariness of everyday life thrilling to action shoot-em-ups like *Spy Smasher,* pulp science fiction fantasies like *Flash Gordon* and *Buck Rodgers* and cliff hangers like *Captain Marvel.* When they acquired the power to make the movies they wanted, they reached back to their childhood memories. *Star Wars* with Luke Skywalker battling the evil Darth Vader is an homage to the Flash Gordon model, complete with sensational crawl titles at the opening. *Raiders of the Lost Ark* was a tribute to the thriller serials of the 1940s. One other component of their theater memories was the animated short cartoon.

Both Francis and George were never that interested in competing with Walt Disney. It must have surprised Lucas to see Pixar, the little computer graphics company he

FIGURE 7.2 Steven Spielberg and George Lucas at the dedication of a new Cinema Arts Building at USC, 2009.

(photo by the author)

formed and nurtured, do so well with animation once out of his corral.[6] George made several starts on his own animation company set in San Rafael. But all they managed to do after several tries was the Gore Verbinsky animated western *Rango* (2011). It did okay Box Office but was never followed up on. Both Lucas and Coppola spent some time developing *Frankenstein* remakes that never quite got beyond the early development stages.

In the 1970s, for many young Baby Boomer artists entering the field burning with a desire to do the kind of beautiful character animation of the Golden Age Hollywood, they grew up watching on TV, only three options presented themselves. Do cheap TV, do cheap commercials or move.

Every so often, an interesting project would pop up, like a Chuck Jones or Peanuts TV special. But they were too few and far between to make a living on. Chuck's crew would work at Hanna-Barbera drawing *Jabberjaws* and *Foofer* until Chuck sent up a Bat-Signal that his new TV project was ready. Then they would all give notice and go work for Chuck at his Sunset and Vine St. office. When they were done, Bill and Joe (Hanna-Barbera) would always take them back. In New York, maverick animator Bill Plympton created independent hand-drawn films like *Your Face, Guard Dog and The Tune.*

The Frank Thomas-Ollie Johnston days, when an animator could spend his entire career in one studio were over. Although nobody thought to tell us boomers, or we refused to believe it was over, Walt Disney seemed to be the only place that offered year-round employment, and even they seemed shaky. For animation artists in cities other than Los Angeles, the situation was worse. Throughout the 1970s, animation work dried up in New York, Chicago and the Bay Area. It was especially acute in Canada, where schools like Sheridan turned out dozens of graduates with no business to take them in, except the National Film Board. And they seemed to be focused on the next celebrity filmmaker from the Iron Curtain.

So, young animators began to look in further and further faraway places, anywhere, to satisfy their craving to work on "good stuff." London, Toronto, Montreal, Prague, Paris, Tokyo, Costa Rica, Salamanca. Anywhere there was a cool project being worked on. Some international films surprised everyone on the world market like *Fantastic Planet* (1968) done in Paris and Prague, or *Allegro Non Troppo* (1976) done in Milan. Others like The *Heavy Metal* movie (1981) by Gerald Potterton, John Korty's *Twice Upon a Time (1983)* or Nelvana's *Rock and Rule (1983)* could not land a wide U.S. distribution deal.

Into this miasma stepped Steven Spielberg.

Steven Spielberg (born 1946) was a young filmmaker from Arizona[7] whose early career experiences mirrored much of what the boomer generation film workers experienced. On his first director job, *"Eyes"* for the series *Night Gallery*, Steven was 23, and his crew were in their 60s.

For a time, he was a protégé of Universal exec Sid Sheinberg and producer Barry Diller, who later was instrumental in setting up Fox Network and greenlighting *The Simpsons* (see Chapter 10). He made friends with another Diller protégé who would one day be important to animation named Jeffrey Katzenberg.

Steven Spielberg's story as one of the foremost directors in Hollywood merits an entire book to itself. Suffice it to say he created our modern concept of the blockbuster movie. *Jaws, Close Encounters of the Third Kind, Raiders of the Lost Ark, Jurassic Park, Schindler's List, Saving Private Ryan*, and more.

Unlike his contemporaries Steven always considered animation a co-equal pillar of the family-friendly movie experience he was trying to bring to audiences. While at Universal, Steven had struck up a correspondence with the old Bugs Bunny director Chuck Jones. Chuck introduced him to his friend Ray Bradbury, the award-winning science fiction writer. When George Lucas was completing *Star Wars (A New Hope)*, he tried to secure the Chuck's 1953 short *Duck Dodgers in the 24th 1/2 Century* to run before the main film. That idea ultimately did not pan out. In his film *Close Encounters of the Third Kind (1977)*, Steven Spielberg was able to get in a clip of a Bugs-Bunny Marvin the Martian cartoon on the TV in his main protagonist's home.

After the Box Office triumphs, *Raiders of the Lost Ark* (1981) and *E.T. The Extraterrestrial* (1982), Steven Spielberg was the king of Hollywood. He expanded into several areas including video games and the TV anthology series *Amazing Stories* (1985–1987). One episode of Amazing Stories was done in animation. It was written and directed by a former young Disney animator named Brad Bird. He called the episode *Family Dog*. It had a 1960s family sitcom vibe with strong animation and good visual humor. A bunch of Brad's old colleagues from Disney Feature pitched in and gave the animation a level of quality high above the usual TV animation fare. Although the Family Dog episode was highly praised, the Amazing Stories series was not renewed for a third season. Steven Spielberg also did *Who Framed Roger Rabbit* with Disney as a co-production. Thanks to Steven's influence with Warner Bros, Bugs Bunny would finally be face-to-face with Mickey Mouse, and Donald Duck with Daffy.

Steven Spielberg wanted to create a Disney-style animation division for his company Amblin. With his Boomer's characteristic reverence for Old Hollywood, he invited a group of retired Disney and Warner Bros animators to his office for advice on starting a production. His conclusion from the meeting was, "What a bunch of angry, bitter old men! None of them could agree with one another."[8] In 1982, one of the competing films E.T. crushed at the summer Box Office was Don Bluth's *The Secret of NIMH*. Steven was shown a copy of *NIMH* by composer Jerry Goldsmith. He reportedly said, "I thought nobody did this type of animation anymore!"[9] Steven and Don Bluth agreed to do a film together. It still took another 2 years to get a good script and start production. In the meantime, Don Bluth created the animation for the videogame *Dragons Lair* and *Space Ace*.

The first film they collaborated on was *An American Tail*, (1986), written by David Kirschner *(Hocus Pocus, Chucky)*. *An American Tail* opened on Thanksgiving weekend 1986 and was an unprecedented smash. Shortly, after it was followed up by *Land Before Time (1988)*. Another huge success that spawned more than a dozen direct-to-video sequels.

These films not only declared a big new force in theatrical animation, but for the first time since Max Fleischer in the 1930s, Walt Disney had some serious competition in the feature animation market. For the Mouse House, this spurred on serious commitment to their animation effort much more than any inner office memo might do. Many argue that The Disney Renaissance might have actually started with *American Tale* than at *The Little Mermaid*.

On *Land Before Time*, Don still managed to get in some classic drama when they staged the death of Littlefoot's mother. Like the death of Bambi's mother a generation earlier, it traumatized millions of kids. Writer Stu Kreiger recalled. "Over the 30 years, I've had countless parents come up to me and say, 'Goddamn you, do you know how many days it took to calm my kid down? Or how many times I had to cry watching the movie with my kid?'"[10]

Steven Spielberg and Don Bluth had three-picture deal but by the third project, creative differences caused them to go their separate ways. Don went on to make several more movies with diminishing success. Steven took the leftover London animation crew from *Who Framed Roger Rabbit* and reorganized them in the London suburb Acton as Amblimation. They created a sequel, *American Tail 2 Fieval Goes West (1991)*, directed by Roger alumni Simon Wells and Phil Nibbelink. This was the final movie work of legendary actor Jimmy Stewart. Next a comedic follow up to Steven's own hit *Jurassic Park*, entitled *We're Back. (1993)*. Spielberg then produced a big screen adaptation of the old Harveytoons favorite *Casper the Friendly Ghost (1995)*. The ILM effects team were jazzed after the success of *Jurassic Park*. Director Brad Silberling got Phil Nibbelink from London and Sheri Stoner from Animaniacs to augment the animation team. *Casper* opened in the summer of 1995 and made $300 million from a production budget of $55 mill. There were expectations for a sequel, but the old problem of securing rights to old characters popped up. Another company challenged for the rights and produced some low-quality knock offs. Amidst all of the legal wrangling, *Casper 2* never materialized.

In late 1994–1995, the great rift in Disney top management caused the creation of the new studio DreamWorks, of which Steven was a central partner along with

Jeffrey Katzenberg and David Geffen. To build DreamWorks Animation, Steven closed Amblimation in London and moved the international crew to Hollywood (Chapter 16). Besides producing series at DreamWorks and Universal, Steven's Amblin was also instrumental in helping Warner Bros reboot its animation department and produce the hit series *Tinytoons, Animaniacs and Pinky and the Brain*.

For all he has done for animation, Steven Spielberg was awarded a lifetime achievement award at the ASIFA Annie Awards in 2014.

NOTES

1   The legendary leaders of CBS and NBC, respectively.
2   NY Times article. *Colorizing Film Classics, a Boon or Bane?* By Leslie Bennett August 5, 1986.
3   Orson Welles had already died in 1985, but director Henry Jaglom reported his quote as he heard it.
4   Hanna-Barbera had sold their company in 1966 to Taft Enterprises but remained as directors. Taft was a company founded by descendants of former U.S. President William Howard Taft. (Source: Wikipedia)
5   In 2025, Warner Discovery.
6   See Chapter 14 CGI.
7   Steven Spielberg was born in Ohio but was raised in Arizona.
8   Steven Spielberg to the author, 1987.
9   Don Bluth, *Somewhere Out There*, pg 222.
10 Stu Krieger quoted in *The Land Before Time Was A Big Box Office Hit—But The Franchise Refused To Go Extinct* by Ryan Scott (SyFy December 2, 2023)

The New Team
To Teach an Old Mouse New Tricks

8

Roy E. Disney[1] was a soft-spoken man with big ears and a warm smile. For a billionaire, he was quite simple in his personal tastes. No gold toilets or penis-shaped rocket ships. When he grew a mustache, he bore an uncanny resemblance to his famous uncle. He even chain-smoked Marlboros like Walt did. Unlike many of his family's second generation who preferred to stay away from the day-to-day running of the family business, Roy liked working at the studio. He began as a part-time editor on the *Dragnet* TV series. Later, he became the producer of the award-winning *True-Life Nature* Series. Roy also had a great talent for business. He set up his own investment company called Shamrock. Its headquarters was near his home in Toluca Lake on the site of the old UPA animation studios. He found he had a talent for navigating the rocks and shoals of big business. All this outside of the family firm.

FIGURE 8.1 Roy E. Disney

(collection of the author)

DOI: 10.1201/b22394-9

The business climate of the 1980s caused by Ronald Reagan's federal deregulation policies was a whirlwind of mergers and acquisitions, speculation, arbitrage and junk bonds. Large corporations swallowed smaller ones. "Vulture Capitalists" would enact a hostile takeover of corporation by buying up a majority of its stock, then firing its officers. Once in control, it would liquidate the companies' assets to pay back the debt accrued to buy it, then bankrupt the company and declare it all a tax write off.

Animation was no stranger to these business practices. Hanna-Barbera Enterprises was owned by Taft Enterprises, who was acquired by Turner Corp. who merged it into Time-Warner. The name Hanna-Barbera almost disappeared but for Cartoon Network protesting fan-based loyalty to the name.[2] Since they began running old HB series, a whole new generation was clamoring for more. Filmation Studios, which produced He-Man and She-Ra, was bought by Westinghouse, who sold it to the Swiss company L'Oreal/Nestle, who stripped its film library for their new European cable stations, then shut them down. It was a dog-eat-dog business climate, but Roy Disney and his partners knew how to play the game.

By the early 1980s, The Walt Disney Company was one of the last of the old Hollywood studios to still have descendants of their founder in charge. Walt's son-in-law Ron Miller was CEO, and Roy's son Roy E. Disney was on the board of directors. Other family members were trust fund inheritors who preferred not to take an active role in running the company. Ron and Roy frequently found themselves clashing over the key decision-making. At times, the arguing became personal. Roy was so disgusted by the direction the board was going in that, for a time, he stopped attending the regular meetings. When people noticed that he was not using the personal parking space[3] reserved for him, others began to use it. One day Roy drove in and saw someone else's car in his spot. He complained loudly enough to get Ron Miller's attention. Ron marched down to the parking lot, and in front of Roy, he pried Roy's nameplate off with his own fingers and flung it over the wall.

After a string of movie disappointments, by 1984, many stockholders were questioning the company's survivability. Behind the scenes, Roy Disney launched a sophisticated plan to oust Ron Miller and his leadership team.

A well-known corporate raider named Saul Steinberg[4] announced in the press his intention to commence a hostile takeover of The Walt Disney Company in order to break it up. Ron Miller had Disney pay Mr. Steinberg $133 million just to make him go away. A tactic known as "greenmail." Roy then confronted Ron with this at the annual stockholders meeting. He pushed through an overwhelming vote of no confidence. The first of its kind at the company. A week later, the board requested Ron Miller's resignation. He complied on September 7, 1984. What was not made public then was that Roy Disney probably had put Saul Steinberg up to the whole thing.

With the Walt Disney Empire now securely under his control, Roy Disney assembled his management team. Frank Wells had been a COO of Warner Bros and now became COO of Disney. They brought over Michael Eisner, his associate Jeffrey Katzenberg, from Paramount. At Paramount, Eisner and Katzenberg had turned around the fortunes of that ailing giant. While Eisner focused on the parks and publications, Jeffrey was put in charge of the film and animation studio. At Roy's suggestion, they hired theatrical producer Peter Schneider to run the animation division, now called Walt Disney Feature

Animation. Roy had been impressed working with Peter on events staged for the 1984 Los Angeles Olympic Games. Peter had no practical experience in animation production, but he was assured that the unit could almost run itself.

They began to immediately to end Walt Disney's "splendid isolation" and bring in the powerful talent of modern Hollywood, directors, writers and composers. Bette Midler, Peter Weir, Paul Mazursky, Billy Joel and Josh Whedon. Don Hahn recalled " The employee parking lot was suddenly filled with Porsches and BMWs."[5] Eisner and Katzenberg in particular used their personal connections to bring in George Lucas and pop star Michael Jackson to develop new attractions for Disneyland like Star Tours and Captain EO. Steven Spielberg was a friend of Jeffrey Katzenberg, and legend has it pulled the treatment of a book named *Who Censored Roger Rabbit?* out of their files for development. Another Katzenberg friend, music producer David Geffen, spoke with them about the potential of movie musicals.

Before they could really effect change, the first problem was what to do with the studio's huge white elephant *The Black Cauldron*. In development for years, costing more than any animated feature to that date[6] and still having story trouble. It was slated for a January 1, 1985, release. But a test screening proved that some of the darker scenes were too upsetting for children. The Motion Picture Board of Revenue gave it a "PG" rating, the first ever for a Disney cartoon. Katzenberg brought in some new editors and cut 12 minutes from the film and released it in July 1985.

After years of publicity declaring what a great comeback The Black Cauldron would be for Disney Animation, what a masterpiece it would be, the film opened weak and quickly fizzled. In it's opening week it placed third in the Box office behind *Pee-wee's Big Adventure* and *The Care Bears Movie*. Even a re-issue of Disney's old *101 Dalmatians* made more money. Professional studio artists know you work just as hard on the flops as you do on the hits. Most of the animators were terribly disappointed.

While the Black Cauldron drama was being acted out, all of the new movie people coming in needed office space to work. And where on the Disney lot was the largest amount of office space? The old animation building. So, on February 1, 1985, the Walt Disney feature animation team except for Ink & Paint was moved from their 1939 building to a collection of anonymous industrial warehouses in Glendale near Disney Imagineering. One building was a repurposed casket factory. The animators took this as a further sign that Disney Feature Animation was being closed down forever. On Flower Street, there was very little space for private offices. The animators squeezed their classic 1939, Kem & Weber oak animation desks and other furniture into bland little open office cubicles. Much furniture was piled up in storage or simply thrown away. One story concerned the office guest chairs, called airline chairs. After *The Black Cauldron* wrapped production, many desks were piled up in an alley outside a soundstage to be rotted away by the elements. In 1989, the Los Angeles Times Sunday Arts section published a feature profiling Kem Weber, the *Streamline-Moderne*[7] designer of that furniture. It mentioned that one of those 1939 airline chairs would easily fetch $1,500 and up on the modern antiques market. The next day the studio security marched throughout the animators' cubicles to catalog each chair and mark it with a special barcode.

WALT DISNEY PRODUCTIONS

INTER-OFFICE COMMUNICATION
P-660 R-1

TO ___ Animation Department Staff   DATE ___ December 17, 1984

FROM ___ Roy E. Disney ___ EXT. ___   SUBJECT ___ Department Relocation

On approximately February 1, 1985, the creative side of our Animation Department will begin a temporary relocation from the Disney lot to new facilities within the Toluca Lake-Burbank area. We anticipate that approximately 120 artists, animation managers and creative support personnel will be moving off lot for a period of two to three years.

Members of Inking and Painting, Camera and other production people within the Animation Department will not be affected by this change, which is designed to provide some much-needed office space in the Animation Building for our expanding live-action motion picture operations.

For those who are affected, the relocation is expected to occur over a period of several weeks and should be completed by March 15. We are currently negotiating a lease agreement for an appropriate site, and we expect to announce specifics on the location and environment available before the end of the week.

All personnel who are affected by the relocation plans will be returning to the studio within two to three years, pending completion of additional office facilities within the complex. The design of these new facilities is already under way.

Once a relocation site is announced, we will begin the process of space planning to assure that the new facilities meet the most productive needs for space, working environments and logistics of animation activities. At that time, we will be looking for ideas and concepts that can enhance the creative processes, and your individual suggestions will be welcomed and encouraged.

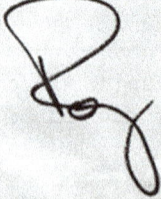

RED:sm

FIGURE 8.2   Memo announcing the move to the warehouses in Glendale.

(collection of the author)

The studio that for decades had promoted from within, now suddenly had to take orders from a stream of fast-talking Hollywood execs. These people had little or no patience for stooped old timers in golf attire explaining, "That is the way we do things here." Most of the ancien' regime's producers and production staff were shuffled off into retirement. Joe Hale, Don Duckwall and more. Eric Larsen, the last of the Nine Old Men on salary, was so disgusted by the lack of respect he felt the traditions of the animation division was being shown that he soon retired. As the studios emphasis leaned toward reviving the Disney musical, the newcomers began to recruit production people from the Broadway and London stage. Kathleen Gavin, Maureen Donley, Max Howard, Ron Tippe, Baker Bloodworth and more. Younger Disney production managers like Don Hahn and Ron Rocha provided a liaison for them to the world of animation production.

In one of their first meetings, Michael Eisner expressed amazement that the studio had abandoned most of its TV animation projects. He ordered an immediate resumption of TV programming and split off its management from the theatrical crew. He mentioned off hand, "My kids love this Swiss candy called Gummy Bears. Why not develop a show around that?" He also wanted to develop a show with the classic characters. Icons like Mickey, Minnie, Donald and Goofy were considered too precious to be exploited, so they reached into their second tier for characters like Chip & Dale and Baloo from The Jungle Book.

On September 23, 1984, the day, Michael Eisner, Frank Wells, Peter Schneider and Jeffrey Katzenberg were shown the story reels for *Basil of Baker Street*, is now thought as the pivotal point in Disney animation's survival. Disney veteran Burny Mattinson (1930–2024) and his team were developing a variation on Sherlock Holmes where the mice living in 221B Baker Street have their own Sherlockian adventures. Normally, while the script is being fleshed out, the storyboard artists illustrate scenes from the movie and film them with temporary voice tracks. Called story reels, they give everyone a rough idea of how the movie will pace. Roy Disney quietly told Burny that the future of Disney Animation was in his hands! Talk about pressure. For 3 hours, Burny took the executives through the development art, and the pinned-up storyboards. "Pitching" the story. The same way Walt Disney and Webb Smith had done it since the 1920s. The executives were polite but fidgety. Burny then ran the filmed story reels on an editing machine, and Eisner and Katzenberg eyes lit up. Live-action producers may not yet have appreciated the potential of still drawings, but they understood reviewing footage. Eisner and Katzenberg saw things like story reels as the way of using their own expertise to influence the direction of the story. Indeed, insiders later confessed to me that the strategic plan was to eliminate the animation team and license off the characters to be done elsewhere cheaply. Roy Disney told Burny afterward, "You may have just saved Disney Animation."

Jeffrey Katzenberg in particular was won over to the potential of animation. He contemplated the potential for animation's ability to make the surreal possible, a way to revive moribund movie genres like the movie musical. He took home Frank and Ollie's book *Disney Animation, the Illusion of Life* and read it cover to cover.

At first, the new management team mixed clumsily. Mirroring Jeffrey Katzenberg's irreverent shoot-from-the-hip style of decision-making, many tossed out comments that the artists thought disrespectful. To the animators used to taking orders from old legends who drew Bambi and Peter Pan, the newcomers adopting the possessive "We at Disney" seemed like interlopers.

In 1985, as *Basil of Baker Street* was being completed, Steven Spielberg released *Young Sherlock Holmes,* a film about Holmes and Watson as teenagers, written by Chris Columbus and directed by Barry Levinson. Despite breakthrough CGI work from the Lucasfilm Graphics Group (Pixar),[8] the film did poorly at the Box Office. So much so that Jeffrey Katzenberg ordered changing the title of Basil to no longer reflect anything Sherlockian. He did not want the project to be caught in the undertow. *Basil of Baker*

WALT DISNEY PICTURES

INTER-OFFICE COMMUNICATION

| TO | ANIMATION DEPARTMENT | | DATE | February 13, 1986 |
| FROM | Peter Schneider | EXT 2630 | SUBJECT | |

Along with the new title for "Basil of Baker Street" it has been decided to re-name the entire library of animated classics. The new titles are as follows...

"SEVEN LITTLE MEN HELP A GIRL"

"THE WOODEN BOY WHO BECAME REAL"

"COLOR AND MUSIC"

"THE WONDERFUL ELEPHANT WHO COULD REALLY FLY"

"THE LITTLE DEER WHO GREW UP"

"THE GIRL WITH THE SEE-THROUGH SHOES"

"THE GIRL IN THE IMAGINARY WORLD"

"THE AMAZING FLYING CHILDREN"

"TWO DOGS FALL IN LOVE"

"THE GIRL WHO SEEMED TO DIE"

"PUPPIES TAKEN AWAY"

"THE BOY WHO WOULD BE KING"

"A BOY, A BEAR AND A BIG BLACK CAT"

"ARISTOCATS"

"ROBIN HOOD WITH ANIMALS"

"TWO MICE SAVE A GIRL"

"A FOX AND A HOUND ARE FRIENDS"

"THE EVIL BONEHEAD"

And of course our latest classic destined to win the hearts of the american public...

"THE GREAT MOUSE DETECTIVE"

FIGURE 8.3   Satirical Disney memo about the renaming of Disney classic movies. 1986. (collection of the author)

Street became *The Great Mouse Detective.* Many of the animators thought the title contrived, like a poor translation of a foreign film. Story artist Ed Gombert wrote a gag memo suggesting they rename every Disney classic in the same clumsy way. So, *Snow White and the Seven Dwarfs* became, *"Seven Little Men and a Girl."* *Bambi* became, *"A Deer Grows Up"* and *The Black Cauldon, "The Evil Black Pot that Dead People Come Out Of."* The memo went around artists' desks, causing many chuckles, but when management got a hold of it, they were furious. There was a vigorous yet unsuccessful search for the author that further alienated the crew. In a cartoon studio, you can be forgiven for many things, except not being able to take a joke.

The Great Mouse Detective* was released on July 6, 1986, directed by two young artists, John Musker and Ron Clements, and two old vets Dave Michener and Burny Mattinson. While not exactly burning up the Box Office[9], the film was a success both critically and financially. I myself was at another studio then. When I saw *The Black Cauldon*, I thought, well, that is the end of that place. But after seeing *Great Mouse*, I thought, well, whattaya know? There is some life left in the old girl after all.

NOTES

1 Roy Edward Disney was called Roy E. to differentiate himself from his father, Roy O. Disney. For a time, he was called Roy Jr, but he disliked the term in preference to Roy E. Disney.

2 In 2024, the Hanna-Barbera brand name was still known, but Cartoon Network was purchased by Warner-Discovery and phased out.

3 Roy's car was recognizable for the personal license plate Pyewacket. The name of the pet cat in the 1958 movie *Bell, Book and Candle*.

4 The Wall Street Saul Steinberg ought not to be confused with the New Yorker cartoonist/illustrator also named Saul Steinberg (1914–1999).

5 Don Hahn, quoted in *Waking Sleeping Beauty*, 2009.

6 The average animated feature then cost around $10–15 million to make. Black Cauldron cost over $44 million.

7 *Kem Weber: Mid-century Furniture Designs for the Disney Studios* by David Bossert.

8 In *Young Sherlock Holmes*, the "Stained Glass Knight" was animated by John Lasseter. He was one of the young Disney animation trainees who left after *TRON* was completed.

9 *The Great Mouse Detective* earned $50 Million in its initial run on its budget of $14 million, although it came behind Don Bluth's *An American Tail*. It later did very well in video cassette sales.

Roger Rabbit

9

I'm not Bad. I'm just Drawn that way.

FIGURE 9.1 The *Who Framed Roger Rabbit* poster.

DOI: 10.1201/b22394-10

Gary Wolf was a writer from Earlville, Illinois. His father owned a pool hall, and his mother worked in a school cafeteria. A decorated Vietnam veteran, after getting out of the service, Wolf dedicated himself to the more pacific pursuit of writing novels. He enjoyed writing stories that played with American pop culture themes. Mysteries, often humorous. In 1978, he wrote a Raymond Chandler noir-style detective story with one key twist. He made his story about a private detective investigating a murder involving a star, except the star is a cartoon character. His tag line was "Help! I'm stuck in a mystery of double-crosses, steamy broads and killer cream pies!" He set his story in the classic period of Golden Age Hollywood where characters like Mickey Mouse and Bugs Bunny were just as popular as flesh-and-blood stars like Clark Gable and Katherine Hepburn. He called it *"Who Censored Roger Rabbit?"* He worked on societal themes where the cartoon characters in Hollywood called "toons" lived in ghettoized communities much like African and Asian Americans were at the time. Also, around the same time, the story was set in the LA trolley-car system was being phased out to make way for the building of freeways.

Roger Rabbit as originally conceived in the novel lived in a comic strip, and many of his words came out above his head as word balloons. Roger was a second-string celebrity who hired burned-out detective Eddie Valiant to investigate why his producers the DeGreasy Brothers would not give him his own comic strip. Roger actually gets murdered in the book, and Valiant searches for his killer based on clues from Roger's last lingering word balloon.

At first, *Who Censored Roger Rabbit* was rejected by every publisher Gary Wolf sent it to. When he protested to one publisher, the man replied that his story was "not categorizable." Gary asked him, "What would you have done if somebody brought you *The Wizard of Oz,* or *Alice in Wonderland*"? He said, "We probably could not sell those either." After 110 rejections, it was at last picked up by St. Martin's Press. The book became a cult classic and went through three printings.[1]

In 1980, the Walt Disney Studio received a copy of *Who Censored Roger Rabbit.* They were regularly inundated with books and scripts from agents, hopeful to be optioned for production. Previous movies like *Mary Poppins, The Love Bug* and *The Rescuers* were adapted from novels. Production chief Tom Wilhite recognized this story as a natural for the animation department and sent it on to young animator Darrell Van Citters. Darrell was just completing a similar type of live-action-animation short film titled *Fun with Mister Future.* Darrell loved the story and immediately set to work creating a test film from it. He got together a number of other young artists who saw it as a chance to develop something out from the disapproving gaze of the older establishment. He reset the story as more about animated cartoon characters than comic strip ones and dropped the word balloon device as unfeasible. By going full Hollywood noir with the story, he could flesh out the character to be similar to a classic character. They shot live-action tests using the studio's city backlot and animator Mike Gabriel as Eddie Valiant. Roger was voiced by then unknown Paul Rubens, who would go on to fame as Pee-wee Herman.[2] Two live-action writers were brought in and began revamping the story. Roger Rabbit goes from being the murder victim to hiring Valiant to clear his name for the murder of his producer. The setting was moved from the 1950s to the 1940s, Raymond Chandler era Hollywood, more like the original novel. Roger's wife Jessica would be a

FIGURE 9.2   The original novel of *Roger Rabbit* by Gary Wolf. (Gary is the man on the cover.) Courtesy of Gary Wolf.

full-on Hollywood goddess, star like Rita Hayworth in *Gilda*.[3] I was working at another studio then, and I recall chatting with a friend at Disney, "Darrell has got them to do this great new story about the murder of a cartoon character." I said that sounds great, to which he replied, "Yeah, but you know they'll never make it. It's too different for them."

Sure enough, after *Tron* and *Something Wicked This Way Comes* disappointed at the Box Office, the conservative faction in Disney upper management regained the upper hand. Tom Wilhite was out, and many of his pet projects like *Brave Little Toaster,*

Where the Wild Things Are[4] and *Roger Rabbit* were shelved. (Late 1983) At various times, Steven Spielberg, Joe Dante, Robert Zemeckis, John Landis, Ron Howard, Terry Gilliam and Michael Apted were each approached about directing the Roger Rabbit, but nothing came of it because up until then Disney was known to not hire top Hollywood directors. And top Hollywood directors had learned not to take an offer from Disney very seriously.[5]

That began to change when the Michael Eisner and Jeffrey Katzenberg team came over from Paramount. After sweeping out most of the producers of the Ron Miller era, Eisner and Katzenberg began aggressively courting and green-lighting top live-action projects. Paul Mazursky, Billy Joel, Gary Marshall, Peter Weir and Bette Midler were brought in and given animator offices on the lot to create big projects. Hit movies like *Pretty Woman, Splash, Down* and *Out in Beverly Hills* were the result. Suddenly, Disney was back in the mainstream movie business again.

Jeffrey Katzenberg was close friends with Steven Spielberg and David Geffen. When they coaxed George Lucas to create a ride at Disneyland (Star Tours) as well as Michael Jackson (Captain Eo), Steven began to seriously look through Disney's library of potential titles. Legend is that he read a screenplay of *Who Censored Roger Rabbit* and said, "Why haven't you guys made this yet?" Steven brought in his protégé Robert Zemeckis who had just scored a huge hit with *Romancing the Stone*, and he was finishing *Back to the Future*. Spielberg decided to co-produce the film, now titled *Who Framed Roger Rabbit*. It would be a Disney-Amblin co-production.

Director Bob Zemeckis had come out of screenwriting and had some big notes for the script. Early versions of Roger made him darker off camera, a spoiled Hollywood star like Jerry Lewis in *King of Comedy*. Bob Z wanted Roger to be more the spirit of innocent fun to contrast against Eddie Valiant as the burned-out, bitter cynic. A better chemistry. Many of these ideas clashed with the incumbent director Darrell Van Citters. Both men were known as alpha personalities. After one disagreement too many, Darrell was taken off the project.

An added benefit of having Steven Spielberg on board was Steven then had great influence with Warner Bros because of his producing the *Tiny Toons* and *Animaniacs* for them. He had been friends with old Warner's animation legend Chuck Jones since he inserted a Marvin the Martian cameo into his *Close Encounters of the Third Kind*. Thanks to Spielberg, they could put Bugs Bunny face-to-face with Mickey Mouse for the first time. The draw of a film with Walt Disney and Steven Spielberg about cartoons started to pull in other legendary characters, Bettie Boop, Droopy, Woody Woodpecker and more. Many of the original voice actors volunteered their services to recreate those classic characters, namely Mae Questel, June Foray, Mel Blanc and Gracie Lantz. But they could not get everything they wanted. King Features would not give them Popeye, Hanna-Barbera would not give them Tom & Jerry and Harvey Comics would not give them Casper. They worried Disney was just out to exploit their intellectual property.

The script was revised to place the setting of the movie in 1947. Specifically, the last year before television sets began to appear in people's homes. Also, the year the Los Angeles transit system of streetcars began to be replaced by freeways and busses. 1947 was also the last year before the UPA graphic design style of the 1950s began to seriously change the look of mainstream animated cartoons.

The role of the detective Eddie Valiant was first offered to Paul Newman, then Dustin Hoffman, Bill Murray, Harrison Ford and Jack Nicholson who all turned it down. Finally, it was decided that English actor Bob Hoskins would do the role. He was known for doing tough-guy gangsters in films like *The Long Good Friday*. He could do a convincing American accent, and he could do the difficult acting opposite an invisible character, since they are added in later. Hoskins agent advised him against doing the part since it was "a kid's film." Hoskins reacted. "Other people talk about going on stage with Lawrence Olivier. I'm going to be in a film with Bugs Bunny, Donald Duck, Mickey Mouse, everybody- The Big Boys. I loved it."[6]

The voice of Roger Rabbit presented a challenge. With 60 years of famous cartoon voices, it could easily have fallen into one cliché or another. He sounds too much like this character or that. Live-action actors attempting to do cartoon voices usually start with an imitation of Pinto Colvig's Goofy or Paul Winchell's Mortimer Snerd. Bob Zemeckis recalled once seeing a standup comedian at the Comedy Store[7] years ago named Charlie Fleischer. Charlie was a very versatile voice actor. He gave Roger a voice that was fun but unique. When Zemeckis suggested he wanted Roger to have a signature speech impediment, Charlie invented the stuttering "Pppppuhlease!" For Roger's lady-love, Jessica, Bob Zemeckis had already used Kathleen Turner in *Romancing the Stone*. She showed she was perfectly capable of producing a smoky, seductive alto voice in her breakout film *Body Heat*. Kathleen joked later about the project. "It was great because I was then pregnant with my daughter Rachel, but I did not have to be on

FIGURE 9.3   Live-action plate animators worked over.

(collection of the author)

camera. I could be sexy with swollen ankles!" Joanna Cassidy, the snake dancer from *Blade Runner*, was cast as Hoskins love interest Dolores. A natural redhead she had to dye her hair black so as not to conflict with Jessica's redhead. She did her own makeup based on Joan Crawford. For the villain Judge Doom, they first screen-tested Tim Curry but passed because they worried he came off too scary. He had to be evil, but in a kookie way, like Captain Hook. They finally decided on Christopher Lloyd who had just completed filming Doc Ballard for *Back to the Future*. Veteran character actors Alan Tilvern and Stubby Kaye rounded out the cast. A special cameo was Raoul J. Raoul, the bad-tempered director of Rogers' opening cartoon. He was played by producer Joel Silver (*Die Hard, The Matrix*), who was famous for his temper.

The live action was filmed half in Hollywood and half in London. In some scenes like Valiant and the kids riding on the back of the streetcar, one side of the street was LA and the opposite side was London. CGI[8] then was not yet good enough to recreate photoreal objects, so when a toon was carrying a gun or a tray, they had to use real props and mounted them on sticks to be handled by puppeteers from The Muppets. Early on, the prop people rigged a small robot to carry things. Like when a weasel is pointing a gun at Valiant. But in the end, his movements were too stiff and mechanical to be believed. The entire Ink & Paint Club was built on a soundstage 12 feet off the ground so Muppeteers could move around below the floor carry the trays of drinks on long wooden dowels. The animators would draw the penguins over them later. Bob Zemeckis insisted we stage things so the humans and toons interacted closely. Grab each other, mess up their hair or necktie. "We're not doing a damn cereal commercial here!" When Roger puts his hands on Valliant's dusty desk, he leaves fingerprints.

The issue of where the animation was going to be done had its own pitfalls. Jeffrey Katzenberg wanted it all done at the Disney studio. Steven Spielberg wanted to set up a unit at Paramount. In meetings, he said that he had been unimpressed with the current Disney animated output and did not think them up to the challenge. Remember, Spielberg is not referring to the classic Disney animation team. They were all retired. He was looking at the crew that did *The Black Cauldron* and *Pete's Dragon*. ILM,[9] contracted to create the visual effects for the movie, said they could do it all up in Marin County. They actually advertised in newspapers for "Walt Disney Quality Animators."

After a lot of wrangling and lobbying by Chuck Jones, the compromise was London. For Hollywood power people, London was like Switzerland. Neutral ground. Both George Lucas and Spielberg had good experiences shooting a Pinewood and Elstree Studios. But what about the animation director? They considered several prom-inent animators like Don Bluth, Bob Kurtz and Eric Goldberg. Producer Robert Watts then showed Spielberg and Zemeckis a 10-minute promo of *Cobbler and the Thief* that Dick Williams was sending around to try and attract investors. Watts said, "Richard was the guy they wanted from the moment they saw the reel. It had to be Richard or nothing."[10] At first, Dick was reluctant to consider taking so much time away from The Thief, but his old friend Chuck Jones changed his mind. "Take the job. Spielberg is marvelous with his people. You'll get your own movie made. You stupid bastard, take the job!"[11]

FIGURE 9.4   Roger story sketch by Richard Williams.

(collection of the author)

What was great about Dick Williams was that he seemed not overly influenced by any one particular drawing style. A Disney look, a Warner Bros look. Many young Disney animators then were into the CalArts Style. Reminiscent of Ward Kimball's TV work in things like *It's Tough to Be a Bird*. Zemeckis was concerned about the characters looking too cliché Disney. Dick Williams relied on his adaptability to draw in different styles. He gave Roger a hybrid design that was made up of several elements. A bit of Bugs Bunny, a bit of Screwy Squirrel and the baggy pants of Charlie Chaplin's Tramp that gave him a triangular silhouette. Max Linder wore kid gloves like all self-respecting mid-century cartoon comedians wore. For Jessica, the inspiration was Tex Avery's sexy dancer Red in the Wolfie films. Add in Rita Hayworth from Gilda and Veronica Lake's long hair down over one eye. William's key animator Russell Hall finalized her design.

The style of the animation would owe much to Tex Avery's manic animation style at MGM than Disney, particularly the "Tex Avery Take." A character reaction so extreme that it was funny just by itself. Avery put himself in contrast to Disney in being the great surrealist in American animation. His characters could come apart or stretch grotesquely to achieve the desired laugh. Animation in the 70s and 80s had been under assault by parents' groups to be more responsible for children. Psychologists claimed there were more random acts of violence in the average cartoon than in a war movie. But to children, it was not real violence but slapstick. A comedy tradition that went back centuries. Whole generations of children watched those cartoons yet never hit each other with hammers or gave each other lit sticks of dynamite. Even so, by the end of the 1980s, there was very little you could do by way of physical comedy. Pressure groups even went back and re-classified classic children's movies like Disney's *Treasure Island* as PG–13. Everything had to be very safe and very dull.

The key factor was just like Indiana Jones was about cliffhanger action, Roger Rabbit was a tribute to those madcap, crazy cartoon shorts of the 1930s–1940s. Bob Zemeckis said, "This is not a kid's movie. I'm not worried about getting kids. It's a cartoon. Kids will go see it anyway. I gotta get young adults, 15–25. They are the ones that go to movies. And they won't pay to see a G rated cartoon." Bob added one swear word into the script to ensure a PG–13. When Roger drinks Valiant's bourbon and goes off like a steam whistle it shatters his whiskey bottle. Valiant exclaims, "Son of a bitch!" That was just enough to earn the rating.

FIGURE 9.5 Jessica Rabbit by lead animator Russell Hall.

(Copyright *Tatler*, collection of the author)

I had come out to London at Richard Williams' invitation to join the animation team in November 1987. I had been doing safe TV series for most of the decade. I read the script the first night and was amazed at all the zany action: Roger getting hit with frying pans, explosions and car crashes. The next day I went up to Bob Zemeckis and asked almost incredulous, "This script is good! Are we really going to do this?" I had become inured to good ideas being watered down and gelded by the Hollywood system. Bob looked at me almost insulted, "Of course we are!" I smiled: "Far out."

Once Dick Williams had finalized Roger Rabbit's design, they did a full animation and effects test. Roger is interacting with Valiant. Roger falling over life action props, Roger doing his first Tex Avery-style take. Zemeckis also wanted to see how the lighting would work to do full-on film noir-style cinematography, which meant in and out of deep shadow. We saw what was needed to match the toons shadowing to the live-action shadows. They learned a lot from the test, but one thing stuck out. The test was done with a "locked-down" camera. Which meant, very little moving camera stuff. Like Ray Harryhausen's classic scenes in *Jason and the Argonauts,* when there was animation, the camera was usually still. But that was 20 years ago. Since then, advancements like Steadycam meant you could be much freer with the camera's movement. As a result, this test seemed to lack energy. Now, one of the Dick Williams' guiding principles was "the best way to do something is the hard way." So, Dick told Bob Z., "Just shoot your movie. We will worry how to match the animation." The result was that when you looked at the rough footage with no animation or effects, it already looked like a fast-paced Spielberg/Zemeckis-style action comedy, and now, we just had to add the toons.

Producer Robert Watts (*Raiders of the Lost Ark*) and Dick Williams formed a unit outside of his own 13 Soho Square studio. This one is in the north London neighborhood of Camden Town. In keeping with the London animation scene of the time, the studio filled up not only with animators from Britain and America, but Canadians, Dutch, German, French, Italian and Hong Kong animators. Andreas Deja, Phil Nibbelink, Simon Wells, David Spafford, Jacques Muller, Frasier McLean, Caron Creed, Alyson Hamilton, Uli Meyer, Raul Garcia, Roger Chiasson, myself and many more. It was a United Nations of toonsters, all fired up with a shared love of classic Hollywood character animation. Producer Don Hahn, one of the few production people from the *ancien regime* to survive the *Katzenpurge,* moved out to London to oversee the creation of the animation. The production team was split evenly between Disney and Amblin people. There were a lot of negotiations to ensure Disney characters did not overly dominate the screen time over the Warner Bros characters. Mickey Mouse has as much screen time as Bugs Bunny. Daffy Duck has as much screen time as Donald Duck. When Mickey and Bugs are descending by parachute, their descent is structured so one does not fly above the other for any length of time.

Bob Zemeckis shot the live action in Los Angeles and London. His cinematographer Dean Cundy and his editor Arnie Schmidt were both Academy Award winners. It was an all A-list crew. Every frame of film was printed onto photographic stats and registered for animation paper. The animators drew over the stats to match to the live action. Each frame was painted, with coordinating effects and shadow levels. Then painted and photographed. The film was shipped across the globe to ILM in San

Francisco where the footage was completed in their Anderson Optical Printer. This was a device that took all the film reels of live action, animation and efx and pressed them together like a large hero sandwich.

At the dawn of digital cinema, when a little company named Pixar was just doing Scrubbing Bubbles commercials, *Who Framed Roger Rabbit* was one of the last movies to be done in the old matte-and-roto system. The process of Hollywood effects movies had been made since the days of *The Wizard of Oz* and *King Kong*. To give the flat-painted characters a feeling of roundness like the live-action people, we had to match the same light that lit them. In the days of *Mary Poppins* (1964), they attempted to solve this by putting a lot of light on the live-action people to minimize the shadows. But film noir was all about figures moving in and out of deep shadow. So, the characters needed the same kind of shadows the live-action figures had. Each toon had to have a set of half-tone shadow and quarter-tone shadow animated onto them. Plus, rim-lights to represent hot spots on their skin. As well as ground plane shadow to make it believable. Glowing effects like sparkles were done by winding back the film and re-exposing the different points. Jessica's sparkling dress in the nightclub scene had as many as 27 runs under the camera. Everything had to register perfectly; otherwise, the characters seemed to be floating off the ground and it would kill the effect. Most of our retakes were about registering to the live-action plates. Bob Zemeckis told us, "We're not making a cereal commercial here! If you don't believe the rabbit is sitting in the chair next to Hoskins, let's not make this movie!" The most mundane looking shots were often the hardest to do. Like Jessica running down an alley at night and casting a long shadow. When done perfectly, you do not notice it. It just feels natural. Nowadays, this shadow and registration problem is all done digitally, but back then, it all had to be hand-drawn and registered by eye. At the time, we thought we were making the most technologically advanced movie ever. But it turned out we were making one of the last of the traditional optical effect movies that harkened back to George Melies. Head of effects at ILM Ken Ralston later confessed to me, "This was the hardest movie we've ever done (at that time,1988)."

While many live-action directors pooh-poohed wasting their time working with cartoon animators, Bob Zemeckis relished the chance. He told us all, "I don't really know how you guys do what you do to create these characters. I am a live-action director. I tell actors where to stand and where to go. So, to me you are all actors with pencils. I am going to tell you where to make them stand and where to make them go." Dick Williams of course led the team and approved the animation, but Bob Z wanted to review every motion test and approve all the acting. He was worried that contemporary Disney animation had fallen too much into style over substance. A character flapping their arms around and crossing their eyes. Trying to imitate what we admired in Milt Kahl's animation. We called it The Head-Waggle School. At the end of each week, a production assistant would walk by your desk announcing "Videos." That meant if you had shot a motion test on ¾ inch videotape that you felt was ready for approval, you gave it to him, and he dubbed it onto one master tape. Then a courier would get it to Bob Zemeckis and Steven Spielberg wherever they were in the world. No internet yet. Bob sent back his notes via fax machine or called Dick Williams directly.

FIGURE 9.6 Gag sketch by Tom Sito of an over-zealous intern disturbing the artist's work. (collection of the author)

Thirty years of emphasis on budget had made most animators reluctant to do big do-overs if a shot was not working out. The days when Walt Disney would cut an entire scene from a film like he did in Snow White[12] were long gone. The mindset then was that if a shot was very difficult and time-consuming to complete, leave it in even if it does not work. It was too expensive to fix. Dick Williams and Bob Zemeckis were exceptions to that rule. Dick was a consummate perfectionist, and Zemeckis' rule was, "If it doesn't work, it's not in my movie." One lead animator had completed the scene of when Hoskins reaches for something to fight Judge Doom with, and he pulls out a "singing sword." It immediately morphs into Frank Sinatra singing "Witchcraft." The animator with three assistants generated up to 500 drawings for the finished scene. But when Zemeckis saw it, he said, "It doesn't look like Sinatra and it doesn't look like a sword. More like a wet noodle." They made him throw it all out and start again, getting the Sinatra caricature pre-approved. What is beyond debate is that the final scene is very good and very funny. I animated the weasels laughing so hard that they drop dead. Zemeckis briefed me, "What I want here is cartoon death. Funny Death."[13]

When the burden of animation production in London grew too heavy, a satellite unit was set up back in LA under the direction of Disney animator Dale Baer. That unit did most of when Eddie Valiant enters Toon Town. Roger was originally budgeted at $30 million. When cost overruns neared $50 million, Disney CEO Michael Eisner wanted to shut it down. But Jeffrey Katzenberg talked him out of it. I did the last shot in the movie, Scene 235/57. When Eddie Valiant, Dolores, Roger and Jessica walk off into the sunset as the happy toons dance around them and Dumbo flies overhead. Bob Zemeckis said he wanted it "to look like the last shot of Hitchcock's *The Birds*, except with toons." James Baxter animated Roger and Jessica. Andreas Deja animated Porky Pig saying, "That's All Folks." The entire scene was designed as a crane shot. Meaning when it began, you were looking down on the heads of Valiant and Roger. Then as the scene progressed, the camera came down to ground level looking up. I asked Dick, "How do I keep all those characters registered to the ground when it is constantly shifting?" Dick smiled. "Keep everybody dancing!" So that's what I did. I had Yosemite Sam with his six-shooters dance a mad little dance inspired by Sean Connery as a street performer in *The Man Who Would be King*. And so forth. Almost 100 characters on 14 separate levels, plus effects. All on ones. When I finally turned in the scene, I collapsed and was sick for a week. But it was done.

A final controversy occurred when Porky Pig is in the iris-out saying, "That's All Folks." The Disney people complained that they were paying for most of the production, and the movie was ending with a Warner Bros character! The solution was to fly in Tinker Bell to tap Porky on the nose with her magic wand. There was little money left in the budget, and most of the crew had moved on. Thinking quickly, production coordinator Steve Hickner had them bring up from the Disney archives the original animation drawings of Tinker Bell from the end of the Walt Disney Presents TV show. That was what was used.

Another issue was the release. Disney chief Jeffrey Katzenberg wanted to revive the name/brand of Buena Vista Pictures. However, Bob Zemeckis was adamant that it not be used. He was concerned that the reputation of Buena Vista then was so bad that it would hurt his films' Box Office. Michael Eisner and Roy Disney were also concerned about it having so many adult-themed jokes in it. The compromise was to release it under Touchstone Pictures, whose name brand was then much better. Thus, it became an Amblin/Touchstone release.

A practice big studios have been doing since the 1930s is to arrange preview screenings with audiences of average people to see if the film appealed to audiences. In exchange for a free movie, they asked the audience to fill out questionnaires and say what they liked and did not like. And in so doing, studio execs could gauge how much money to put into advertising. The test screenings for films like *The Little Mermaid* and *Toy Story* were so good that they excited the advertising execs that they had a hit on their hands. That is when they say the film has a good buzz about it. The problem with a film like Roger Rabbit was that the most complex and impressive composite[14] shots were usually the last to be completed. Director Robert Zemeckis was known for making changes up to the last minute. The Roger Rabbit print for the preview screenings went out to audiences with many important effects shots only half done. The audience saw scenes of empty chairs moving and pencil test footage. And they usually do not understand the difference. We would get comments from them like "We liked the scenes in color." Studio chiefs were stunned when the film got poor grades from the audience. Eisner, Katzenberg and Spielberg had to take a leap of faith and gamble that the finished film would be better received than this preview predicted. At the time, a cousin of mine said to me, "Are you guys worried that you got another *Howard the Duck?*" George Lucas' first big-budget flop. I replied, "No. I think they are more worried about it being a *Young Sherlock Holmes.*" A well-made film with breakthrough effects work that very few went to see.

Who Framed Roger Rabbit premiered at Radio City Music Hall on June 19, 1988, and opened nationwide three days later. A bunch of the crew came out from London, LA and San Rafael to rendezvous in New York for the premiere. Afterward, we all went up to the Rainbow Room to celebrate.

On opening day, I went down to the Ziegfeld Theater in Rockefeller Center with great anxiety. The critics liked it. We all could see it was good. But the ultimate test would be the public. Would they like it? I still remember sitting in an empty theater watching my first movie project, Richard Williams' *The Adventures of Raggedy Ann & Andy.* Would this be another exercise in heartbreak? When I came out of the subway onto the street, I immediately saw police barricades. The crowd waiting to get in was six rows deep and snaked down the block. This was a massive, Star Wars-sized crowd! Once inside, the people laughed and hooted in all of the right places. The end credits were greeted with thunderous applause. I teared up. You could not have written a better Hollywood ending.

Who Framed Roger Rabbit grossed over $11 million in its first weekend, a record then for a Disney film. Grossing $156,452,370 in the US alone, it was the Box-Office smash of 1988. When Eddie Murphy's hit *Coming to America* came out, he was asked about the other films he was competing with. He joked, "Ask me about the damn rabbit!"[15] When it was released in England a few months later, the London magazine Time Out trumpeted, "At last. Bucks Bunny!"

FIGURE 9.7 Roger Review in the NY Post, June 1988.

(collection of the author)

At the Academy Awards, *Who Framed Roger Rabbit* won three Oscars, Sound editing, etc. and a special Oscar to Richard Williams for the animation.[16] The film confirmed what studios began to suspect after the success of *An American Tail* and *The Great Mouse Detective.* That there was a huge audience for good quality character animation. The kind of fun cartoons created in the 1940s. Studios began to rethink rebuilding their animation units.

Afterward, several attempts at a Roger Rabbit sequel were begun, but getting all that talent to all agree a second time proved difficult. Bob Zemeckis was already back on to *Back to the Future 2.* He said he did not want to spend the second 10 years of his directing career making sequels to his first 10 years of films. Dick Williams wanted to get back to his epic *Cobbler and the Thief.* Disney animation in the short run began doing a series of Roger Rabbit shorts to run in front of Disney releases. The first short *Tummy Trouble* ran in front of *Honey I Shrank the Kids'* with animated titles done by another Disney alum Bill Kroyer. It beat out the opening of *Indiana Jones and the Last Crusade.* This aggravated Steven Spielberg who said why am I getting my ass kicked

FIGURE 9.8   Some of the Animation Crew celebrating Roger's Oscars, LA 1989.

(collection of the author)

Front row: Steve Hickner, Joe Haidar, Katherine Bell (Dick's mom), Richard Williams, Natasha Williams, Vera Lanpher and Pat Sito. Second row: Mark Kausler (behind Joe), Jacques Muller, Dave Spafford, Andreas Deja, Carl Bell (eyes closed) and Dorse Lanpher. Next row: Franz Vischer (hidden), James Baxter, Kenneth Williams (Dicks dad), Debbie Spafford and Joe Ranft. Back row: Alex Williams, Hans Bacher, Mark Gordon-Bates, Roger Chiasson, Tom Sito and Nik Ranieri.

by a character I half own? He asked that the next Roger Short, *Trail Mixup*, come out in front of one of his movies. Disney's said no. In the breakdown of negotiations, Roger's sequel was put aside. The final stroke was the untimely passing of Eddie Valiant actor Bob Hoskins in 2014 and Richard Williams in 2019.

But you cannot keep a good rabbit down. Roger and Jessica's antics continue to entertain newer generations of kids, and Gary Wolf continues to create new stories for them. Just like *Who Framed Roger Rabbit* taught us all to love the old Hollywood cartoons again, someday a new reboot might bring Roger back.

NOTES

1 Gary Wolf quoted in *Pulling a Rabbit Out of a Hat, The Making of Who Frame Roger Rabbit*, by Ross Anderson, University Press of Mississippi.
2 Paul Reubens had graduated from CalArts with Van Citters and many of the other Young Disney animators.
3 Gary Wolf said he also was inspired by the beautiful dancer Red from Tex Avery cartoons like "Red Hot Riding Hood".
4 Disney never actually had the rights to make *Where the Wild Things Are*. Author Maurice Sendak was very protective of his books. They were creating a test in the hopes of convincing him when the project was shelved.
5 Just before the Eisner change-over the Ancien Regime had made some tentative moves toward attracting A-list live-action talent. Carroll Ballard (*The Black Stallion*) directed the film "*Never Cry Wolf*" for them that became a sleeper hit. Ron Howard's *Splash* was also put into production just before the change.
6 Quoted in Anderson, *Pulling a Rabbit Out of a Hat.*
7 The Comedy Store was an improv club on the Sunset Strip started in April 1972 by Mitzi and Sam Shore and Don Ward. It was the premiere comedy club on the west coast where many famous comedians got their start.
8 CGI - computer generated imaging.
9 ILM - Industrial Light and Magic. George Lucas's movie special effects team.
10 Ross Anderson, *Pulling a Rabbit Out of a Hat.*
11 Ross Anderson, *Pulling a Rabbit Out of a Hat.*
12 The Soup Eating Sequence was cut from *Snow White.*
13 Robert Zemeckis to the author, 1988.
14 When a scene of animation with effects is combined with live action and reshot in the optical printer, the finished scene is referred to as a composite shot.
15 Quoted in the *NY Times*, Aug 1988.
16 The Best Animated Feature Oscar category would not exist until 2001. Animated Short films have been getting awards since 1932. Occasionally, the Academy would award a special Oscar for special achievement like to Walt Disney in 1938 for *Snow White and the Seven Dwarfs* and to John Lasseter in 1995 for *Toy Story.*

The Little Mermaid

10

Now all you gotta do is make the fish sing.

By 1989, The Walt Disney Studio was starting to feel pretty good about itself. Back in 1984, when Roy Disney's management team took over and started renovating, the House of Mouse was seen by Hollywood as a backward industry joke. Now it was back on top. Box Office receipts had tripled, and the stock price increased fivefold. This was due to a string of live-action hit films at Touchstone like *Down and Out in Beverly Hills, Pretty Woman,* new attractions at the park like *StarTours* and an aggressive slate of TV shows on the new Disney Channel. The studios return to TV animation, initially scoffed at "Walt Disney suddenly wants to be Hanna-Barbera?" now created solid hits like *Darkwing Duck, Gummi Bears* and *Gargoyles.* The studio was also still basking in the success of *Who Framed Roger Rabbit? (1988),* the Oscar-winning blockbuster of the previous year that had re-acquainted the public with the kind of high-quality character animation not seen in decades, and most baby boomers recalled from their childhood.

But one could make the argument that the success of *Roger* was not happening due to Disney animation, as much as it was the magic touch of Steven Spielberg and his talented protégé' Robert Zemeckis. It was Spielberg's influence with Warner Bros that had brought them to the table to work out a deal, so that for the first and only time in history, Bugs Bunny could meet face to face with Mickey Mouse. Bob Zemeckis was then the wunderkind of Hollywood with hits like *Back to the Future* and *Romancing the Stone.* *Roger Rabbit* might be ascribed to his ever-growing list of successes. But Zemeckis was not interested in making a sequel. Steven Spielberg had also co-produced *An American Tail* and *The Land Before Time* with Disney rival Don Bluth and was now building his own animation studio in London called Amblimation to create animated features to compete directly with Disney.

What about Walt Disney Feature Animation? Roy Disney had declared the animation division to be the heart and soul of the Walt Disney Company. Other studios were having some successes, but no one in the industry seriously believed this animation revival was for real until Disney had a breakout hit. They had always led the way.

After initially being skeptical about the need to keep their animation division, Walt Disney Studio Chairman Jeffrey Katzenberg had now come around to embrace the creation of animated features. *The Great Mouse Detective* had done well in 1986. Now due

96

DOI: 10.1201/b22394-11

to his friendship with music producer David Geffen, Katzenberg conceived of a pairing of Broadway musical stage with an animated film. By the 1980s, the movie musical had long fallen out of favor with audiences. Attempts to revive the grand Hollywood musical with films like *Hello Dolly (1969)* or Ross Hunter's *Lost Horizon (1973)* brought yawns from the Rock & Roll generation. A modern movie audience found the sight of inner-city gang members dancing pliés in *West Side Story (1961)* to be quaint but absurd.[1] A testament to more innocent times. The only movie musical in those days to find an audience was the John Belushi/Dan Aykroyd send-up of Chicago rhythm & blues called *The Blues Brothers (1980)* and the midnight cult film *Rocky Horror Picture Show (1975)*.

Disney creative producer Jeffrey Katzenberg had been a Hollywood insider for years. In conversations with his friend, producer-musical agent David Geffen, they talked about reviving the lost era of the Disney filmed musical. The surreal world of animation seemed to Katzenberg a natural fit for the type of hyper-metaphor fantasy seen in staged musical numbers. The great Disney animator Ollie Johnston once said, "Disney animation is not about copying life. It is about caricature of life." In musical theater, you needed to exaggerate slightly to project your emotions to reach the back of the theater. In animation, we call that pushing the pose. In live-action cinema, it looks a bit trite and overdone (*Paint Your Wagon*). But it suits animation perfectly.

After the first run Box-Office failure of films like *Pinocchio* and *Fantasia*, the Walt Disney animated musical had limped through the 1940s, only to roar back on top with 1949's musical *Cinderella* and 1951's *Peter Pan*. They then lapsed again in the 1960s until *101 Dalmatians*, *Mary Poppins* and *The Jungle Book* (1967).

Now to a world that had experienced Janis Joplin, the Stones and Woodstock, the innocent Disney hokum of animals bouncing to Dixieland jazz seemed sadly out of step. The studio that once had been filled with excited young artists, by the 1980s had grown stodgy. Conservative, middle-aged people making films for a narrowing niche audience. Floyd Norman recalled about *The Jungle Book*, "The old guys really felt they were doing something hip and fresh, using all that dated jazz music." The in-studio employee dress code ensured most men looked like they bought their clothes in a golf pro shop. It was not until 1977 that women were allowed to wear jeans to work. In *The Jungle Book (1967)*, the main character Mowgli encounters a flock of vultures that looked and sounded like the hit pop band The Beatles. But when they sang, out came an old barbershop quartet. Walt Disney argued that this rock & roll group The Beatles would probably be forgotten in a few years anyway. Walt's rule since the 1930s was that film music had to be timeless, so as not to date the film. This is what makes *Snow White and the Seven Dwarfs* feel as fresh now as it did in 1937. But by the age of Psychedelic Rock, Punk and Disco, Disney films like *Robin Hood (1973)* and *The Aristocats (1970)*, with syrupy ballads heavily orchestrated and backed by the 1950s vintage Disney chorus, came off hopelessly corny. In a 1987 market study of teenagers, most of them declared that they would not be caught dead watching a Disney animated movie.

At first, Disney studio's chief exec, Jeffrey Katzenberg thought the answer was to introduce more modern composers to the Disney musical. The Disney Records group scored a big hit with *Stay Awake (1988)*, a collection of classic Disney songs reinterpreted by modern musicians like Tom Waits and Dollie Parton. I was at an Oscar party that year and heard one top Disney director say to another "Do you know what the new guys wants to do next? Oliver. Not Oliver Twist, but that stupid musical from 1970!" Be careful what you make fun of. Jeffrey announced *Oliver & Company*, a reworking of the classic musical *Oliver,* with music by top pop icon Billy Joel, directed by George Scribner. Bette Midler did a voice, as well as Cheech Marin, who in 1969 had been banned from Disneyland for being too much of a drugged-out hippy-stoner for them.

When *Oliver & Company* premiered, it was a modest success ($74 million domestic), but the sulky animation crew felt the subject matter was still not up to the level of sophistication of *Who Framed Roger Rabbit.* Jeffrey even held an impromptu meeting with the crew to order them to stop criticizing *Oliver* in the press before the film even came out. He made his point with his characteristic bluntness "We're not going to throw out 60 years of tradition in family films just because you guys want to draw fuck cartoons!" Clearly, Disney could not do a musical as raunchy as *Rocky Horror* and still be Disney. Fox, Universal or Warner Bros might get away with it. They did not seem to carry all of the burden of Americana that Walt Disney had so carefully built. It was as though Uncle Sam, apple pie and the bald eagle were all under studio contract. *Oliver & Company* not only opened well, it came out on the same day (November 18, 1988) as Steven Spielberg's second collaboration with Don Bluth, *The Land Before Time*, and outdid its Box Office. But while *Land Before Time* spawned 17 profitable direct-to-video sequels, *Oliver and Company* made its money and quickly disappeared.

The problem remained how to do a musical that satisfied modern tastes, yet still adhered to the strict cultural brand that is Walt Disney? The answer came in the team of lyricist Howard Ashman and composer Alan Menken. American musical theater itself was then in the midst of a depression. The only successes on Broadway seemed to be British imports like Andrew Lloyd Weber's *The Phantom of the Opera* and Cameron Mackintosh's *Les Miserables*. The only interesting stuff seems to be the Off-Off Broadway independents like the WPA Theater, above a donut shop. Ashman & Mencken were a throwback to the great writing teams like Rogers & Hammerstein and Compton & Green. Instead of everyone on stage stopping in their tracks to sing a song, their musical numbers actually advanced the story. Their songs had a hip freshness that was not based in negative iconoclasm or social criticism. Their initial pairing in 1979 Kurt Vonnegut's *God Bless You Mister Rosewater* was a modest success, but their next effort, the musical version of the Roger Corman 1960 cult film *The Little Shop of Horrors* was a huge success. It was called the freshest American musical in years. Roy Disney and Jeffrey Katzenberg reached out to Ashman & Mencken to write an animated musical for animation. Jeffrey with his usual intensity even interrupted Ashman in the middle of his Passover Seder to ask if he was coming out to LA. "Howard, the combination of the talent of Howard Ashman and the Walt Disney name is a home run waiting to happen!"

Producer Don Hahn in his documentary about Ashman called "Howard" theorized that Howard Ashman always felt like a bit of an outsider in mainstream Broadway and Hollywood, and people who did animation had that same vibe. He concluded "One of the last great places to do Broadway musicals is in Animation."[2] So, they all clicked right away.

FIGURE 10.1   Close-up Scuttle, "I can't make out a heartbeat."

(Courtesy of Walt Disney Pictures. collection of the author)

The initial treatment for *The Little Mermaid* had been done by John Musker and Ron Clements. Both had come up through the Cal-Art's Disney Animation training program, had done storyboard work and then earned their first directing experience on *The Great Mouse Detective* (1986). In January 1985, Ron Clements was rooting around in a children's book section of a local bookstore when he happened upon a copy of Hans Christian Andersen's *The Little Mermaid*. Rereading the old story, he became intrigued by the possibilities.

Ron & John did a pitch to the studio brass at one of the "Gong Shows." The Gong Show was a concept brought over by Michael Eisner from Paramount Studio. All of the creative heads would hear new ideas for films pitched from the staff. If they liked one, it went into production. If they did not like it, it got gonged (a'la the 1980s Chuck Barris' *The Gong Show* on TV). At that meeting, Ron & John's proposal for the Little Mermaid initially was gonged because the studio was concerned it would come off looking like a poor imitation of their recent live-action hit *Splash,* starring Tom Hanks and Darryl Hannah.[3]

But production VP Jeffrey Katzenberg was intrigued with the story. It stuck with him. He reread Ron's treatment that night and by morning was all for putting it into production. He made sure that it was one of the properties Ashman and Mencken would see. Now supposedly, somewhere deep down in the Disney studio archives, there is a yellowing memo where Walt Disney himself had listed all of the ideas that should never be made into animated films, and *The Little Mermaid* topped that list. But Ashman and Mencken were intrigued by the possibilities of Hans Christian Andersen's lonely little siren, who surrendered her voice for love.

After all agreed *The Little Mermaid* would be the project, the normal Hollywood thing to do would be to engage a top movie screenwriter. But Musker and Clements claimed they could write the script themselves. Katzenberg gave the nod, and by years end, they turned in a credible first draft. They were then sent to meet with Howard Ashman in New York City. They had never worked with a Broadway lyricist, and Ashman had never worked with Disney animators before. But they quickly hit it off. "You had us at Jamaican Crab" Ron smiled.[4]

Commuting between Burbank, Cal and Dobbs Ferry, NY, the three began to rework the story, closely interweaving the music and prose dialogue. "Ashman was doing more than write lyrics to songs," lead animator Duncan Marjoribanks recalled "he was really creating a libretto for the entire film."[5] During one disappointing focus group of some of the story reels, Ashman helped rewrite the key scene where Ariel's father King Triton relents and is won over to her wanting Prince Eric. They also arrived at the decision to change the story's ending, where the mermaid dies and turns into seafoam. This tragic ending was the main reason old Uncle Walt had initially dismissed the fairytale as good subject matter for a film.

Recording the music tracks took place in New York City on some dependable recording stages to assure easy access to veteran Broadway talent. Veteran actors Pat Carroll, Kenneth Mars, Rene Auberjenois and Sam Wright were brought in to add their voices. Buddy Hackett was to be the seagull Scuttle. Howard Ashman specifically called his friend Jody Benson to come in and audition for the voice of Ariel. They had worked together on his failed 1986 musical *Smile*. Jody Benson recalled: "Anytime I told somebody what I was working on, they said, 'Oh that's too bad you're doing a cartoon.' Like my career had really tanked. So, I just stopped telling anybody about it. Then when the movie came out, everybody was saying 'why didn't you tell me?' but they had been acting like my career was going down the toilet, basically."[6]

Howard Ashman was a stage director and performer in his own right in addition to being a lyricist. Often on the rough tracks the artists worked from, it was Howard singing while Alan Mencken accompanied on the piano. Howard personally directed the recording of the main songs for Mermaid. Instead of remaining sequestered within the engineer's booth, he remained standing next to Jody during her recording, giving her notes like "here intensity of feeling is better than noise (meaning the kind of vocal projection required to reach the back seats of a large theater)."[7] As an animator, after I returned to LA from London and doing *Roger Rabbit*, I was given a cubicle on *Mermaid* very close to the sound editor's room. At first, it was an ordeal having to listen to hour after hour of Buddy Hackett improvisation on Scuttles' lines. *"A-jeesh, huh! Ugh! Okay Ariel! Hang in dere, kid! Sheesh! Oooh!"* and so on.

The first sequence that went into animation production was the song "Under the Sea." Animator Duncan Marjoribanks had started early on the production while most of the main crew was still completing *Oliver and Company*. A native of Canada, Duncan had initially been turned down by Disney in the Ron Miller years because the management then was loathe to go through all of the immigration visa issues. Duncan made it down to Hollywood anyway, and after a lot of TV and commercials, he did yeoman's work on Brad Bird's first film *Family Dog* (1986). This led Brad to recommend the tall, softspoken Canadian to his former CalArts schoolmates Musker and Clements. Duncan did some test animation of Sebastian, the little crab, that was so good, he was promoted to be the lead (directing) animator for that character. As animators from Roger Rabbit returned from that project, they were given new assignments on Mermaid. Andreas Deja did the father King Triton, Tony Fucile created Ariel's sidekick Flounder, Matt O' Callaghan did Chef Louie and Prince Eric. Rob Minkoff was originally slated to create the villainess Ursula. But after a few scenes, he desired to move on to directing Roger Rabbit shorts, so the lead position was assumed by the Okinawa-born Ruben Aquino.

Glen Keane had tired of being known for doing dastardly villains like Ratigan and Sykes. He requested to do Ariel herself, seen then as a challenge for his abilities. He was backed by another top animator, Mark Henn. A contemporary recalled, "Glen's Ariels resembled his wife Linda, who had a slender long neck and arms. While Mark's Ariels had a bit more baby fat on them." Mark said, "She should look like a teenage girl on the edge of womanhood, unsure but determined."[8] Some of the artists enjoyed a healthy competition of who was producing the most completed footage per week. Glen and Mark were always neck and neck in output. When a production assistant posted the week's footage totals, Mark was usually the first to pop out of his office to check to see how he was doing in the ranking.

I animated Ursula's victims, called the Polyps, some Sebastian, but mostly a lot of singing fish. I also created the bishop who tried to marry the sea witch Vanessa to Prince Eric. I had drawn him as a doddering old man who had to stand on a box to be eye-level with the couple. This arrangement caused an internet sensation, years later, because some people claimed his knees protruding from his robes were actually a male erection! That this was some kind of sick joke of a perverse animator to corrupt children. I had to make a deposition in a lawsuit brought against Disney by a Southern Baptist Church group alleging the said seduction of the innocent. It was all just a tempest in a teapot.

Many times, your ability to generate a lot of animation was depended upon the department before animation, the layout department, delivering enough new scenes for you to get a momentum going. I was getting nervous about the song sequence Seq. 11- *Kiss the Girl* because the layouts for a key scene were lagging behind schedule. It involved a long tracking shot following a number of sea creatures swimming around Ariel and Eric's rowboat as dragonflies buzzed overhead. Such camera work required meticulous planning timed to the tempo of the song before an animator could start drawing. So, I waited. Finally, layout artist Daniel St. Pierre dumped the thick completed scene folder on my desk and smiled "There. Now all you gotta do is make the fish sing."

Animated film production is famous for the way we fuss over the minutest details. Designer Rowland Wilson and art director Michael Peraza created a beautifully colorful world under the sea. Rowland Wilson was a well-known illustrator and cartoonist for Playboy magazine. When it came to the design of Ariel, Rowland suggested that she look like a being that had never seen the surface world or sunshine. In some of his earliest designs, he drew her with a light blue skin color and turquoise eyes. Jeffrey Katzenberg was against this because he thought it would be off-putting to the audience, who could not relate to such an alien-looking creature. The decision was made to keep the skin tone a more Caucasian-cream color.

FIGURE 10.2 *The Little Mermaid* animation crew.

(courtesy of the author)

Then, there was a big argument about making Ariel a redhead. Some actually argued "Everyone knows mermaids are blonde!" But that would make her look too much like the Daryl Hannah in *Splash*. Plus, the red hair–green fishtail was more color-complimentary. Another debate was over Ariel's clamshell top. The issue was whether to create a seaweed bra-string that tied around the back. Some argued that this drew attention to the fact that her top was lingerie, and the clams should just stay on with magic. Others said clamshell pasties would cause even more distraction, like the way the topless pixies of *Beethoven's Pastorale in Fantasia* still cause endless snickering among the pubescent kids. The final decision was to keep the bra string. Even if after the film's debut, we received a letter of complaint from a Washington State nudist colony. "Ariel's clam shells are restrictive, sexist, hint at S&M, and she cannot check herself for breast cancer."[9]

Matt O' Callaghan was given Prince Eric to develop. Jeffrey wanted us to model Eric with the dark eyebrows and smile of actor Tom Cruise. He turned out to be a difficult character to build, as many perfect hero types are. At one point, Jeffrey pointed out in a meeting "I don't believe she could ever fall for him. And if the love-story doesn't work, the movie doesn't work." Matt chafed under the restrictions of doing what at first seemed such a typically bland hero. After all, who recalls the prince in Cinderella or Snow White? In the opening number, a rollicking sea shanty, he did not want him to be doing nothing while the ship's crew toiled away doing all of the real work. So, he had him pulling on ropes like one of the guys. The attending of his manservant Grimsby was the only nod to his status as a nobleman. Matt also disliked the idea of him playing a small flute when thinking. This music was what first caught Ariel's attention. Matt felt it was unmanly. "Why not have him on deck playing a cello?" he proposed tongue firmly in cheek. Giving him a dog (Max), ably animated by Russ Edmonds, helped to humanize him as well. All of this focus on Prince Eric's character lifted him from being evolving from a cookie-cutter prince to a warm, appealing character.

The Little Mermaid was Walt Disney's final animated feature to be painted with traditional paints on acetate sheets called "cels." This technique had been the way animated cartoons had been done since the dawn of film a century earlier. The Walt Disney Company maintained a paint lab that mixed its colors from vats of powdered pigment. Although drawings were xeroxed onto the cels, the underwater bubbles had to be hand-inked the way they were in the 1940s. The amount of labor needed usually made Ink & Paint the largest department in terms of sheer numbers. Michael Eisner had sought to save some money by sending a percentage of the painting work to China. This had been done very successfully with the animation work on the Disney television series.

The two artists sent to supervise in Shenzhen were Bethann McCoy-Gee and Leo Sullivan. While they were working there, the student movement protests resulting in the 1989 Tiananmen Square crackdown occurred. Bethann recalled "All TV and telephone communications with the capitol (Beijing) ceased, but through word of mouth we had heard something terrible was happening. I lived in an apartment building that was half Chinese and half foreigners. As the police crackdown continued, every day I went to get my mail I noticed another name on the mailboxes was missing. I asked the landlord 'Where is Mr. Chen? And he replied' . . . who?" I thought this is bad and getting worse! Leo and I contacted the American Consulate in Shanghai and received the kind of response no one ever wants to hear, "If the worst happens, we can get you out." We had visions of us like the Iranian Hostages in 1979 or like in Beirut being on camera holding up today's newspaper saying how well treated we were. "Forget that Jack! We want out NOW!"[10]

Back in California, the producers had visions of tanks rolling over piles of precious animation art. No one had thought to make copies of the drawings before shipping! Bethann and Leo were eventually able to get home with most of the animation drawings, but some scenes were lost. Any further overseas work was curtailed, and no further animation was shipped without it first being photocopied and carefully cataloged. The Walt Disney Studios had been dabbling in computer graphics since the late 1960s. Chief engineers Bob Lambert and Dave Inglish proposed utilizing the newest computer technologies to paint the animated characters. "We took some old (Black) Cauldron elements and sent them to Pixar to be scanned and painted using their imaging software. It came back with no degradation of quality. We put together the financials and pitched the concept to the studio. This would allow us to keep everything here."[11] The work of 500 Chinese painters could be done digitally by no more than a dozen local painters, and the selection of colors would be vastly increased. Roy Disney was not only convinced but he also sold the idea to his colleagues in corporate. Roy told his partner Frank Wells "Frank, I want to spend ten million dollars on something we may not see a dime from initially. "[12]

FIGURE 10.3 *Little Mermaid* storyboard featuring Ursula.

(collection of the author)

The system would be called computer animated production system (CAPS). It would not only be a paint and surfacing system but also a production router for the scenes. After entertaining several bids from various computer graphics producers, they made a deal with a little company owned by Apple's Steve Jobs called Pixar. Pixar's Renderman software was a top-line standard for big VFX films like James Cameron's *Terminator II Judgement Day*. And their engineers had experience developing digital paint systems since the days of Xerox PARC and New York Institute of Technology in the 1970s. The deal came at an important moment for Pixar's fortunes as well because even though they made a number of award-winning shorts, the company, for the most part, was living off of Steve Jobs' personal checks. The occasional Scrubbing Bubbles or Listerine commercial could not keep them going much longer. Everyone there feared if one day Jobs might tire of his new toy and unload them. This rapid infusion of cash from The Big Mouse down south ensured their survival.

In 1989, Pixar's team joined with Disney's in-house scientists to create the CAPS. Not only would the system have to be developed to fulfill the specific needs of Disney Animation, but the artists also had to be trained to use the system. Animator Randy Cartwright was of that rare breed of traditionally trained artist who embraced the new technologies. He helped as a conduit between the eggheads and the artists. Only a decade earlier, you needed a PhD in mathematics just to turn on such a system. "It got to where we had a painter up and using the equipment in an hour."[13] Development went smoothly; one in-house joke drawing done anonymously was a color test of Ariel's breasts popping out of their clamshells. Boys will be boys.

But CAPS would not be ready in time to affect much of the final completion of *The Little Mermaid*. The very last scene of the movie, Ariel and Eric sailing off as King Triton and the mer-people wave farewell, was the first all CAPS painted scene. The bulk of the artwork was completed by a dedicated team of traditional painters and checkers, the finest in the business.

While the animators toiled and pencil sharpeners whirred, sections of the unfinished movie were put before the public through focused test-screenings. The average person-on-the-street does not always comprehend the future potential of animated films. We artists can foresee the look of the finished picture, but for now, all the audience could see was raw footage of pencil tests and story drawings. We inevitably got comments like "we liked the parts in color." One such test screening nearly yielded a tragic result.

One of the key sequences is the beautiful song *Part of Your World*, where in the privacy of her hideaway, Ariel opens up about her hopes and dreams. Howard Ashman explained, "It's usually the third song in a musical, where the little lady sits down on a trashcan or something, and sings about what she wants."[14] Glen Keane had created a virtuoso performance planning the sequence and animating the character to Ashman & Mencken's beautiful melody.

But when shown to a test audience,[15] much of the sequence was still in black and white pencil test. Many children present, not understanding what they were seeing, shifted restlessly in their chairs. One boy dropped his popcorn tub and turned his back on a key moment of the song to retrieve the loose kernels. Another kid yawned. Sitting in the rear, Jeffrey Katzenberg grimly came to the conclusion that *Part of Your World* was killing the stories pace and so must be cut from the film. Howard Ashman and Glen Keane immediately leaped to its defense. Howard thundered "OVER MY DEAD BODY! THIS SONG IS THE HEART OF THE WHOLE MOVIE!" After a spirited argument, Jeffrey reluctantly agreed to allow *Part of Your World* to remain in the film. In the final weeks of production when Glen was in England beginning *Beauty & the Beast*, Jeffrey was still trying to get part of the darker colors of Ariel repainted "She looks like a frog." He grumbled. When it was pointed out how much more these changes would increase the budget, he again backed down.[16]

Walt Disney's *The Little Mermaid* opened on Friday, November 16, 1989. Disney traditionally opened their holiday season releases around November 18 because it was the anniversary of the 1928 short film *Steamboat Willie*, the birth of Mickey Mouse. This was for good luck, and November 18 was the week before American Thanksgiving the traditional beginning of the holiday season. Mermaid opened well ($6 million) but then something interesting happened. The following week, instead of its Box Office dropping, as was often the case, it doubled. The next week it doubled again and kept doubling. Obviously, word of mouth was carrying the film, and parents and children were seeing it again and again. It seemed to leave all of the competing films behind. As an experiment, the studio held a screening for adults only and saw it had become a date movie. Sold out, with nary a moppet in sight. The *Little Mermaid* soundtrack quickly climbed to the top of the Billboard charts.

Critics were exultant. Roger Ebert of the Chicago Sun Times said, "Walt Disney's 'The Little Mermaid' is a jolly and inventive animated fantasy—a movie that's so creative and so much fun it deserves comparison with the best Disney work of the past." Janet Maslin of the New York Times called it "the best animated Disney film in at least 30 years."

Jeffrey Katzenberg jubilantly predicted that *The Little Mermaid* would be the first animated film to earn $100 million dollars in the Box Office. Long time, animation veterans were skeptical. Up to then, animated films had never made the kind of monster profits that a *Star Wars* or an *ET the Extra Terrestrial* did. And Disney had not attempted a full-on cartoon musical in over 30 years. In the 1970s, if an animated film made back its cost in domestic Box Office, that was considered a success. Overseas Box Office and ancillary sales like toys and cable TV sales were where the studio made their real profits. Also, conventional wisdom at the time was that a film in which the lead character was a girl would not perform as well. That little boys would not go to see a film with a girl as the hero. $100 million for a cartoon just seemed like pie-in-the-sky wishful thinking. But *The Little Mermaid* outdid all of the analysts' estimates. The final domestic Box Office for its original run was $111, 543, 479.[17]

The Little Mermaid did something no one had seen at Walt Disney since the days of The *Jungle Book* (1967). It gave the studio an undisputed, smash hit musical. This had an unexpected effect from few remaining retired elderly Disney animation veterans. They were outwardly supportive and happy for the studio. But some were not a little envious that their little protégés had created a classic that could be compared to their masterworks. They really felt that their level of artistry would never be equaled in their lifetime. Now everyone was calling Ariel the equal of Snow White and Cinderella. "That's not a mermaid, it's more like a jellyfish"—grumbled one old timer.

Instead of releasing the film in other countries with subtitles, Disney generated new prints with voice tracks in French, Spanish, German, etc. Supervised by Ashman and the production team, instead of contracting an outside dubbing house. This attention to quality increased the impact of the film fourfold. When *The Little Mermaid* opened in Denmark, Ron Clements and John Musker sat in the royal box with the queen of Denmark, Margarethe II. Hans Christian Anderson was a sacred institution in Denmark, and a statue of the Little Mermaid in Copenhagen harbor is the most beloved monument in the country. Disney had done a careful redubbing of the movie into Danish and had hired a local pop star who was called the Danish Madonna to be the voice of Ariel. Still, Ron and John anxious waited to see if Danes would embrace the handling of their national myth. When the credits rolled and the house lights came up, the Danes reacted with a thunderous standing ovation. Queen Margarethe said it was wonderful. Ron Clements asked her if she minded that they changed the ending to a happy ending. The Queen laughed "Oh, Anderson (Hans Christian Anderson) never could write a good ending. He just has everyone die!"[18] At that year's Academy Awards, *The Little Mermaid* won two Oscars for Best Score and Best Song "Part of Your World." The song that had almost been dropped from the film. These were Disney's first musical Oscars since The *Jungle Book* (1967).

The Little Mermaid was not just a hit; it was a phenomenon. Around the world, people went multiple times, and when it came out on home video, they watched the videos until they wore out. Little girls around the world wanted to be Ariel. To the amazement of Disney marketing executives, Little Mermaid toys and merchandise were selling as strongly 4 years later as they were in 1989.[19] My mother called me to say that they had worn out their video copy watching it. I do not think that up until then, I had ever worn out a video cassette myself.

Great Mouse Detective and *Oliver & Company* were hopeful signs; *Who Framed Roger Rabbit?* could be considered a special one-time case. But after *The Little Mermaid*, Walt Disney Animation really seemed back, and animation was now the talk of the town. Crosstown rivals like Paramount, Universal and MGM that had not thought seriously about animated film in decades, now began to plan their own animated movies. What was equally satisfying was that these successes were high-quality productions, where few compromises were made to economize. Studios that tried to recreate their success but did it on the cheap were unsuccessful. A new era of high-quality animation has been inaugurated. Much like late 1930s Hollywood with *Snow White* and *Gulliver's Travels*.

At the crew party at the Beverly Hills Hotel, the animators basked in all of the success. After so many years of struggle. Being told they would never do anything as good as the old guys. Here was a success that would stand next to anything the Golden Age Generation had done. One artist gestured over to old production manager Ed Hansen. He said *"Hey Tom. There's old Ed Hansen. Let's go thank him for not hiring us in the 1970s, so we didn't have to work on any of those movies like Pete's Dragon!"*

But would this last?

NOTES

1 In 2021, When Steven Spielberg remade *West Side Story*, it flopped at the box office.
2 Howard Ashman quoted in *Howard*.
3 Waking Sleeping Beauty, documentary.
4 Waking Sleeping Beauty, documentary.
5 Duncan Marjoribanks quoted, interview on "The Animation Guild" podcast, July 2013.
6 Jodie Benson quotes in 2010 interview Part of His World, Remembering Howard Ashman. http://howardashman.com/blog/featured_posts/?guest=jodi-benson
7 John Musker recollection in Remembering Howard Ashman. http://howardashman.com/blog/10-questions-for-john-musker/
8 Mark Henn quoted in *Waking Sleeping Beauty*.
9 Ron Clements to the author, 1989.
10 Bethann McCoy-Gee to the author, August 1990.
11 David Inglish, quoted in *Moving Innovation: A History of Computer Animation* (MIT Press, 2013) pg 226.
12 *Waking Sleeping Beauty*, documentary.
13 Randy Cartwright, quoted in *Moving Innovation: A History of Computer Animation* (MIT Press, 2013) pg 227.

14 Howard Ashman quoted, *Waking Sleeping Beauty*.
15 Filmmakers have been using test-audiences to gauge audience reactions since the days of silent films. Charlie Chaplin or Walt Disney would sit in the back of an audience and note what they laughed at and what they did not. In the mid 1930s, Professor Boris Morkovin of the University of Southern California started the idea of handing out index cards to the audience to gauge their likes and dislikes.
16 Glen Keane to the author, 1989.
17 Box Office Mojo.com
18 Ron Clements to the author, 1989.
19 Howard Green to the author, 1994.

Cowabunga!
The Simpsons

11

The Simpsons created an audience for prime-time animation that had not been there for many, many years. . . . As far as I'm concerned, they basically re-invented the wheel. They created what is in many ways—you could classify it as—a wholly new medium.
—*Family Guy* creator Seth MacFarlane

One day in 1985, Polly Platt, the executive vice president of Gracie Films,[1] walked into James L. Brooks' office holding a newspaper comic strip. James L. Brooks was the producer and director well known for TV hits like *The Mary Tyler Moore Show, Taxi* and movies like *Big* and *Broadcast News*. Polly had an equally distinguished career as an art director and producer.[2] She pushed the comic under Brook's nose and said, "Have you ever seen this?" It was a nine-panel cartoon from the free L.A. Weekly newspaper titled *"The Los Angeles Way of Death,"* drawn by somebody named Matt Groening. "People all around the office cut out his gags and post them on the fridge or their desks. This might make an interesting animated series." Jim Brooks had come to rely on Polly's instinct, since in the past, she had discovered people like Cybill Shephard and Wes Anderson. He agreed to call in this Groening fellow to discuss the possibilities of a show. Initially, nothing came of that first phone call, but Brooks kept that drawing framed on his wall. More importantly, he filed the idea away in his mind.[3]

In the era when the big three networks CBS, NBC and ABC dominated television broadcasting, the most important time slot a TV show could hope for was called Prime Time. 8:00–11:00 PM Eastern/Pacific and 7:00–10: 00 PM. Central/Mountain. Demographics showed that it was the time when most families would be home, after dinner, centered around their TVs. When Ed Sullivan debuted The Beatles on his Sunday primetime show in 1964, it got 37 million viewers, a third of the population of the USA. Back in the 1960s, it was not uncommon to see many animated comedies running in prime time.

The Flintstones, The Jetsons, Top Cat, Rocky and Bullwinkle, all did their first runs as primetime shows.

But as the kid audience for cartoons on Saturday mornings grew, the primetime audience diminished. Advertisers did not want to pay the same rates for cartoons as they paid for live-action series. They felt they were for kids and so should be in the daytime. One by one, animated shows slipped away from evenings. The last one I recall seeing was Creston Studios *Calvin and the Colonel* around 1970. Hanna-Barbera tried to launch new primetime series like *The Huddles* (1970) and *Wait Till Your Father Gets Home* (1972–74). But both failed to attract an audience.

Animation went into the "Saturday Morning Ghetto" until the mid-1980s. In 1983, studios like Filmation and Marvel, trying to get around the stranglehold of the three networks, created syndicated package deals for regional media stations. Instead of Saturday mornings, they ran weekdays after 3:00 PM, when the kids came home from school. *He-man and the Masters of the Universe, She-Ra: Princess of Power, Jem, G.I. Joe* and more. Since 1980, the new pay-cable stations like HBO and MTV were experimenting with animation.

Rupert Murdoch was an Australian newspaper mogul who had made a name for himself by riding roughshod over the Fleet St press barons in London. He then set his sights on America. He arrived in 1974 and quickly gobbled up fabled old publications like The New York Post, The Village Voice and The Wall St. Journal. Then in 1985, Rupert made a surprise move into broadcasting by purchasing the Hollywood movie studio Twentieth Century Fox. Like his contemporary Ted Turner, Rupert Murdoch wanted to challenge the television networks at their own game. He wanted to create a fourth network, The Fox Network. It was an audacious plan. Nothing of the kind had been attempted since the DuMont Network rolled over and sank in 1956.

Sir Rupert brought in Barry Diller to helm his effort. Diller had risen from the mailroom at William Morris to at one time head ABC Network and then Paramount Pictures.

The Fox Broadcasting Network debuted October 9, 1986. Its initial efforts did not do so well. *The Chevy Chase Show, the Joan Rivers Show* and a political sitcom *Mr. President* with George C. Scott and Madeleine Kahn. All failed to find an audience. The Fox Network lost $95 million dollars in its first year. NBC chief Brandon Tarticoff scoffed that Fox was a network with a coat hanger for an antenna.

Fox Broadcasting director Barry Diller knew he had to do something different or perish. He deliberately cut back on censors and the standards & practice types. He said they were doing it to save money, but industry insiders thought it was a ploy to attract viewers with more edgy, adult material. The first show of this type, the sitcom *Married With Children*, started to attract viewers. One episode was titled *"Her Cups Runneth Over"* where Al and a friend go to a lingerie store to buy Peggy her favorite bra. A Michigan housewife named Terry Rakolta organized a grassroots boycott citing the show's obscenity that amounted to nothing except to give them more press exposure. The Fox Network quickly gained a reputation for being the brash, iconoclastic alternative to standard network fare.

Barry Diller had worked before with James L. Brooks and Gracie Films on the hit show *Room 222*. In 1987, Diller brought in Jim Brooks to build a comedy show around Tracey Ullman. Tracey Ullman was a British sketch comedienne who did impressions of famous women. She and her producer husband had recently moved to Hollywood to try their luck. Brooks recalled "I saw original talent, and how often does that happen to you?" Brooks and Ullman worked out a format for the proposed show. It would consist of Ullman's comedy sketches, with something between the segments and commercial breaks. They considered how to transition from one sketch scenario to another. A decade earlier, the British sketch show *Monty Python's Flying Circus* had found that going to black and silence in between sketch scenes created dead zones that killed the energy and pace of a show. So, animator Terry Gilliam cut up some magazine illustrations and improvised clever animated interstitials on a down shooter camera. They became the

21

FIGURE 11.1   Matt Groening's cartoon: "The Los Angeles Way of Death".

(Courtesy the L.A. Weekly)

show's signature. Jim Brooks conceived the idea of using several different cartoonists to generate short, animated interstitials. One was M.K. Brown's *Dr. N!Gotatu* in a rotation. She had come from The National Lampoon. Then Brooks recalled his meeting 2 years earlier with that *Life in Hell* guy.

Matt Groening moved from his native Portland to LA in the 1980s. After disappointing attempts to break into the cartoon animation business there, he channeled his frustration out in a quirky comic strip he created entitled *Life in Hell*, published by the free independent newspaper the L.A. Weekly. He was living in a shack in Venice Beach. Jim Brooks and Polly Platt decided their characters in *Life in Hell* just might match the quirkiness of Tracey Ullman's style of humor.

However, Matt Groening balked when Fox first asked him to sell them the rights to his *Life in Hell* characters. "I had been drawing my weekly comic strip, *Life in Hell,* for about 5 years when I got a call from Jim Brooks, who was developing "The Tracey Ullman Show" for the brand-new Fox Network. He wanted me to come in and pitch an idea for doing little cartoons on that show. I soon realized that whatever I pitched would not be owned by me, but would be owned by Fox, so I decided to keep my rabbits in *Life in Hell*, and come up with something new. Groening was worried if the show did not work, he would lose the one property that was paying his bills. Groening was on the spot, so while waiting in the Gracie Films offices, he conceived a sitcom similar to the old animated series *The Flintstones,* but with a more modern, hipper, dysfunctional take on the American family.

He called it *The Simpsons*. Matt drew the first designs on a napkin. Homer was the name of Groening's own father, Marge was his mother with her beehive hairdo and his sisters were Lisa and Maggie. At first, he was going to call the boy Matt, but decided on Bart, which was an anagram of brat. He liked the name Simpson from a character in Nathaniel West's *Day of the Locust*. It also seemed funny to him, "Simp." The family lived in the town of Springfield. Matt Groening has always been coy about admitting which town was the original inspiration, Springfield, Massachusetts, Springfield, Illinois, etc. He actually took it from the 1950s TV sitcom *Life With Father*.[4]

FIGURE 11.2   James L. Brooks.

(Courtesy of Venice Magazine Dec. 1997)

James L. Brooks swung over the same voice acting team working on his other interstitials onto voicing *The Simpsons*, Julie Kavner, Yeardley Smith and Dan Castellenata.[5] Actress Nancy Cartwright had gone to Tracey Ullman's production offices to apply for a different gig. When upon her arrival, she learned that part had already been cast. But the casting director noticed on her resume that she could do little boy voices. He sent her over to speak to Brooks. She did although at one point, she thought she was there to read for Lisa and Julie Kavner for Bart. Julie suggested, "I think we should switch." They did, she read, and Brooks immediately hired her to be the voice of Bart Simpson. He did not bother to audition anyone else.

They hired young animators David Silverman, Wes Archer and Bill Kopp to animate the interstitials through the animation house Klasky-Csupo. David Silverman came out of the UCLA film school as an independent, experimental animator. Instead of checking into a large Saturday Morning factory like Hanna-Barbera, David and Wes worked at several little fringe studios, like a company that created animated laser-light shows on the sides of buildings. His friends (including your author) urged David to stop wasting his time and "get a real job" in a real studio. But when he came to animate *The Simpsons*, he took to the quirky little designs and created quirky little animated actions for them to do. Like when Bart and Lisa drink soda pop and have a belching contest, David created clever odd geometric mouth shapes and effervescence bubbles flying about. In one segment, the Simpson's children watch cartoons on TV. An issue bedeviling parents' groups and other culture warriors at the time was the amount of violence in cartoons. The team created a show within the show called *Itchy & Scratchy*. Based on older 1950s cat-chases-rat pursuit shorts like *Tom & Jerry* and *Herman & Katnip*, but outrageously more violent. Matt Groening had expected his initial sketched designs would be given a makeover. But David and his friends liked animating them just as loose and funky as they were. Designer Georgyi Peluce gave Bart and his family their distinctive bright yellow coloring. These oddball little sequences were quirky, like something never seen before on American TV. *The Tracey Ullman Show* premiered on April 5, 1987. While never becoming a ratings juggernaut, it was an early critical hit for Fox and earned them their first Emmy Awards.

After a few weeks, the other cartoonist's interstitials faded away, and it was all *Simpsons*.[6] Even Tracey Ullman herself began to see the Simpson's character was getting more attention than she was. People began to urge James L. Brooks and Barry Diller to spin off Homer, Bart and his family into their own show. Brooks recalled, "At that year's Christmas Party, celebrating the first year's success of the (Tracey Ullman) show, one of the animation directors (David Silverman) came up to me and said, 'Jim! You don't know how much animators want to do this as a primetime series! There hasn't been an animated series on primetime in twenty-five years!'"

But they were hesitant. A nighttime cartoon aimed at adults seemed pretty risky. A 1976 study by the National Ad Council had determined, "Animation is too expensive and time consuming to ever be profitable." Garth Ancier, President of Fox Entertainment at the time, claimed that there were a lot of corporate people at Fox who wanted to cut them, mainly due to the price of animation. "It cost $15,000 a week to make the animated bumpers."[7]

FIGURE 11.3 The original *Simpsons*'s directors 1989 (Clockwise from top left): Wes Archer, David Silverman, Matt Groening, Rich Moore and Mark Kirkland. Missing: Bill Kopp

(Courtesy of David Silverman)

Associate producer Paul Germain had an idea. He brought Brooks and Diller down to Tracey Ullman's live studio set. He showed them that they were using a collection of the Simpson's interstitials to warm up the studio audience instead of the usual live comedian. Watching this audience of adults howling with laughter at these cartoons finally convinced Diller and Brooks that a primetime cartoon series could work.

The Tracey Ullman Show never really caught on with the American audiences and by May 1990 was canceled. Tracey herself was not a little miffed that the cartoon on her show was getting more interest than she was. In 1992, she sued Twentieth Century Fox seeking profits related to the merchandising to create the show. "I breast-fed those little devils."[8] Animator Brooke Keesling recalled, "Tracey Ullman shopped at the music story Music Plus in Studio City, where I worked as a teenager. I once told her I loved her show, and my favorite parts were the animated interstitials . . . that went over like a lead balloon (as you might imagine)."[9] Ullman lost her lawsuit but moved on to a very successful career creating shows for HBO and Showtime and appearing in movies.

So, the decision was made to turn *The Simpsons* into a regular series. Now it was one thing to do brief snippets of quirky observational comedy, quite another to create a full-on TV series with recurring plots and ensemble characters. At least 6 hours of programming a season.

James L. Brooks was a veteran writer-producer, with a dozen Emmy Awards and hit movies, but animation was a new thing for him. Fortunately, one of his old collaborators was Alan Burns, a writer he met on the set of the *Mary Tyler Moore Show*. Among his many titles, Alan Burns had been a writer-director on the classic Jay Ward cartoon *Rocky and Bullwinkle*. Burns explained to him Jay Ward's philosophy of successful TV animation. Stay away from complex pantomime comedy like in Warner's Looney Tunes and focus instead on strong writing and tracks. *Rocky and Bullwinkle* were never known for their character animation. It was mostly animated in Mexico on a shoestring budget. Old animation legend Chuck Jones first impression of the Simpsons was "Really good radio." That you could turn off the picture and still laugh. But the adult-oriented writing and voice acting were so good, nobody seemed to mind.

James L. Brooks had said, "This is not going to be a cartoon series. It will be a sitcom done in animation." He and producer-writer Sam Simon passed over the usual stable of cartoon writers in town and began to assemble a killer team of comedy writers. People who would later go on to success on shows like *Cheers, Saturday Night Live, The Daily Show* and others. John Vitti, Al Jean and Jeff Martin. John Swartzwelder and George Meyer created a sensation with an online comedy magazine entitled *Army Man, America's Only Magazine*. They later went on to write for *Seinfeld*. Conan O'Brien was a Simpson's writer. Ricky Gervais and Seth Rogen later wrote the episodes they did a voice in. What Jim Brooks was doing was bringing The Harvard Lampoon, *Animal House* style of iconoclastic comedy writing to network cartoons. Brooks and Simon introduced a convention common in live-action comedy shows, but not used in standard TV animation. The large writer's room where writers could knock around ideas and otherwise improv. Comedy writers would come to describe *The Simpsons* writers' room with the same awe and reverence that they once reserved for Sid Caesar's *Your Show of Shows* in 1955 or *Saturday Night Live* in 1975.[10]

One particular writer did his best work in the morning in a local coffee shop, smoking cigarettes while sipping his brew. When the City of Los Angeles passed an ordinance banning smoking in restaurants, he had a vinyl cushion and linoleum coffee-shop booth reassembled in his garage. That way he could keep his creative juices flowing.

The Simpson's animation team moved into offices at 729 N. Seward St. in Hollywood, which used to be the studio of legendary Looney Tunes director Bob Clampett. Bob's wife and partner Sody Clampett was there to welcome them on the first day and wish them luck. They had created their own quirky, irreverent TV series *Beanie & Cecil* in 1962. Wes Archer set to work refining the designs so numbers of different artists could draw them the same "on model," while still maintaining the essence of Groening's style. What Matt called "Potato-chip lip."

The animation production house contracted to handle the production was Klasky-Csupo. After the first few seasons, it was shifted over to Film Roman.[11] To help pull the growing storyboard team together, they hired Disney animator Brad Bird. He brought in storyboard experts Jeff Lynch and Jim Reardon.

Danny Elfman was hired to write the music for the show. Elfman, formerly of the band Oingo-Boingo, had just broken into film scoring with clever soundtracks for Tim Burton's *Pee-wee's Big Adventure* and *Beetlejuice*. For reference for what he was looking for, Matt Groening sent Danny a mixtape he made that contained the opening of Fellini's *Juliana of the Spirits,* a Frank Zappa jingle for an electric shaver, parrot sounds and the theme from *The Jetsons*. Somehow, Elfman digested all that and produced the Simpson's Theme Song the world knows today. The opening sequence the animators designed was much like the classic opening title sequences for cartoon shows like *The Flintstones, The Jetsons* and *Top Cat.* Matt Groening wanted it to seem conventional at first, but then he suggested a little twist. He explained his inspiration was the opening of the Dick van Dyke Show, which had Dick enter the room, greeting everyone, then he falls over an ottoman. The team began to add witty variations to the opening montage leading to the Simpson's family all assembled on the couch to watch TV. This became the famous Simpson's Couch Gags. The first season had five different gags. The next season even more. It was not until episode five that audiences saw them just simply sit down. David Silverman explained that later whenever they found a completed show had run short, they could expand the couch gag to make up the time.

By the 1980s, many studios used overseas contractors to keep their production costs down. First in Australia and Japan. Later, mostly in Taiwan, mainland China and Korea. Shows sent overseas had to be meticulously plotted out. The Korean artists were paid on volume more than quality; the more work they turned in, the more they got paid. And many did not know English. So many did not bother to interpret confusing instructions; they just drew them as written. The first Simpsons sent over was handled by a veteran American animation director accustomed to pushing things out cheaply, even if the quality suffered. He changed or tossed out dialogue he did not care for without telling anyone. Standard practice then for low-budget TV animation. The kiddies never seemed to care.

When this first show *"Some Enchanted Evening"* was screened at Gracie Films for Brooks and the producers, they were thunderstruck. The animation was sloppy, the staging was bad, dialogue was missing and the jokes were not landing. When the episode ended, there was dead silence in the room. Jim stood up and said, "Do you think we can just thin out the ranks a bit?" That was the signal for the large crowd that had packed the theater to slip out, just leaving the essentials. The editor recalled "The room emptied out so fast it created a vacuum." Jim then exploded, "What the fuck was that? This is not funny! We can't show this shit!" Barry Diller said, "What have you done?" When another Fox exec said "Look, we'll get it fixed." Diller snapped "What do you mean? How are you going to fix that? Out of sync, you can fix." All their initial reservations about attaching their names to a dumb kiddie cartoon seemed justified. Animation producer Margot Pipkin recalled "Gabor's and my stomach just went pppfft . . . because we worked so hard and so long to get that one done."

There was a tense interval through the next week waiting for the second show to come in, *"Bart the Genius."* Matt Groening confessed he could not sleep that week. That episode could spell the end of his career designing animation. It would be the dealbreaker. The whole project's future depended on it. This is where David Silverman came into his own as a director. He put in long hours personally redrawing and retiming storyboards. When the completed footage of *Bart the Genius* came in and was cut together, everyone gathered in the screening room to see the result. By contrast, this show was terrific. Everything they had hoped for. For once, David Silverman's experience not having worked in low-budget hack-productions paid off. The show had a fresh, iconoclastic style not seen before in an animated series. Barry Diller decided to hold back that premiere episode and launch the series with the holiday special *"Simpsons Roasting On An Open Fire,"* which was also directed by Silverman.

One of the novel changes to animated TV shows James L. Brooks introduced in *the Simpsons* was retakes. In doing TV animation on a budget, the conventional thinking was that if some jokes did not land, or some shots did not work, too bad. When the show came back from overseas, completed in color, that was it. There was little money or inclination to do many retakes. Re-dubbing lines does not work in animation like it did in live action. Brooks brushed aside those concerns. If a scene was not working, he would have it rewritten and re-animated, even if it was already in color. While a typical half-hour show of *He-Man* cost around $450,000, a Simpsons episode could go over $2 million. But the attention to the quality paid them back in dizzying success.

Barry Diller and James Brooks screened the finished Simpsons opener for senior Fox Studio execs. Diller recalled "No one in the room was laughing except for Jim Brooks and me. No one had done an animated sitcom since *The Flintstones*, and it was like 'What is this?' But we put it on (the air). And it grew more successful week after week."

The first Simpsons episode to air was the holiday special, *Simpson's Roasting on an Open Fire* on December 17, 1989. It scored the second highest rating ever for a Fox program. On January 4, 1990, the show then went on to its regular timeslot, where viewership kept doubling week after week, until by May 1, it owned its timeslot and was among the top 20 shows on television. This was when Fox Broadcasting was still only reaching 4/5ths of the country. By the end of the first season, Newsweek said "*The Simpsons* has emerged as a breakaway ratings hit, an industry trendsetter, a cultural template, and among its most fanatical followers, a viewing experience verging on the religious." Postproduction head Brian Roberts recalled, "We went from zero to a thousand overnight." Kirk Wise, the co-director of Disney's *Beauty and the Beast* recalled, "During my time at Walt Disney feature animation, almost every Monday morning story meeting began with a recap of Sunday's episode, with all present recounting their favorite jokes and approximating all the voices. When Mr. Burns sang a parody of 'Be Our Guest' it was one of the proudest moments of my career!"[12]

Within a few years, *The Simpsons*, combined with additional hit shows like *In Living Color* and *The X-Files*, made Fox a major power in TV broadcasting. The Fourth Network was at last realized. Barry Diller remembered, "In terms of ratings and financial terms, it really built the network, but also in terms of giving Fox its attitude. Some of that was already there with *Married With Children,* but *The Simpsons* is by far the networks most successful show." Many things they said became national pop phrases, like "Eat my shorts, Cowabunga" and "Don't have a cow, man." In 2001, the academic dons of The Oxford Dictionary of the English Language accepted Homer's expletive "D'oh!" as a new addition to the lexicon.[13]

As the success of the series grew, the animators were encouraged to get more elaborate with the couch gags. They invited famous artists to do a couch gag in their own unique styles. Bill Plympton, John Kricfalusi and Disney animator Eric Goldberg. Al Jean created one based on M.C. Escher. Legendary elusive street artist Banksy had seen the episode "*Exit Through the Gift Shop*" directed by Karen Johnson. He liked it so much that he volunteered to design a couch gag. In the second season in 1990, they introduced a special Halloween episode entitled *the Simpsons Treehouse of Horror.*

It also proved to be so successful that it became an annual institution. Audiences are expecting more outrageous and surreal stories each year.

In the Presidential election of 1992, embattled incumbent President George H.W. Bush tried to run on a platform touting "Family Values," to cover for his poor handling of the economy. In a speech to the National Religious Broadcasters Association, President Bush declared, "We are going to keep on trying to strengthen the American family, to make American families a lot more like the Waltons, and a lot less like *the Simpsons*." The Simpson's creative team immediately took up the challenge, and a week later, the opening couch gag showed the family watching the president's speech. After Bush's wisecrack Bart replied, "Hey, we're just like the Waltons. We're praying for an end to the Depression, too." That year, President Bush was defeated by Bill Clinton.

The breakout success of *The Simpsons* encouraged Fox to invest in more prime-time animated series with adult content like Seth MacFarlane's *Family Guy* and Mike Judge's *King of the Hill*. Matt Groening created a new show about the future called *Futurama*. He initially sold the idea as "Simpsons in the Future." Where before no TV producer in his right mind would ever consider a primetime-animated series, by 1991, rival networks had six animated series in production. Simpson's showrunners Al Jean and Mike Reiss initially tried to create a Krusty the Clown spinoff that did not work

FIGURE 11.4   Seth MacFarlane and his *Family Guy*.

(Courtesy of Seth MacFarlane)

out. They then created a show around a Siskel & Ebert-style TV film critic voiced by Jon Lovitz. *The Critic* debuted on ABC on January 6, 1994. It later moved to Comedy Central. Wes Archer moved on in 1997 to direct *King of the Hill, Bob's Burgers* and *Rick & Morty*. David Silverman went on to stints at DreamWorks and Pixar before returning to Springfield. In 2007, he directed *The Simpsons' Movie*. It did over $500 million at the Box Office. After Arlene Klasky and Gabor Csupo lost *the Simpsons* production to Film Roman, they started their own series about life from a little child's point of view (they have six children). That show, *The Rugrats* (1991), became a huge success and spawned sequels and feature films. In 1998, *The Rugrats Movie* became the first non-Disney animated feature to top $100 million in first-run Box Office.

The Simpsons continues to be a success year after year. Staff left, new people came in, yet it still keeps going. Before *the Simpsons*, the animated show with the longest run was Hanna-Barbera's *The Flintstones* at seven seasons. *Rocky and Bullwinkle* was five seasons, *Scooby Doo three*. In 2016, *The Simpsons* surpassed *Gunsmoke* as the longest-running TV program ever.[14] It has amassed bushels of industry awards. Season after season, year after year. Five years, 20 years, 30 years and more. The public never seems to get enough. It is not just the greatest show in TV animation, it is the greatest show in television, period. In 2021, Fox Network's President Michael Lyons called *the Simpsons,* along with *Family Guy* and *Bob's Burgers* "The Mount Rushmore of Animation."

NOTES

1 James L. Brooks had named his company Gracie Films after comedienne Gracie Allen (1895–1964), the partner of George Burns in the radio show *Burns & Allen.*

2 Polly Platt (1939–2011) was the first woman art director accepted into the Art Director's Guild. Her movie credits include *The Last Picture Show, What's Up Doc?, Terms of Endearment and Broadcast News.*

3 In another account an assistant to Fox executive Ken Estin first brought the *Life in Hell* cartoon to their attention.

4 "Matt Groening reveals the location of the real Springfield". By Claudia De La Roca *Smithsonian Magazine* May 2012.

5 Hank Azaria was later brought in to replace the guy doing the voice of Mo.

6 They made about nine Dr. N!GoDatu interstitials.

7 Quoted in "Tracey Ullman's Dislike of *the Simpsons* Nearly Led it to an Early Grave" by Michael Boyle and Hannah Shaw-Williams, *Slash Magazine.*

8 Ullman Loses Simpsons Suit (*Variety*, October 22, 1992).

9 Brooke Keesling to the author, December 2023.

10 Steven J. Cannell created a similar writer's room for his animated series *Fish Police* and *Capitol Critters.*

11 Film Roman was started by old Warner Bros animator Phil Roman. He spun his company off from Bill Melendez Productions (*A Charlie Brown Christmas*) when they began to develop TV specials based on the *Garfield* comic strip.

12 Kirk Wise, to the author, December 2023.

13   Dan Castellaneta took the term "D'oh" from Scottish-American comic actor James Finlayson (1887–1953). A foil for Laurel & Hardy in their 1930s film comedies, he was a master of the double-take. He was known for saying "D'oh-ooh" in exasperation. Matt Groening suggested Dan shorten the phrase to simply D'oh!

14   *Meet the Press* (NBC, 1947) is actually the longest continuously running TV show, but it is a news format interview program, not an entertainment show.

Toontown Boomtown

Television 1989–1997

12

As previously mentioned in Chapter 2, up until the 1980s TV viewing meant The Big Three networks: CBS, NBC and ABC. They had a chokehold over all mainstream TV viewing. That began to break up in the 1980s with the rise of cable TV and syndication.

In the early 1980s, Lou Scheimer, the head of an animation studio named Filmation, worked out a deal to bypass the networks entirely and release his new series *He-Man and the Masters of the Universe* to syndicated local TV stations during the week. Producer, voice actor (and Lou's daughter) Erika Scheimer recalled:

> "Producing kid's shows for syndication was a completely different ball game than making them for the networks because the networks only aired its children's shows on Saturday mornings. My Dad (Lou Scheimer) believed that there was a market for cartoons to be aired after school, five days a week. So instead of just making 13 episodes of a show per year, Filmation would now produce 65 shows per year; that's 5 shows per week times thirteen weeks of new shows. Wow, what a difference that made."

He-Man and the next series *She-Ra: Princess of Power* were huge successes not only in viewership but also in selling toys for Mattel. The shows hit just as the first big video game craze had subsided and children wanted to play with physical toys again. Soon other studios like Marvel began producing shows in syndication, G.I. Joe, GEM, the X-Men. Meanwhile as mentioned in Chapter 11, the Fox Network's success with series like *the Simpsons* and Family Guy moved the American audience into the perception that adults

DOI: 10.1201/b22394-13

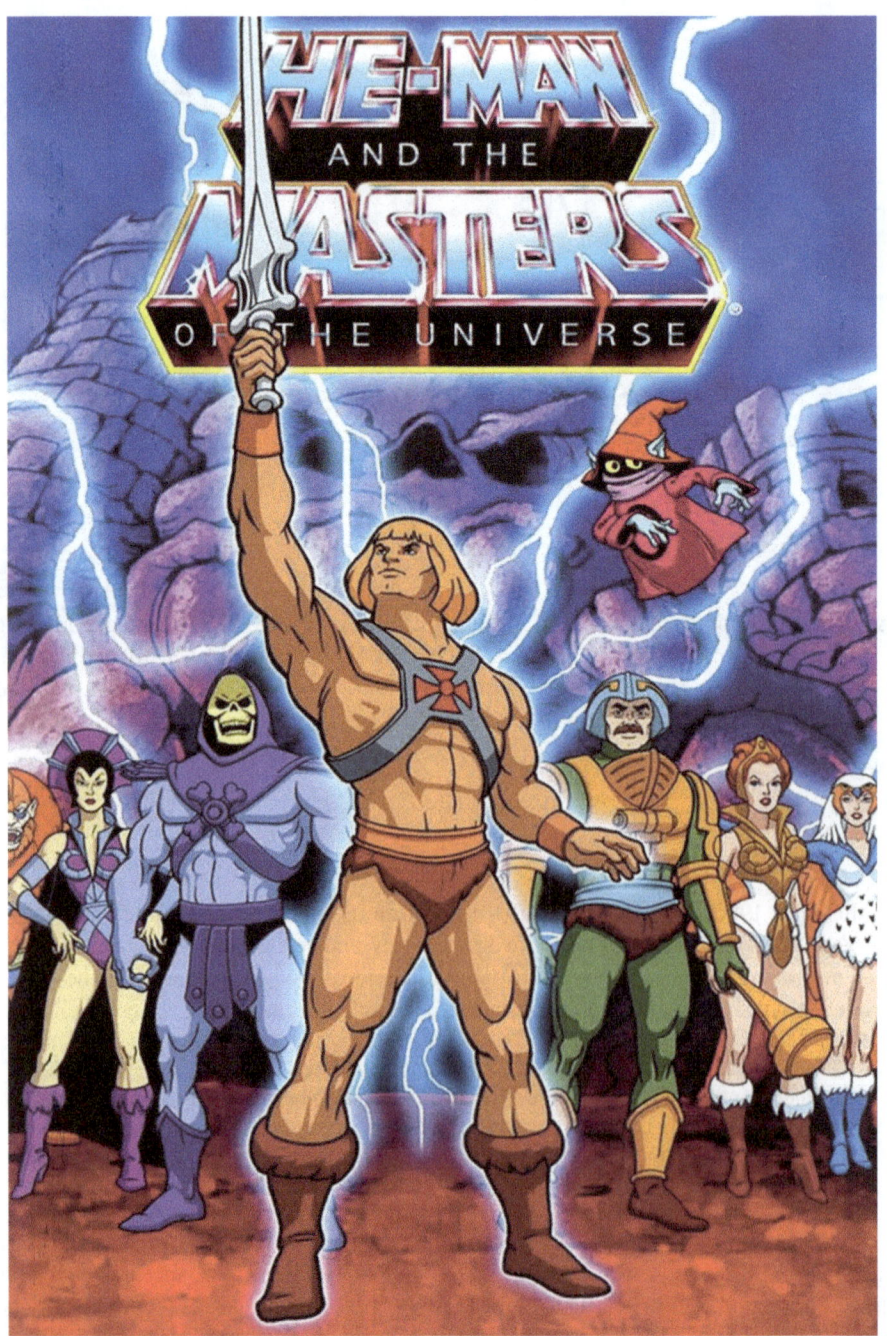

FIGURE 12.1 *He-Man and the Masters of the Universe.*

(collection of the author)

might like to watch cartoons too. *The Simpsons, Family Guy* and *Southpark* in prime time finally buried the old cliche once and for all that adults would not watch cartoons at night.

In 1972, The Home Box Office (HBO) started as a cable service to get first-run movies into rural homes where analog network reception was bad. HBO was soon joined by other cable stations, Showtime and Cinemax. First, hooking audiences with softcore adult movies in the privacy of your home. Then, first-run hit movies before they went to regular TV channels. Then Ted Turner's stations TBS, TCM, Cartoon Network and Nickelodeon. Walt Disney started Disney Channel for all their content, and Warner Bros began the WB network. All of these stations grew to offer higher-quality programing like *The Sopranos* and *Game of Thrones*. In defense of their empire, the networks responded with cheap reality TV shows.

MTV, the all-rock music channel, spent the 80s at the forefront of pop culture, showcasing the finest in interesting and artistic rock videos. Michael Jackson's *Thriller*, Peter Gabriel's *Sledgehammer*, Herbie Hancock's *Rockit* and Aha's *Take On Me*. Early CGI like Rebecca Allen's *Adventures in Success* and Dire Straits's *Money for Nothing* were breakthroughs in their time. MTV's titles were animated by NY Studio J.J. Sedelmaier and Buzz Potemkin of Buzzco. But by the 1990s, MTV sensed that the fashion for music videos was fading. They were losing audience to rival channels like Turner and Disney. After 1996, as the internet grew more and more of the audience away to watch things on independent formats like YouTube. Animation always had a place, but it needed to be hip and cutting-edge in the MTV tradition. Colleges ran festivals of edgy shorts like *Mike and Spike's Sick and Twisted Animation Festival*.

FIGURE 12.2 *Johnny Bravo* and creator Van Partible.

(Courtesy of Van Partible)

On June 2, 1991, MTV launched a collection of short series at late night called *Liquid Television*. Its first show was Peter Chung's sexy cyberpunk *Aeon Flux*. Two years later, Mike Judge created *Beavis and Butthead* in a blackout short called *Frog Baseball*. It became a phenomenon and spawned a regular TV show and movies.

In 1994, show runner Mike Lazzo teamed up with old Superfriends designer Alex Toth for a novel idea. Taking one of the HB's 1960s classic superheroes Space Ghost and giving him his own late night talk show. Space Ghost interviewed live-action film stars like Emma Thompson. The villains of the show Zorak and Moltar were his announcer and bandleader. The show was written to appeal to adult Baby Boomers who grew up on the original show. *Space Ghost Coast to Coast* became a hit and ran for years. It spawned spinoffs like *Aqua Teen Hunger Force* and *Harvey Birdman, Attorney at Law*. All for the evening primetime animation market.

Fred Seibert was a programming exec at MTV, Cartoon Network and later Hanna-Barbera. When it came to animation, instead of taking pitches from existing studios, he advocated creating showcases for new talent. "Do what they did when cartoons were great. Make shorts, one at a time. If they are good, make more."[1] His 1995 show, *What a Cartoon!* provided an incubator for future hit TV series. They resulted in shows like *Dexter's Lab, Cow and Chicken, Courage the Cowardly Dog,* Van Partible's *Johnny Bravo* and *Craig McCracken's Powerpuff Girls*. Many of whom originated as student senior projects.

———————

Over on the other side of town, The Walt Disney Studio in 1984 facilitated a rebirth of their TV animation division under Gary Krisel. He oversaw an ambitious slate of new TV series shown on their cable station, Disney Channel (later ToonDisney). They began with a show based on Eisner's original inspiration Gummi Bears, and followed up with the Wuzzles. Both became successes. Initially told they could not use the classic characters like Mickey, Donald and Goofy, they created series around second-tier characters like Scrooge McDuck and Chip and Dale. The Ducktales show originally began in syndication, then moved to cable. It was a great success and spawned the 1990 movie *Ducktales the Movie: Treasure of the Lost Lamp*, directed by Bob Hathcock.

After *Rescuers Down Under*, Disney Feature management had concluded that maybe doing sequels in the main studio was not such a great idea. In 1994, only 2 years after the initial run of Disney's *Aladdin*, the studio came out with a sequel, *The Return of Jaffar* directed by Tod Stone, Toby Shelton and Alan Zaslov. The preproduction was done in LA, but the show was animated in Australia and Japan at a third of the cost. It was a great success and was soon followed by more sequels like *Beauty and the Beast 2 Belle's Magic Christmas*.

At the same time, Warner Bros Animation was finally reopened after being in a coma for years. The television animation was revived after doing *Tiny Toons* (1993), *Animaniacs* (1993), *Pinky and the Brain* (1995) and *Freakazoid* (1995). These shows played very well on Kids WB.

FIGURE 12.3   WB *Batman Beyond.*

(courtesy of Warner/Discovery)

But what really gave them momentum was getting into the growing Batman craze. Warner Bros and DC comics had been affiliated since 1968 (when they were both acquired by Kinney National, who had changed their name to Warner Communications). Cartoonist writer Bruce Timm had worked around the studios for a few years until he settled at Warner Bros. and with fellow writer Paul Dini launched *Batman: The Animated Series.* Together they both created the character of Harley Quinn. They also created the *Superman Animated Series, Green Lantern* and *Justice League* series. All of these shows were made to augment and interact with the Dark Knight series of Batman, Joker live-action feature films. The animated *Batman: the Mask of Phantasm* directed by Eric Radomski and Bruce Timm is considered one of the best Batman series, including the live-action movies.

Legendary animation director Ralph Bakshi (*Fritz the Cat*) had an old association with Terrytoons before they ceased operation in the late 60s. In April 1987, Ralph approached Judy Price, the head of CBS programming with some ideas for TV series.

Price rejected them all and asked if he had anything else. Grasping at straws, Ralph mentioned he had the right to Terrytoons' old star, Mighty Mouse. He could do a reboot for modern times. Judy agreed to buy that series. Turns out Ralph did not actually own it. CBS had bought the show in 1955 and had completely forgotten about it. " I sold them a show they already owned, so they gave it to me for nothing!"[2] Ralph produced the series in his own wild, unconventional style, but more importantly, like Eric Larson with the young Disney artists, he brought under his wing and trained an excellent group of young animators who would turn much of TV animation on its head. Bruce Timm, Jim Reardon, Lynne Naylor, Tom Minton, Rich Moore and a wild young Canadian named John Kricfalusi.

John Kricfalusi (or John K) learned a lot about production and iconoclasm under Ralph. After *Mighty Mouse*, John sold Nickelodeon a new show featuring a chihuahua and a cat called *Ren & Stimpy*. John had invented the characters in his final year at Sheridan College. Through his company Spumco, he assembled a strong team of writers and artists who were drawn (pun intended) to his chaotic comedy style. Very influenced by Bob Clampett's work at Looney Tunes and Jim Tyers' wild animation at Terrytoons. The kind of crazy, surreal humor most animators wish they could do, before they are reined in by the business types. John himself voiced Ren in a mad version of Peter Lorre from *The Maltese Falcon ("You Fat, Bloated EEDIOT! I'll KEEL U!!")*. *Ren & Stimpy* premiered on August 11, 1991, with the Nicktoons slate alongside *Rugrats* and *Doug*. They received great critical acclaim. Simpson's creator Matt Groening called *Ren & Stimpy* "The only good cartoon on TV other than *the Simpsons*." The Nicktoons slate doubled Nickelodeon's ratings, and for a time, *Ren & Stimpy* was the most popular show on TV.

But as they went into the second season, cracks began to show. John K's increasingly erratic behavior started to get on the producers' nerves. His insistence on holding back and changing things already approved wreaked havoc with their deadlines. It seemed like John was almost provoking his employers to react. Finally, they did. Nickelodeon fired John K in September 1992 and replaced him with his co-director Bob Camp. Spumco was reorganized, and the season was completed. But the energy seemed to drain away. There was no third season. Most of the veterans of the show went on to very successful careers on other projects, thanks in part to their association with *Ren & Stimpy*. John Kricfalusi went on to create some of the first original shows for the internet like *Weekend Pussy Hunt* and *The Goddamn George Liquor Program*. In 2018, he withdrew from the industry entirely due to a personal scandal.

Trey Parker and Matt Stone were two film students at the University of Colorado at Boulder. In 1992, while animating on other student's films, they decided to make a gag Christmas Card. Deliberately crudely stop-motion animated with construction paper, it was of a group of little kids swearing up a storm while they watched Jesus duke it out with Santa Claus. Called *"The Spirit of Christmas,"* they did not even bother to put their names on it. Just the names Kranken-Blass, a joke on Rankin Bass, the original creators of *Rudolph, the Red Nosed Reindeer*. The following year, they were in LA looking for work. They showed it to Fox executive Brian Graden. He thought it was so funny, he asked if he could send copies out to his friends as his holiday card. After this, it went viral.[3] No internet yet, so people were sending each other VHS cassette copies.

FIGURE 12.4   *South Park* pilot "The Spirit of Christmas".

I was working at Dreamworks on *The Prince of Egypt* when I was given a copy from a friend in Steven Spielberg's office, who got it from George Clooney. Clooney thought it was so funny he was dubbing off six cassettes at a time and sending them to friends all over town. You could not plan a better ad campaign. MTV and Fox passed on the series originally as being too crude, but Cartoon Network took it. South Park debuted on August 13, 1997, and immediately shot up in the ratings. In a few weeks, they were on the cover of *Newsweek*.

In the past, the conventional wisdom in the US had been that successful cartoons had to appeal to "ages 6 to 60." Many classic cartoons in the 1930s and 1940s had been intended as much for adults as they had been for children. Postwar, the perception had shifted to the idea that cartoons were only for children. The success of *The Simpsons* and the big Disney musicals in the 1990s proved that adults liked cartoons also. While adult humor programs segued off from general audience animation, a third branch blossomed in the 1990s as well. Animation specifically aimed at younger viewers and preschoolers.

FIGURE 12.5   *Peppa Pig.*

Designing creative content specifically for preschoolers went back to the late 50s with ventriloquist Shari Lewis, *Mr. Rogers' Neighborhood*, *Kukla, Fran and Ollie*, *Ding Dong School*, among others. Later in the 60s, the Children's Television Workshop created *Sesame Street* specifically to give young viewers a start on learning. *The Electric Company*, *Via Allegre* and *Zoom* soon followed. Such program specificity has been the norm in England and Japan for years,[4] but in America, it failed to gain a foothold beyond the nonprofit public stations.

In the 1980s, when the Walt Disney Company re-entered the television market by creating Disney Channel, they planned content for a 24-hour cycle. Cartoon Network and Nickelodeon began to plan for the 24-hour cycle, so 6:00 AM to 12 pre-school shows, 8:00 PM to 4:00 AM, including Adult Swim, *Phineas and Ferb*, and *Peppa Pig*.

NOTES

1   Fred Seibert quoted in "Happy 30th Birthday, What a Cartoon!" *Animation Magazine* May 2025.
2   *Unfiltered: The Complete Ralph Bakshi,* pg 210.
3   "How *South Park* was Born" by James Hibberd, *Entertainment Weekly* May 2014.
4   The BBC's *For the Children* was first broadcast in 1946.

Toontown Boomtown

13

Animated Movies 1989–1997

We were living the dream. We went from rock bottom to creating the greatest movies ever.
—Don Hahn (*Waking Sleeping Beauty*)

Following up on the Oscar-winning success of *The Little Mermaid*, Walt Disney Animation went on an aggressive production schedule. They created overlapping teams of animators hoping to turn out one, if not two big feature releases a year. The studio staff numbers rose higher than they were in 1958 when they were completing *Sleeping Beauty*. They began to expand the role of their new studio in Orlando from just doing limited edition display cels to actually working on sections of the productions being done in California. Based on the good experience they had using outside studio Richard Williams, they engaged Richard Purdum's studio to develop *Beauty and the Beast* and greenlit Tim Burton and Henry Selick's *Nightmare before Christmas*. Disney purchased the Paris studio of brothers Paul and Gaetan Brizzi to become Disney France. They purchased Hanna-Barbera's old studio in Sydney, Australia, for TV production work. They also inked a deal with a little Bay Area computer house called Pixar to develop a film (see Chapter 14).

The next film on the production schedule was a sequel to the 1977 film *The Rescuers*. Set in Australia, it was called *The Rescuers Down Under*. Directed by Hendel Butoy and Mike Gabriel. This film would be the first film to be colored and filmed entirely in digital. The CAPS[1] system (see Chapter 14). Art director Maurice Hunt designed the boy hero of the film Cody to be a cute indigenous Australian. But before any scenes could be animated, the studio changed Cody to a blonde-haired white kid. The reason given was the native kid would have "too little audience appeal." We argued, "Uh, Mowgli? He's not a white kid. *Jungle Book* did okay." But orders are orders. *Rescuers Down Under* was to be a movie set in Australia where we never see an indigenous

DOI: 10.1201/b22394-14

Australian. Maurice (also called Pixote) left the project and went on to create beautiful work on *Fantasia 2000, Emperor's New Groove* and Ted Turner's *The Pagemaster.*

Despite early hiccups, *Rescuers Down Under* turned into a great film. Since the Bear Fight Sequence in *Fox and Hound*, Glen Keane had developed a custom of taking one scene and storyboarding it all and animating it with his trademark dynamic style. On the crew, we called it "The Glen Scene." On *Rescuers*, Glen chose the scene where Cody befriends the eagle Marahute. Together they go on a wild ride over waterfalls and canyons. This was not only exciting, but it was planned to test the capabilities of the CAPS system to handle difficult camera movements.

Rescuers Down Under was paired with a short featurette, *Mickey's Prince and the Pauper* directed by *Oliver & Company's* George Scribner. This was a chance to reacquaint the public with the classic Disney characters. Art director Thom Enriquez wanted to recreate the beautiful color palette of the 1937 Mickey short *The Brave Little Tailor.* Even down to securing the same type of Kodachrome film stock. While Rescuers was the first all-digital shoot, the Mickey film would be the final Walt Disney cartoon to be hand painted on acetate cels and photographed on downshooter cameras. Even with the Mark Twain novel to work from, we still had problems with the story to work out. At one point, George brought in Ward Kimball for advice. Ward Kimball was one of the last of Walt's Nine Old Men. He was retired, famous, wealthy, and in his 80s. So, he had nothing to lose by being frank. He told us what we needed to hear. "Guys. If you can't describe your story in one sentence you haven't got a story. What was the story of Bambi? A deer grows up. War and Peace? The trials and tribulations of two Russian families during the Napoleon's invasion. So, what is the story of Prince and the Pauper? Two kids get into trouble by changing clothes. That's all!" He was right. And that was helpful.

As an animator, it was great to work with those classic old characters. It is like you are a parking valet and someone leaves you a Porsche to park. They just handle well. I found Mickey Mouse was a particularly tricky design to draw. A 1928-character Ub Iwerks designed with simple circles; over the decades, it had been modified again and again by master draftsmen to the point where nobody could agree on the proper design. We knew we wanted to get back to the Fred Moore-style Mickey of *Brave Little Tailor* and *The Sorcerer's Apprentice.* It was common to see Andreas Deja, Mark Henn and Dale Baer standing in the hallway debating the size and positioning of Mickey's ears.

After *Rescuers Down Under* came *Beauty and the Beast.* In the Spring of 1988, when I was working to complete Roger Rabbit, producer Don Hahn tossed a script at me. "Whattaya think? Walt Disney presents *Beauty and the Beast.*" I said cynically, Beauty and the Beast is mostly about two people having dinner. One has a dog nose. "What's animation-y about it?" Don replied, "The cups and dishes are all going to sing and dance." I replied, "So what? That was done in Sword and the Stone." Yet despite my initial skepticism, *Beauty and the Beast* turned into a major Disney classic.

I was involved with the first crew in London led by Richard and Jill Purdum. Dick was a terrific animator in his own right, for a time Richard Williams' right-hand man. But he struggled to comprehend the kind of aggressive producer types we have in Hollywood. Even the Disney ones. From his commercial experience, he believed that when you got an approved script, you followed it to the letter. At Disney Feature, the first draft script was merely a jumping off point. A first salvo. And our initial script had not really thought about the music, while Howard Ashman and Alan Mencken were excited to rewrite it all as a big musical. Pretty soon Dick and Jill withdrew from the project, and the project returned to Burbank. Story artists Kirk Wise and Gary Trousdale took their place directing. Jumping into a troubled project, undergoing big changes and it being their first direction, they did a masterful job. One lasting result from our European sojourn is that we fixed the setting as rural Loire Valley in France in 1709. This was because it was a rare sedate period in French court couture. Between the big curly wigs, frills and makeup of Sun King Louis XIV, and the big, powdered wigs, frills and makeup of Louis XVI. The Beast's castle was a combination of the château of Chambord, Chenonceau and Azay-le-Rideau. The two big heroes on *Beauty and the Beast* were Howard Ashman and Glen Keane. Howard basically rewrote much of the script in his lyrics. The opening number, Belle's Song ("Little town, it's a quiet village. Every day, like the one before . . ."), Howard basically lays out the setting and characters. "I'm Belle. I live here. I don't like it here. I'm Gaston. I like Belle. She doesn't like me. I don't care, I'm going to get her anyway." Etc. Glen Keane started designing the Beast while we were still in London. He was very aware that previous versions of the character were just a man with a dog snout or fur-like Lon Chaney's Wolf Man of the 1940s. Glen designed him with the back legs of a wolf and the neck of a buffalo. When he was rushing or excited, his animal instincts would get the better of him, and he would run on all fours. For his face, he combined a mandril, gorilla and boar's teeth. He played for a time with a boar's snout, but ultimately reasoned a lady would not fall in love with a guy with a pig nose. Sections of the film were done at the Florida Studio where animator Aaron Blaise followed Glen's lead to give the Beast a likable yet intimidating personality.

FIGURE 13.1 *Beauty and the Beast* crew lunch.

(By Tom Sito, collection of the author)

As we were working to complete Beauty and the Beast, we saw less and less of Howard Ashman. Producers explained, "Oh he just hates LA and would rather work out of his home in New York." We weren't told he was very sick with HIV/Aids." He was literally composing on his deathbed. Howard died just a few months before Beauty opened. He was 40. On the end credits, we placed this dedication: "To our friend, Howard, who gave a mermaid her voice and a beast his soul, we will be forever grateful. Howard Ashman (1950–1991)."

One novel idea Jeffrey Katzenberg worked out with studio publicist Terry Press was to screen the unfinished workprint of *Beauty and the Beast* at the 1991 New York Film Festival as a work-in-progress. Those of us who work in animation know the beauty of rough drawings moving are almost as lovely as the finished product. But here we let the public see it, and the impact was electric. It caused a great excitement in the film community.

Beauty and the Beast opened at Thanksgiving 1991 and was a huge hit. It grossed $217 million domestically and $473 million worldwide. It won two Oscars and became the first animated film to be nominated for Best Picture. Only narrowly losing out to *The Silence of the Lambs*.

FIGURE 13.2 *Beauty and the Beast* gag drawing.

(Collection of the author)

Beauty Makes History With Oscar Nominations

Disney's 30th animated feature, *Beauty and the Beast*, has garnered the first Best Picture Academy Award nomination ever for an animated film. In addition to a Best Picture nomination, the Academy of Motion Picture Arts and Sciences bestowed five other nominations on *Beauty and the Beast*. A complete list follows:

Best Picture of the Year
Achievement in Music (Original Score)
Achievement in Music (Original Song–
                        Beauty and the Beast)
Achievement in Music (Original Song–*Belle*)
Achievement in Music (Original Song–
                        Be Our Guest)
Achievement in Sound

Commenting on the announcement, Producer **Don Hahn** called the film's nomination "validation of animation as a legitimate way to tell a story." The nomination for Best Picture marks only the third time that a Disney film has been nominated for such an Oscar. The first one was *Mary Poppins* in 1964 and the second was *Dead Poets Society* in 1989.

Watch for complete coverage of the 64th annual Academy Awards in the April 3 issue of the *Newsreel*.

┌ Congratulations ──────

to The Walt Disney Studios, Feature Animation and each and every individual who has contributed to the success of Disney's 30th animated feature–**Beauty** and the **Beast.**

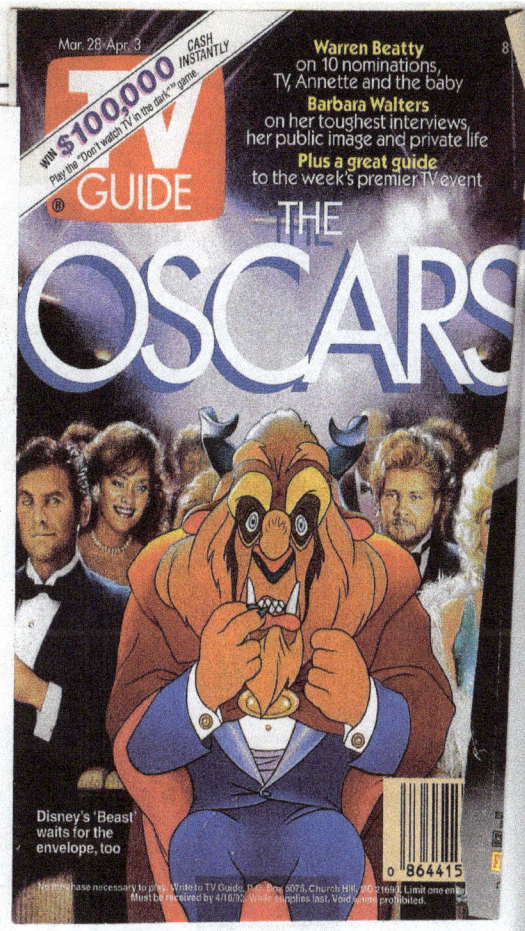

FIGURE 13.3 *Beauty and the Beast* TV guide cover.

(Collection of the author)

On April 18, 1994, Disney's first theatrical musical based on one of their animated films, *Beauty and the Beast: A New Musical*, opened on Broadway. It would run for over 13 years and became the fourth highest earning show on Broadway. It began Disney's practice of turning hit animated musicals into hit Broadway and West End musicals. It was overseen by Tom Schumacher, one-time animation producer, later our own Broadway impresario.

When Howard Ashman died, he had been working on several songs for the next project, *Aladdin. Little Mermaid* writer directors Ron Clements and John Musker who took on the project conceived of it as more of a broader comedy than the previous two stories. They wanted to cast Robin Williams to be the Genie and allowed for his broad style of improv humor. Lead animator Eric Goldberg designed the Genie based on the flowing design style of 89-year-old caricaturist Al Hirschfeld. "I look on Hirschfeld's work as a pinnacle of boiling a subject down to its essence, so that you get a clear, defined statement of a personality," explains "Aladdin" supervising animator Eric Goldberg, who was in charge of the madcap Genie. "There's also an organic quality in the way one line will flow into another: It may go along the back of a neck, down the spine, across the behind and the down the leg—all in one single line that is very, very elegant. I wanted the Genie to have that kind of elegance."[2] Al Hirschfeld himself traveled to California to meet us all and see the work. A few years later, a documentary was done about him titled *The Line King*.

FIGURE 13.4   Eric Goldberg and Al Hirschfeld.

(collection of the author)

Eric took a speech from one of the Robin Williams's comedy albums and animated a test. It included some of the crazy visual transformations he intended to do. That convinced him.

Robin Williams in *Aladdin* opened the floodgates for Hollywood stars to do voices in cartoons. There had always been a notable celebrity or two in animated films in the past. Bing Crosby in *Ichabod and Mr. Toad* (1949) and Judy Garland in UPA's *Gay Pur-ee* (1962). But for most of its history, animation had been too low profile and too low paying to make it worth a big celebrity's notice. After *Goodfellas,* when Joe Pesci was approached to provide a voice for WB *Quest for Camelot,* he is reputed to have said about the offer: "What? You mean I do not get my normal rate and then you guys go out and make kazillions of dollars with this movie? F*** you. My time is better spent playing golf." (Eventually he did the part, and he did get paid his rate.) After Robin celebrities did start getting paid their rates, and did start taking roles.

Robin's imitations of famous people were funny but presented a few issues for the directors. Turning into Arnold Schwarzenegger and Jack Nicholson was one thing, but at one point, he turned into Ed Sullivan. Ed Sullivan (1901–1974) was a big name on TV in the 1950s and 1960s well known to Baby Boomers. But would anybody under the age of 60 know Ed Sullivan? But when it was shown to test audiences, the children laughed anyway because he turned into a funny man.

Another issue was when the Genie is free and Aladdin and Jasmine fly off together on the carpet, the peddler at the beginning comes back to sing a reprise of the song Arabian Nights, then reveals himself to be the Genie. But at every test screening, as soon as the Genie, Aladdin and Jasmine flew off, the entire audience cheered and stood up to leave. Musker and Clements sat looking at all of the posteriors shuffling past them. Ron said, "I think they are telling us this is the end of the movie." And so, it was.

After *Aladdin*, the Disney feature animation crew broke into teams, one to do *King of the Jungle*, soon to be renamed *The Lion King*, and one to do *Pocahontas*. A third team was developing the sequel to *Fantasia*. The Orlando studio was gearing up for *Fa Muhlan,* later simply *Mulan*.

A sequel to *Fantasia* was a passion project for Roy E. Disney. He said his uncle never intended the first *Fantasia* (1940) to be a one-shot film. Walt Disney wanted The Concert Feature to be an ongoing series. Every time you would go back to the theater, there would be new sequences interspersed with some older sequences like a traditional concert. Jeffrey grumbled, " The first one didn't make any money,"[3] but Roy insisted. So, a team was formed around director Hendel Butoy. Maestro James Levine of the Metropolitan Opera of New York led The Chicago Symphony Orchestra. His early pieces like *The Pines of Rome* with whales was done as an early exercise for the studio's CGI unit to flex their muscles. *The Steadfast Tin Soldier* set to a Shostakovich piano concerto. I was a classical music nerd, so I made a lot of jokes like let us do Gustav Mahler's *Kindertotenlieder* (songs on the death of children). The response I got was a weary look. "Very funny, Sito." Finally, I was put on *Noah's Duck*, the sequence set to Elgar's *Pomp and Circumstance*, which was suggested by Michael Eisner. They wanted a Donald solo piece to partner with Mickey's *Sorcerer's Apprentice*. *Fantasia 2*, later *Fantasia Continued*, and finally, *Fantasia 2000* was in production for a number

FIGURE 13.5   *Animation Magazine's Aladdin* issue. 1992

(courtesy *Animation Magazine*)

of years. After I had left the production, Eric Goldberg had the idea to do the masterful *Rhapsody in Blue* by George Gershwin using the drawings and designs of Al Hirschfeld. The only major change the Disney censors insisted on was that he remove the cigar from Gershwin's teeth as he played. (Is Lampwick paying attention?).

Eric was also instrumental (pun intended) in getting them to animate an idea by legendary story artist Joe Grant about a flamingo playing with a yo-yo set to Saint-Saëns's

Carnival of the Animals. Joe Grant (1908–2005) was the only artist on the project who worked on the original Fantasia as well as the sequel. Later Paul and Gaetan Brizzi created the beautiful finale set to Stravinsky's *Firebird Suite.*[4]

Both *The Lion King* and *Pocahontas* went through the usual growing pains and changes. Songs dropped and added. Rewrites. Directors were swapped out. *The Lion King* was directed by Rob Minkoff and Roger Allers. *Pocahontas* by Eric Goldberg and Mike Gabriel.

The Lion King had songs created by Elton John, melodies Elton created on his Casio keyboard. To orchestrate his tunes, the studio looked to a German born composer named Hans Zimmer who had just created an impressive score for a South African film called *The Power of One.* Hans brought in African musicians Lebo M, a Zulu chorus, and Ladysmith Black Mambazo. The African sounds supercharged the images to transport any and all to the grasslands of KwaZulu. Jeffrey Katzenberg was so impressed that he moved up the completion of the opening song "Circle of Life" and released it into theaters as the film's trailer.

That Spring in Las Vegas theater, marketing and distribution people gather for an annual convention called Show-West, where the Hollywood Studios announce their upcoming releases. Many celebrities appear to ornament the show. That year, Jeffrey Katzenberg was on stage to speak about The Lion King accompanied by a trained lion.[5] The lion had been on stage with Jeffrey several times before and felt very comfortable with him. Lions are really not much different than kitty cats in their behavior. When they like you, they think nothing of playfully batting you with their paws. Except they are huge compared to a person. So, while Jeffrey was making the case for the movie, the lion was hugging him and batting him and finally hit him in the face so hard his glasses

FIGURE 13.6   Jeffrey and the Lion, gag drawing.

(collection of the author)

broke and it split his lip. "I had blood trickling down my shirt. People are screaming. Trainers tugging his chains. I'm covered in orange fur and lion spit, all the while calmly telling people what a great movie this is going to be."[6]

The studio also took another gamble and opened *The Lion King* in the summer, instead of the holiday release. Audiences were accustomed to seeing a Walt Disney animated movie around Thanksgiving. Summer was for the blockbusters with Arnold Schwarzenegger and Tom Cruise, but the studio was confident.

The Lion King opened on June 15, 1994. This film became the toon blockbuster of all blockbusters. Up to almost a billion dollars just in its first release. It was the apex of the animation renaissance. It was not just the highest-grossing animated movie for all time. It was the highest grossing movie period, until 1997 when it was eclipsed by James Cameron's *Titanic*. Two years later, The *Lion King* went to Broadway as a musical resculpted by stage director Julie Taymor. It became a monster hit of musical theater. In 1980, the single largest income earner for the entire Walt Disney Company was their theme parks. In 1995, it was an animated film.

Studios like to follow a winner, and as it was with sound and color, at this time, high-quality animated features were in. Competitors that had dismissed animation long ago suddenly were staffing up and releasing new films. Just in 1991, you saw *Ducktales the Movie, Jetsons: The Movie,* Don Bluth's *Rock-a-Doodle, The Nutcracker Prince, Dragon Ball Z* and the German film *Werner the Wizard of Booze*. On that film, the animators in Berlin took time off to go dance on the Berlin Wall as it came down.

FIGURE 13.7   *FernGully: The Last Rainforest.*

(courtesy of Bill Kroyer)

In 1992, Bill Kroyer, the former young Disney animator who did *TRON* and won awards for his short *Technological Threat*, came out with his film *FernGully: the Last Rainforest*. It had a beautiful look and a strong environmentalist message. Art directed by Ralph Eggleston who later did *Finding Nemo, Wall-E* and *Inside Out* for Pixar. Music by Sheena Easton, Elton John and Tim Curry. Animator Kathy Zielinski did a masterful job animating Tim Curry as the bad guy Hexxus singing his song "Toxic Love."

In 1992, that same year as *Aladdin* and *FernGully*, Miyazaki did *Porco Rosso*, Ralph Bakshi did his own animation-live-action combo *Cool World*, starring Kim Bassinger and a young Brad Pitt. Independent NY filmmaker Bill Plympton released his feature *The Tune,* and Tom Wilhite, the producer who tried so hard to get the old Disney leadership to move into the future, released *Bebe's Kids*. Based on the comedy of Robyn Harris, it was the first animated feature directed by an African American, Bruce W. Smith. Bruce would later animate Dr. Facilier for Disney in *Princess and the Frog* and design and produce his own TV series, *The Proud Family*.

FIGURE 13.8 *Space Jam.*

(courtesy of Warner Discovery)

FIGURE 13.9   Warner Animation Crew gag shoulder patch 1997.

(courtesy of Doug McCarthy)

In 1996, Warner Bros completed the rebirth of its animation division with *Space Jam*. Directed by Joe Pytka, it featured the basketball great Michael Jordan meeting Bugs Bunny and Daffy Duck. Directed by Joe Pytka, the animation was directed by Tony Cervone and Bruce W. Smith.

The press declared Animator to be the hot new career in Hollywood. Animators were getting agents, getting signing bonuses and demanding higher salaries. Everyone wanted to do animation. It seemed like the party would never end.

Or could it?

NOTES

1 CAPS meant Computer Animated Production System. Co-developed by Randy Cartwright, Jim Houston, Dylan Kohler, Dave Wolf and a team from Pixar. CAPS was used on Disney 2D animated films until 2007, when it was replaced by a newer generation of Toonboom Harmony.

2 Eric Goldberg quoted in "Aladdin's Inspiration? They rubbed Hirschfeld" by Charles Solomon (*Los Angeles Times* November 8, 1992)

3 *Fantasia* (1940) did not show a profit until 1969.

4 Initially composer Igor Stravinsky was dismissive of the way his Rite of Spring was handled in the 1940 Fantasia. In a 1950 Sat Evening Post he called the visuals "imbecilic". But that did not deter him selling Walt Disney the rights to his Firebird Suite that same year.

5 Don Hahn, *Waking Sleeping Beauty*.

6 Jeffrey Katzenberg quoted, address to the Disney animators, your author included.

The Digital Revolution

14

I think we just saw the future of animation.

—Bill Hanna

In the late 1970s and early 1980s, you saw them at film festivals like Filmex and Mike & Spike's Sick and Twisted Festival of Animation.[1] After a long day enjoying clever animated features and shorts from around the world, they were usually the last film of the evening. The computer films. CGI.[2]

FIGURE 14.1 *Hunger* by Peter Foldes (1974).

(Courtesy of the National Film Board of Canada Archive)

DOI: 10.1201/b22394-15

Strange, experimental. Done by people none of us pencil pushers never heard of. Chuck Csuri's *Hummingbird* (1968) and Peter Foldes's *Hunger* (1974). Crude, geometric graphics wiggling painfully across the screen like some radioactive erectors set. The computer operating systems were given screen credits as prominently as the humans. The math nerds who championed this stuff kept telling us these films were primitive now, but they were the true future of filmmaking. But traditional animators all just laughed them off. Why spend tens of thousands on advanced graphics to emulate what an animator could do with a 39-cent Blackwing pencil? Cast iron Mickey Mouse, stainless steel Betty Boop. Who wants to watch that? We traditional animators would leave the theater that night smiling at these simple little films, but little did we realize these were the first rumbling of a seismic shift that would change all of our lives forever.

Outside of science fans, if the general public thought at all about computers, it was as the large, impersonal machines used by *James Bond* villains. 1960s sociologists like Alvin Toffler warned of "Future Shock." That a push-button world was coming, where automation would put skilled craftsmen out of work and reduce all of us to mindless keyboard slaves. The idea that you might use a computer to create art seemed crazy, like drawing cartoons with a missile. Yet, many scientists and entrepreneurs anticipated the potential of communicating visually using these new electronic brains.

Initially, there was no master plan. No corporate strategy. No President John F. Kennedy declaring to the public, "It will be the stated goal of this nation to create a computer animated film within ten years!" The research divisions of tech giants like IBM, Xerox and Bell Labs dabbled in it. They hired experimental artists who wanted to create art by nontraditional means. It was many years before movie and animation studios would consider using computers. Their emergence on the world scene coincided with the mid-century economic collapse and retrenchment of old Hollywood. With studios selling off their assets, computers seemed too remote, too pie-in-the-sky, and way too expensive to be seriously considered.

There was no single Walt Disney figure who built the entire industry by himself. Computer graphics imaging, or CGI, was born in the minds of dozens of visionaries on their own. Research scientists, math geniuses, beatniks, hippies, military people and avant-garde filmmakers. All with a common dream. Sharing ideas, publishing research papers and moving from company to company. Many were working on their own after hours, without their supervisor's knowledge. The first commercially retailed computer game, the Magnavox Odyssey, was developed by Ralph Baer at a small New Hampshire company that contracted with the military to make gunsights for helicopter gunships. Where there was no social network to freely exchange ideas and breakthroughs, they created their own, SIGGRAPH.[3] In these conventions, each new breakthrough was shared and improved upon in the spirit of a research lab. People freely discussed possibilities, published research papers, and showed off their latest discovery. Engineers sat in a darkened theater in intense anticipation. When an image appeared of a glass of milk with a candle behind it, the audience erupted in cheers like someone had scored the winning touchdown at the Super Bowl. That film demonstrated software to solve the problem of translucence. Certain surfaces like milk, marble or human skin absorb a certain amount of light as it reflects it. Another small step forward toward the eventual goal of photoreal imaging.

These visionaries broke down into two main groups: scientists and engineers who wanted to create art, and artists who wanted to tell stories in nontraditional ways. At first, experimental filmmakers thought that the way to make electronic art was to bend and shape beams of light. These were called oscilloscope films because they mostly used repurposed post-World War II military surplus oscilloscopes and sonar monitors. These had limited success and were soon abandoned in favor of using pixels. Invented in 1956, these were little lights, turned on and off like the bulbs in a Broadway electric billboard. Ken Knowlton of Bell Labs used clusters of binary code, zeros and ones, to create images like the ink spray on a newspaper. Then in late 1962, at MIT[4] Ivan Sutherland, a graduate student on an ROTC scholarship was allowed to use a large TX2 computer that had been decommissioned by the Air Force. He had 8 months to create his thesis project. He decided to focus on graphics. Sutherland wrote SKETCHPAD, the first software for a computer to draw lines instead of zeroes and ones. Ostensibly, it was designed for military engineering projects like designing retractable bridges. But he added an element of drawing and moving organic shapes like a human leg and an eye blinking. His final treatise contains the prophetic comment, *"Sketchpad need not be used only for engineering purposes. For instance, it might be nice to make a cartoon."*[5] Years later, when student Alan Kay asked Ivan if he realized the immensity of what he was inventing? Sutherland smiled, "I didn't know it was hard."

Ivan Sutherland went on to team up with a like-minded researcher named David Evans at the University of Utah. In the late 1960s, major American universities were centers of student anti-war demonstrations and strikes. Utah seemed to offer a peaceful refuge from the turmoil of the times. There, they set up a graduate program focusing exclusively on computer graphics that attracted acolytes from around the world. Many of the graduates of their program went on to important careers in computer graphics. Ed Catmull, Ralph Guggenheim, Bill Reeves and Jim Clark, who became the tech backbone of Pixar, Bui Dong Phoung who created Phoung Shading, Jim Blinn designed the Voyager spacecraft flight simulations and Nolan Bushnell founded Atari Games.

In France, Pierre Bezier created software that became the basis of CADCAM (Computer Aided Design) that greatly expanded an engineer or architects' ability to design industrial objects like cars and planes.

At the same time, in Westbury, NY, there was a president of a small technical college named Dr. Alexander Schure (1920–2009) who liked to dream big. He was an engineer who grew wealthy selling post-war army surplus technology and real estate. He sold New York City the land that Lincoln Center was built on. At first, Dr. Schure[6] tried to become the next Walt Disney by starting a traditional animation studio on his campus, The New York Institute of Technology (NYIT). He scraped together a team of traditional animators left over from Paramount and Terrytoons and set to work, making a musical of the popular children's story *"Tubby the Tuba."*

When a salesman tried to sell him on the concept of computer graphics, Schure was inspired to explore the combination of his two favorite subjects, entertaining children and technology. He began to dream of creating the first animated movie drawn with computers. A full 20 years before such a thing became possible.

Dr. Schure spent millions of his own money on state-of-the-art equipment, and he hired all of the burgeoning young talents in computer graphics research then available, including Ed Catmull, Ralph Guggenheim and a young nonconformist from Texas named Alvy Ray Smith. While working for NY Tech, this team developed many of the digital tools essential to the creation of modern computer animation. 2D Rendering, fractals, inverse kinematics, alpha-channel, motion capture and more. In addition, collaborating with the traditional animators from Tubby gave the young scientists an appreciation of how the cartoon production pipeline worked. Ed Catmull designed a program to create 2D-drawn inbetweens between keyframes automatically called Tweening.

One thing Alex Schure was not good at was directing an animated feature.[7] When *Tubby the Tuba* was completed, it was so bad that no studio would release it. At the crew screening, one animator stood up and shouted, "I wasted two years of my life on this!" One positive lesson learned that Ed Catmull took away from this debacle was how to better redesign the animation production pipeline for computers. New York Tech was the first time professional animators ever interacted with computer techs. Now, Catmull, Alvy Ray Smith and the CGI team sat down to estimate the task before them. How practical would it be to create a 90-minute animated feature film digitally? They calculated that just to render the frames would take 7 years, even if the computers were going 24 hours a day, 7 days a week.[8] They began to feel like they were just spinning their wheels performing an impossible task. A Flying Dutchman of a lab, doomed to never make it to port.

Then one day in late 1977, a friend named Richard Edlund[9] showed up at their office. He sported a big gold belt buckle that read LUCASFILM. He said George Lucas, the Star Wars creator, was building his own CGI unit and needed people like them. Ed, Alvy and the team jumped ship from NY Tech and relocated across the country to Industrial Light and Magic (ILM) George Lucas' dream factory in the San Francisco suburb of San Rafael.

There they became the LucasFilm Graphics Group. They figured out how to do movie editing digitally (Editdroid) as well as the VFX[10] optical printing process. They created new rendering software to enable digitally lit elements to blend in seamlessly with live-action scenes (Point Reyes). Realizing that since NY Tech, they needed to bring in seasoned animators to collaborate with, Ed and Alvy hired a young animator who had just left Disney named John Lasseter. John was steeped in all of the training of classic Disney personality animation, but he was excited for the potential of computers. Alvy said "John wasn't afraid of it. He really got it."[11] But the problem now was that once editing and opticals[12] were digitized, George Lucas was satisfied. He really was not that interested in creating original cartoon movies digitally. Remember at that time, animated movies did not make the kind of monster Box Office a *Star Wars* or *Raiders of the Lost Ark* did. And the traditional VFX artists of ILM were not any happier to see these computer guys compete for their jobs as the traditional animators of NYIT were. Ed and his team tried to impress George about the potential of 3D VFX by creating an all-digital efx scene in the second Star Trek movie, "*The Wrath of Khan.*" Called "*The Genesis Effect,*" it visualized how this device, put on a dead planet, could generate a hospitable climate and atmosphere capable of sustaining life. Alvy called it "Our sixty second audition to George." The sequence came out beautiful, and the filmmakers of Paramount were overjoyed. But to their chagrin,

George Lucas barely noticed. The next day after the screening, he poked his head into Alvy's door and said, "Nice camera move." That was it. And the traditional visual effects artists were grim. At the crew screening of "Wrath of Khan," when they saw the Genesis Effect, many grumbled, "Well, there it is. we'll all be out of jobs soon." Some crumpled the complimentary poster they were handed and stuffed it in the trash bin in the theater lobby.[13]

Since the beginning of cinema, animation and live-action special effects had worked side by side on separate tracks. Even under the aegis of a main studio like Universal, they were separate teams, separate companies, separate cultures. Life action movies attempting special shots like lightning,[14] death rays or magic would occasionally bring on an animator or two to help. In Shoedsack and Cooper's classic *King Kong* (1933), Willis O'Brien and his team created beautiful stop-motion animation of Kong and the other beasts. Roy Seawright and Arthur Lloyd created the stop motion *March of the Wooden Soldiers* in Hal Roach's 1934 film. And in 1956, when Cecil B. DeMille redid his classic *The Ten Commandments,* Walt Disney loaned him his 2d effects animators to create the pillar of fire and the inscribing of the tablets. That same year, another Disney freelancer, Josh Meador, animated the scary Id Monster for MGM's *Forbidden Planet.* In 1963, stop motion master Ray Harryhausen created the famous skeleton battle in *Jason and the Argonauts.*

But beyond these exceptions, in the main live action and animation, communities lived and worked apart. Because of the emphasis on children's entertainment in the 1950s, the mainstream film world tended to look down on animation as not a serious career. There were people who did animation, and then there were people who worked on "real" movies. Animators came to think of themselves as the bastard child of the film business. Animators had to battle skeptics at the Academy who wanted to discontinue the animation Oscar. Celebrities asked to hand out the animation Oscar had to be warned not to act like sulky kids made to sit at the children's table. When *Beauty and the Beast* earned a Best Picture nomination at the 1992 Academy Awards, many actors openly expressed their annoyance. "Well! Maybe we should all be cartoons now!" Paige O'Hara, the voice of Belle, had to take out a full-page ad in Variety defending the film. But as CGI became more believable and more user-friendly to artists without a science degree, special effects coordinators began to see it as the next frontier in cinema. As the software improved, the vfx became less about toy spaceships on strings and more about people animating them on computer consoles.

The 1980s was a boom time for computer graphics. Creating and moving graphics on a computer required much more memory than writing or computation. The invention of silicon chips in 1980 so increased the computational power of computers that the kind of graphics that once required a supercomputer the size of a bus could now be done on a tabletop workstation. The federal governments' anti-trust suits against IBM and Bell Telephone freed up a lot of advanced technology for general use. Steve Jobs of Apple took computers out of the lab, put them in a plastic box and marketed them like appliances. The public's fascination with electronic video games like Pong and Donkey Kong, first as video arcade games, then on home computers, spurred further industry growth. Computer animation studios, not aligned to one corporate giant, proliferated like mushrooms. Digital Domain, Boss Films, Bob Abel & Assoc., Rhythm & Hues, DeGraf Wahrman, Mainframe, Banned from the Ranch[15] and many more. All promising glittering digital marvels, and many keeping a traditional animator or two around in case their overloaded computers crashed.

In 1985, Steven Spielberg directed *Young Sherlock Holmes* about the adventures of Holmes and Watson as teenagers. It featured the Stain Glass Knight scene, animated by John Lasseter at Lucasfilm. Unfortunately, only 30 seconds long. In 1986, the Nick Castle film *The Last Starfighter* boasted the first effects movie with 100% digital effects. A spaceship battle with no miniatures, no toy rocket ships on strings. In 1992, the film *Lawnmower Man* utilized game engine software to create the first virtual reality sex scene. All of these films were breakthroughs, but for weak script or a good budget failed to catch the attention of the public.

A Canadian named James Cameron moved down to California to study physics and English at Cal State University, Fullerton. One day, he saw *Star Wars* and that convinced him he should enter the movie business. His drawing ability[16] got him work on John Carpenter's *Escape from New York* (1981). There he first began to see what computers might be able to do on science fiction fantasy films.

He got his first big break writing and directing the Arnold Schwarzenegger hit *The Terminator* (1984). Afterward, he focused on Sci-Fi action movies with simple stories but strong characters and breakthrough effects. One ILM artist mentioned Cameron would bring in storyboards of shots he had no idea how to accomplish and just told ILM to figure it out. Each film he did was a step forward in digital effects. *The Abyss* (1989), *Terminator 2 Judgment Day* (1991), *Titanic* (1997) and *Avatar* (2009). In 1993, he formed the CGI studio Digital Domain with Scott Ross and Hollywood SFX makeup master Stan Winston.

FIGURE 14.2 *Jurassic Park* (1994).

In 1993, director Steven Spielberg decided to create a movie version of Michael Crichton's best-seller *Jurassic Park*. It worked on the idea that emerging gene theory would make it possible to bring back real dinosaurs from DNA from blood preserved in amber. A rogue billionaire builds a theme park on an island where people could visit the dinosaurs. As expected, they get loose, and mayhem ensues. Spielberg told his team at the outset, "I don't want to just make another monster movie like Godzilla here. I want you to be able to see the dinosaurs feeding, panting and sweating and sleeping. Like a big National Geographic program."

The ILM effects team of Phil Tippett began to stop-motion animate the dinosaurs like they had done the Taun Tauns on *The Empire Strikes Back*. In classic Ray Harryhausen style, except with added digital go-motion, motion blur is added. Initially, Spielberg liked it, but he said it still felt too "go-motionly" to him. Meanwhile, maverick ILM CGI artists Steve "Spaz" Williams, Walter Dippe' digitally animated a heard of gallimimus skeletons on their own in their spare time and got it in front of Spielberg. Steven said it blew his mind. He asked Phil Tippett what he thought of the test, and Phil murmured, "I think I've just become extinct."[17] Steven liked that line so much he wrote it into the movie. After that they did many of the main dinosaur effects shots in CGI. Once they committed to doing the dinosaurs all CGI, they ran into the problem that there was now too much work for only two animators to finish. A compromise was created where they wired a stop-motion rig with sensors like a little motion capture suit. This way the veteran stop-mo animator can articulate the rig frame by frame, and the data would move the dino on the computer. All told that there were only 6 minutes of pure CGI in the entire movie; they steal the film. *Jurassic Park* was the monster hit film of the year. Not since the original *Star Wars* had a movie so held the public's fascination. And the digital dinosaurs were the talk of the Hollywood.

The famous TV animation studio Hanna-Barbera had been sponsoring a program at Cornell University to develop a digital ink and paint system. It was first used on their feature-length reboot of the 1960s series *The Jetsons*. Its lead scientist Marc Levoy[18] moved west to lead the setup of the digital system. They tried to interest Disney animation in their system but enough of the Nine Old Men were still around to dissuade the execs from using it. While creating their Jetson's reboot, they hired the young studio Kroyer Films to create the animation of the Jetson's flying cars. Eighty-year-old animation director Bill Hanna was given a demonstration of their system by young animator Bill Kroyer. He was amazed at the speed with which they would effect changes. Hanna later said to a friend, "I think we just saw the future of animation."[19]

The late 1980s saw several important movies combining character animation with live action. *Who Framed Roger Rabbit?* created an opportunity for Mickey Mouse and Bugs Bunny could meet face to face. Warner Bros' *Space Jam* and Ralph Bakshi's *Cool World*. The effect was good, but all three films never let you forget that the "toon" characters were hand-drawn 2D figures living in a 2D cartoon reality.

In 1986, George Lucas decided to sell off his computer graphics group, now calling itself Pixar.[20] Steve Jobs of Apple Computers decided to buy it because he wanted to see full-color computer graphics on his home computers. He had told his skeptical engineers that one day people should be able to watch a full-color movie on their home computers. In their only face-to-face meeting about the deal, George Lucas warned Jobs about the Pixar team "Watch out for them, they are hot to make animation."[21]

Steve Jobs took the Pixar team from San Rafael across San Francisco Bay to a new facility in an Oakland neighborhood called Richmond. For the next few years, Pixar lived a hard-scabble existence doing commercial spots like Johnson's Scrubbing Bubbles, medical films and other stuff while they honed their craft through a series of shorts. (*Luxo Jr, Tin Toy, For the Birds, Geri's Game.*) Each short highlighted a new breakthrough they achieved. Even though these shorts brought them a lot of attention and won many awards, they did not bring in a lot of money. At the end of every month, Steve Jobs had to open his personal checkbook to keep the lights on. That all changed in 1989.

In 1982, The Walt Disney Studio had taken an early lead in CGI by making the film *Tron*. Directed by Steven Lisberger, it boasted to be the first digitally animated film. It did use the digital work of several outside studios like Bob Abel & Associates, Triple III and Magi. Young Disney-trained animators like Bill Kroyer, Jerry Rees and John van Vliet oversaw the work. Although it used some CG, the animation still had to be printed out on acetate cels and hand-painted in the old-fashioned way. When *Tron* failed to score at the Box Office,[22] Disney abandoned the idea for a decade.

After the change of management in 1984, Roy Disney set Bob Lambert (1957–2012) and his team working to develop a digital ink and paint system for animation. Roy Disney smiled as he told his skeptical partners, "I want to throw two million dollars into something we may not see a dime back from." They were making progress, while the smaller, more nimble CGI houses like Rhythm & Hues seemed to be moving faster. So, Disney entertained outside bids for the creation of a digital paint system. Among the contenders, Pixar's Ed Catmull and Alvy Ray Smith were able to draw on all their experiences at NYIT, Xerox Parc and Lucasfilm to propose a complete paint production system with the high-quality Walt Disney expected. For instance, thanks to their time at NY Tech, Ed and Alvy had already worked out how to scan hand-drawn pencil animation, the backbone of Disney's production method. Roy Disney signed with Pixar to develop not only their ink & paint system but also their production tracking system. Part of doing an animated feature was keeping track on every one of the 1,500 individual cuts as they moved through the various stages of the production pipeline. Called CAPS (Computer Animation Production System). The Pixar people worked hand in glove with Lambert's team in Burbank.

The first all digitally painted animation was the very last shot of *The Little Mermaid*, where all of the mer-people are waving goodbye to Ariel and Prince Eric as they sailed away. Their next film *Rescuers Down Under* (1990) would be all digital paint, while the short *Mickey's Prince and the Pauper* would be the last Disney animation traditionally painted with brushes, paper and mixed acrylic paint. With Mermaid, the artists had to limit Ariel's colors to one set of day colors, one set of night colors, and a special set for when she is illuminated by the magic lights of Ursula's cauldron. While on Rescuers, artists could art-direct every shot with a color palette that was nine times greater than the color palette of Disney's *Pinocchio*. Considered by animators the pinnacle of 2D animation. The CAPS system also made difficult camera depth-of-field shots easy. The sort of shot that Disney had developed the massive multiplane camera for was now routine. The famous multiplane camera system, once considered the ultimate in animation technology, now became a museum piece.[23]

While still keeping character animation the realm of traditional pencil artists, Disney explored more and more ways to make use of their computer systems. For *Beauty and the Beast* (1991), it was Belle and the Beast waltzing through a digitally moving ballroom with dancing plates and cutlery. For *Aladdin*, it was the talking Cave of Wonders (poses aided by animator Eric Goldberg). In *The Lion King*, it was the Wildebeest Stampede, and in *Treasure Planet*, it was Long John Silver's prosthetic arm. Each film was a step forward in the evolution of digital cinema.

Meanwhile, from the success of their paint system in 1991, Disney concluded a three-picture deal with Pixar to create feature films.[24] They would share some artists, but in the main, keep their management team independent from the Mouse House in Burbank. They were taking a slow approach to long-form animated film. Their 1988 short "Tin Toy" won them their first Academy Award. Their original idea was to create a holiday TV special based on it. "*Tinny's Xmas*." When the Pixar team met studio production chief Jeffrey Katzenberg, he dismissed the TV special idea. "If you are going to go to all the trouble to build and rig models and locations, you might as well go for a feature."

The old industry saying goes, "Animation can do anything, except save a bad idea."[25] While Ed Catmull oversaw the perfecting of the technology, director John Lasseter focused on the story with his hand-picked storyman Joe Ranft. Joe was trained by many old Disney story artists and contributed to classics like *Who Framed Roger Rabbit* and *Nightmare Before Christmas*. Joe trained a superb team of story artists, as well as inviting up to help legendary story people like Joe Grant who worked on the 1937 *Snow White*, Floyd Norman and Robert Lence.

As they began preproduction, they realized that the character design of Tinny was too limited to get a full performance out of. His hands were always attached to his accordion. The bass drum and cymbals are always on his back. The dropped the idea of Tinny but kept the setting of toys in a kid's room. They created the conflict of an old toy cowboy with a pull-string voice meets a new space ranger toy. At this time, the best animated features were musicals. Beauty and the Beast, The Lion King, all boasted catchy, award-winning songs. John Lasseter deliberately decided to avoid it being a musical to not seem cliché. He hired composer Randy Newman to write music for the film, but beyond the main song "You got a friend in me." Most of the rest are orchestral soundtrack.

As Toy Story was being completed, some Disney studio execs resented the independence Pixar enjoyed from the main studio in Burbank. They began to say those computer people do not know how to make a long film. Not enough musical numbers. And that computer stuff could never be warm, cuddly and charming like a hand-drawn character was. John Lasseter and his team had to speed up the completion of a good character scene to quiet the skeptics down south. They picked the first confrontation between Woody and Buzz on Andy's bed. For the annual Disney stockholders meeting, where new projects were hyped, they showed the completed "Army Man Sequence" voiced by former Marine drill sergeant R. Lee Ermey.[26] It brought down the house. All dissent went silent after that.

After almost 10 years of funding Pixar's efforts, Steve Jobs was beginning to consider selling off the company to Microsoft. After all, he had dropped $50 million of his own money into that well and had not seen a penny back yet. Then the numbers started to come in on test audience reactions to Toy Story. Steve was told that it was going to be a serious hit. The decades long dream of CG pioneers like Dr. Schure to create the first digital feature length cartoon at last premiered on November 22, 1955.

Toy Story was a monster hit. It has been said that Steve Jobs bought Pixar as a multimillionaire, but *Toy Story* and the subsequent films made him a billionaire.

The one-two punch of *Jurassic Park* then *Toy Story* convinced the world that digital imaging was now THE way to make movies. Digital producer Sherry McKenna said, "Before those movies, if you told a producer let's make this next movie with computers, the producer would say That's ridiculous!."[27] After those movies, if you told your producer that let us make the next movie without using any computers, he would say, "That's Ridiculous!"

FIGURE 14.3 Walt Disney's *Dinosaur* (2000).

(Courtesy of the Walt Disney Company)

In 1988, Paul Verhoeven and Phil Tippett sold Walt Disney studios on a film project using CGI entitled *Dinosaur*. However, the growing interest then in 2D hand-drawn movies turned the studio's attention away from untried CGI, so Verhoeven and Tippett moved on to other projects. After the success of *Jurassic Park*, the Disney Studio dusted off its Dinosaur project as a new film for their growing CGI team. Called The Secret Lab, it combined what consisted of the feature animation's CGI unit, combined with a digital effects house called Dreamquest.[28] The tale of the iguanodon Aladar and his lemur friends went through a long story process and several directors until settling with Eric Leighton and Ralph Zondag. Ralph had worked on Don Bluth's original *Land Before Time*. Trying to make the dinosaur world as realistic as possible, at first, they opted not to have the animals talk. Any story points were done as voice-over narration. But when they screened the first test to Michael Eisner, he said, "But . . . but . . . why aren't their lips moving?" That was it. The dinosaurs had to talk. And the films dark, violent tone was softened for a family audience. Originally, the film ends with the great comet collision that kills off all of the dinosaurs except the little marsupials. Aladar sacrifices himself shielding the lemurs, who would someday evolve to be the human race. That was changed to make the dinosaurs and lemurs leave the island after an asteroid destroys their home. But they all make it to safety and live happily ever after. Despite some critical complaints, *Dinosaur* opened in 2000 and made a splash with audiences, garnering a hefty $350 million worldwide.

Still the innovations kept coming. In 1997, James Cameron made *Titanic*, an epic movie where the digital scenes blended in so seamlessly with the real people that it took a trained eye to spot the difference. Even the ocean water was mostly digital. In 1999, George Lucas released his long-awaited follow-up to the Star Wars trilogy, *The Phantom Menace*, which was filmed and projected digitally. Celluloid film, which had been the way movies were made for over a century, was now obsolete. *Slumdog Millionaire* (2008) was the first movie shot digitally to win a Best Picture Academy Award. Venerable old film-producing and processing companies like Eastman Kodak, CFI and Technicolor filed for bankruptcy.

Animation camera services, using downshooter rigs that used to retail for $40–80,000 now told museums if you came with a truck to haul it out you could have it. All through the back alleys of Hollywood, you saw dumpsters overflowing with unwanted 35-mm and 16-mm film cans and reels. The old animation studio, that smelled of bond paper, pencil shavings, acetate celluloid, kneaded erasers, hot-splice and Bestine thinner, was gone, never to return.

NOTES

1   Craig "Spike" Decker and Mike Gribble were two California hippie promoters who put out compilations of independent and experimental shorts to colleges around North America.

2   CGI stands for Computer graphic images.

3   Special interest group on graphics, chartered by Mies Van Dam in 1972. With branch chapters around the world.

4   MIT, the Massachusetts Institute of Technology. Founded in 1861 as a polytechnic university focused on practical science and technology. Under Dean Vannevar Bush, it was one of the very first American schools to seriously work on the development of computers.

5   *Technical Report No. 29, Sketchpad, a Man-Machine Graphical Communication System.* By Ivan Sutherland, The MIT Museum Archives, Cambridge Ma.

6   Alex Schure earned doctoral degrees in engineering and education from NYU. Although he surrounded himself with academics with equal credits, everyone referred to him as Dr. Schure.

7   Tubby initially did have a more experienced producer named Al Brodax (The Yellow Submarine) and director named Sam Singer (Courageous Cat & Minute Mouse, Bucky & Pepito). But creative differences with Schure caused him to quit.

8   Ed Catmull quoted in Moving Innovation, *A History of Computer Animation*, by Tom Sito (MIT Press 2016).

9   Richard Edlund (b. 1940) is an Oscar-winning visual effects pioneer who worked on *Star Wars A New Hope* and *Raiders of the Lost Ark*. He helped build ILM and Boss Films.

10   VFX, the modern acronym for visual effects, also called SFX, for special effects.

11   Alvy Ray Smith quoted in Sito: Moving Innovation, *a History of Computer Animation*, pg 70.

12   Opticals was an industry term then for complex matte shots completed on an optical printer.

13   Australian VFX artist Peter Greenwood to the author, 2010.

14   To this day in all movies when you see a lightning bolt, it was created by an animator.

15   Legend has it Banned from the Ranch got its name from two VFX workers who were fired for drunkenly breaking into George Lucas' private office in Skywalker Ranch during an office party. After they left, they formed a company and gave it that name. They contributed to some pretty big effects movies like *Titanic* and *Twister*.

16   In *Titanic,* the drawing Jack does of Rose is James Cameron's own drawing. The close-up of DiCaprio's hand drawing is actually Cameron's hand.

17   Phil Tippett went on the start his own digital VFX studio and create hits like *Starship Troopers* (1997).

18   Marc Levoy later became a fellow at Adobe Industries.

19   Quoted in *Mr. Inbetween, My Life in the Middle of the Animation Revolution* by Bill Kroyer.

20   The name Pixar was originally for the new rendering computer they created. It was adapted from a faux-Spanish word "pixer" to make images. They changed it to Pixar because it was phonetically more pleasing, like "radar."

21   Issacson, Walter, *Steve Jobs*, pg 145.

22   *Tron* came out the summer of 1982 in the midst of a traffic jam of classic hits like *E.T. The Extra Terrestrial, John Carpenters' the Thing* and *Star Trek 2 the Wrath of Khan.* As well as Don Bluth's *The Secret of Nimh.*

23   As of 2020, there are only three multiplane cameras still in existence. One in the Disney Burbank Studio TV animation building lobby, one at the Walt Disney Family Museum in San Francisco and one in storage.

24   Walt Disney Studios had been known for keeping all their productions done "in house" but by the 1980s had opened to using outside vendors. The CG work on TRON (1982), Tim Burton's "A Nightmare Before Christmas", animation for the parks, etc.

25 Don Bajus quoted in Animation Magazine July 1984.
26 Marine Sgt. F. Lee Ermey (1944–2018) was originally brought on the movie *Full Metal Jacket (1987)* to be a technical advisor. Director Stanley Kubrick was so impressed with his delivery, he gave him a key role and allowed him to improvise his dialogue. Ermey stole the movie and had a long career acting in war movies.
27 Sherry McKenna to the author, 2013.
28 Dreamquest was started in 1979 by Hoyt Yeatman, Fred Iguchi and Tom Hollister. They had won back-to-back Oscars for *the Abyss* and *Total Recall.*

The Fall and Rise of Stop Motion 1993–2022

15

Hmm . . . did I shoot that frame already?
—Ray Harryhausen animating seven skeletons fighting
simultaneously in *Jason and the Argonauts*

One of the unforeseen results of The Digital Revolution has been the growth of 3D stop-motion films and TV shows. Stop-motion animation means creating a 3D puppet or statue of clay, latex, resin or other materials and articulating it frame by frame. Stop-motion animation began at the same time as hand-drawn animation. James Stuart Blackton, who made experiments for Edison, animated a stop-motion trick film, *The Haunted Hotel*, in 1908. In 1914, Russian etymologist Ladislas Starevitch created *The Ant and the Grasshopper.* This was considered the first narrative story done in stop motion.

In 1925, Willis O'Brien animated dinosaurs for Arthur Conan-Doyle's *The Lost World.* This was the first of what the Japanese call a Kaiju movie,[1] where a giant monster runs amok in a modern city. Hungarian George Pal and Czech Jiri Trnka created wonderful films with puppets. Famous examples of stop-motion include Willis O'Brien's *King Kong*, George Pal's Puppetoons, and Ray Harryhausens' masterful fantasy movies like *Three Million Miles to Earth*, *Sinbad and the Eye of the Tiger* and *Jason and the Argonauts.* In the 1950s, Czech animator-director Karel Zeman created whimsical steampunk fantasies based on nineteenth-century prints that interacted with real humans, the 1950s and 1960s, Art Klokey created the TV stars *Gumby* and *Davey and Goliath.* In 1960 Arthur Rankin Jr and Jules Bass formed Rankin-Bass. Despite being NY-based they recorded in Canada and animated their films in Japan. In 1964 their version of *Rudolph the Red Nosed Reindeer* became a seasonal favorite and had run almost continuously ever since. They followed up with other specials like *Frosty the Snowman* and *Mad Monster Party.* In the 1970s, Will Vinton in Portland Oregon won an Oscar for his stop-motion film *Closed Mondays* (1974), and James Picker for his spoof of then-President Jimmy Carter, *Jimmy the C* (1977).

The animators who create stop-motion have always had a curious relationship with their pencil and stylus using brothers and sisters. Like people who speak Attic Greek to

DOI: 10.1201/b22394-16

people who speak Ancient Latin. Equally admirable, yet different. Because stop-motion characters blend into live-action films more easily than hand-drawn work, before digital the stop-mo world has often been tied more closely to the live-action visual effects community. In previous decades, the live-action filmmakers' disdain of animation as kid's stuff did not feel the same way about stop motion. Especially when they needed a flying saucer, fire-breathing dragon or a Martian war machine to augment their opus.

In 1993, when Steven Spielberg's *Jurassic Park* (ref chapter 14) turned the film world digital, many assumed stop motion would go the way of tintypes and stained glass. Stop Motion Magazine recalled, "Producers all over started to abandon hand-made everything from hand puppets and stop motion animation, all the way up to environments and matte paintings which had been a staple for filmmaking since the early days."[2] Even venerable old Ray Harryhausen was doubtful about their future. When asked how he felt about the success of *Jurassic Park*, he smiled with his characteristic modesty, "I think as a stop-motion animator, I and all my colleagues should find a very high cliff and jump off."[3]

Yet among the boomer generation, there were those who felt the charm and immediacy of stop motion was too interesting to be cast aside. While digital smoothing of stop motion (go-motion) made the realistic movement more natural to the human eye, like in *Dragonslayer* (1981), another school of thought wanted the nostalgia of the older clunkier movement they loved as children. Like Rankin/Bass' *Rudolph the Red-Nosed Reindeer* (1964), or Davey and Goliath (1961). Part of its charm was its hand-crafted simplicity. Paul Reubens (1952–2023), aka Pee-wee Herman made a career out of acting like a host of a 1950s children's show. This style of humor appealed directly to old baby boomers than children. Reuben's show Pee-wee's Playhouse ran on CBS and Adult Swim from 1986 to 1990. He employed the New York studio Broadcast Arts (later Curious Pictures) to create little scenes of stop motion to augment his program. In his first feature film, *Pee-wee's Big Adventure* (1985), he hired the Chiodo Brothers (Steven, Edward and Charles) to create the Large Marge scene.

To direct his feature, he chose a former Disney artist from the CalArts animation program named Tim Burton. Tim Burton's playful take on the classic gothic horror genre was a bit too macabre for the older Walt Disney management to handle. He completed a short *Frankenweenie,* about a kid trying to revive his dead pet dog a 'la Dr. Frankenstein. The Disney studio then fired him for wasting the company's money, but Paul Reubens immediately put him in the director's chair for his movie, *Pee-wee's Big Adventure.* On a budget of $8 million, the film made $40 million just in the USA alone. Tim Burton went on to direct a number of highly successful films in his own unique design style. *Beetlejuice* (1988), *Batman* (which revived interest in the character, dormant since 1969), *Edward Scissorhands* (1990).

In the past, animators once they moved into mainstream live-action movie making tended not to look back. Such was the case with Gregory LaCava (1892–1952) and Frank Tashlin (1913–1972). Tim Burton however has kept his interest in animated films, particularly stop motion. When the Disney Studio now asked him to make his idea *The Nightmare Before Christmas* a reality, he accepted. He had actually been sketching ideas for it as early as 1983 when he was a concept designer at Disney on *The Black Cauldron.* He was too busy to direct this himself, but he engaged another old CalArts

FIGURE 15.1   Animator Chris Oakley working on *Pee-wee's Playhouse.*
(Courtesy of Chris Oakley)

FIGURE 15.2   Tim Burton and Henry Selick on *The Nightmare Before Christmas.*
(Courtesy of the Walt Disney Company)

Disney Program animator named Henry Selick to take the helm while he produced. *The Nightmare Before Christmas* was a huge hit and has since become a holiday staple.

In 1972, two teenagers at the University of Bournemouth dabbled in claymation. They made short animated scenes for the hearing-impaired children in the BBC1 show *Visions*. They decided to go into business for themselves and maybe one day make a feature film. They set-up shop in their hometown, the southern English seaport of Bristol and called themselves Aardman Animations Limited. Aardman was a character from their show. Peter Lord explained that the name "Aardman was a teenage joke. A combination of Superman and Aardvark. We just thought it sounded funny."

They animated small projects for television and attracted more like-minded people who wanted to animate for them. They scored a high profile hit with Peter Gabriels rock video " Sledgehammer" (1986). "Sledgehammer" won awards and has been declared MTV's number one animated video of all time. One of the animators on Sledgehammer was a fellow named Nick Park.

Nick Park was born in 1958 and conceived of the characters Wallace and Gromit while finishing his degree at the National Film and Television School. He joined Aardman in 1985. Aardman was just doing a series of shorts for Channel 4 using "vox pops[4]" candid interviews of people on the street. The encouraged Nick to direct one. His completed short, *Creature Comforts* won multiple awards including Aardmans' first Academy Award. This success gave him the impetus to complete *Grand Day Out*. It premiered in 1989. It was an immediate success and introduced Wallace and Gromit to the world.

FIGURE 15.3   Aardman's *Wallace & Gromit: The Curse of the Were-Rabbit* (2005) Courtesy of Aardman Animation, Ltd.

Nick Park, Peter Lord and the Aardman team continue to generate award-winning stop-motion films that are popular around the world. In 2000, they paired with Dreamworks to do *Chicken Run,* the most successful stop-motion movie ever. Then *Flushed Away,* 2006.

In Portland, Travis Knight took over the faltering Will Vinton Studio in 2005 and renamed it Laika for the Soviet doggie astronaut. Henry Selick came over for a while to direct *Coraline*, then Laika turned out *Boxtrolls,* and *Kubo and the Two Strings.*

Other live-action directors tried their hand at making stop-motion films like Wes Anderson (the *Fantastic Mr. Fox* (2009) and *Isle of Dogs* (2018). In 2005, Seth Green and Matthew Senreich created *Robot Chicken*, a rude but funny adult satire of pop icons all done in stop motion. In 2022, live-action director Guillermo Del Toro (*Pan's Labyrinth*) with Mark Gustavson directed a new take on *Pinocchio* that was an Oscar-winning hit that even bested an attempted Disney live-action remake. That same year, *Marcel the Shell with Shoes On* was released in the US written and directed by Dean Fleischer Camp. Animation by the Chiodo Bros. It was a sleeper hit and earned an Academy Award nomination.

In recent years, there has not been a time when there were not at least three or four stop-motion feature films in production around the world.

Peter Lord said, "Well, there is something about working with the materials. There is a fundamental difference between working with your hands and your arms and your fingertips, and working on the keyboard. I don't know . . . For all of us animators at Aardman now, we are trained in this craft, just the like a musician or a painter, it's all hand and head, hand and brain."[5]

NOTES

1 Ishiro Honda, the director of the first Kaiju movie *Godzilla* (1954) said he got inspiration from O'Briens' *King Kong* and Harryhausen's *20 Million Miles to Earth.*
2 *Stop Motion Magazine*, June 4, 2016.
3 Frank Gladstone to the author.
4 Vox pops meant "vox populi" Latin for the voice of the people.
5 Peter Lord quoted in "An Interview with Peter Lord by Wendy Jackson" (*Animation World Network*, May 1997).

The Retreat of Hand-Drawn Animation

16

"From the bottom of my heart, you've been a wonderful crew . . ." Traditional *Thank you speech of a movie director to his(her) crew at the end of production. It usually meant you were about to be laid off.*

—Old film industry lore

On April 3, 1994, a few weeks before Walt Disney's *The Lion King* came out, Disney exec Frank Wells went skiing.

Wells was an executive who loved skiing on challenging mountain slopes. Today he had hired a helicopter to take him to a summit in the Sierra Nevada mountains. Clint Eastwood was due to go with him but canceled at the last moment. As his helicopter climbed to the mountain ranges summit, loose snow blowing from an escarpment was sucked into the engines air intake manifold. This caused the engine to stall and the helicopter to crash. Nobody on board had a chance. Frank Wells was 62.

Frank Wells was COO[1] of the Walt Disney Company, but more importantly, he was the central link in the top management. He was very good and soothing over ruffled egos and finding workable compromises. Now that he was gone, there was no filter between the various alpha personalities vying for power. Michael Eisner and Jeffrey Katzenberg began to argue openly, and Roy Disney in his low-key manner seemed to signal he was tired of both. The code-name studio execs used to describe these altercations was "Mom and dad are fighting again."[2]

After Frank Wells' memorial, everyone assumed Jeffrey Katzenberg would move up to his CEO position, especially Jeffrey. But Michael Eisner delayed making the announcement. The ever-impatient Katzenberg began to press Michael to make the decision. He even confronted Michael in his hospital suite while he was recovering from quadruple bypass surgery. Finally, at the Telluride Film Festival, Michael told Jeffrey he would not be moving up. That Michael himself would assume the joint roles of chairman and CEO. Jeffrey was stunned. Michael and he had come up together working for Barry Diller in the 80s. In late July 1994, while the world was packing theaters to see *The Lion King*, Jeffrey Katzenberg announced he was leaving Disney.[3]

DOI: 10.1201/b22394-17

Jeffery's friends director Steven Spielberg and music producer David Geffen invited him to now join them in a partnership to found a new studio. The first new major studio in Hollywood created since RKO in 1928.[4] They bought a lot to build a studio in Glendale near the Disney animation and imagineering. The Disney Company immediately bought all the land around it so it could never expand. In our first meeting, we were addressed by all three partners about the studio's mission. One animator said afterward, " What I got out of that was here is a studio where we can all live our dreams . . . . and we have to kick Disney's ass."

DreamWorks took on Disney in all aspects. Disney did animated musicals, and DreamWorks did musicals. Disney had a relationship with the CG house Pixar, so DreamWorks bought its Silicon Valley sister PDI (Pacific Data Images). Disney had animated TV series like *Duck Tales and Gargoyles,* so DreamWorks made series like *Father of the Pride, Toonsylvania.* Disney had a live-action global disaster movie *Armageddon,* so DreamWorks had a global disaster movie *Deep Impact.* DreamWorks made a movie based on Central American native culture called *The Road to El Dorado,* so Disney had a movie set in Central American native culture called *The Emperor's New Groove.*

Just a few weeks before Disney Pixar released its film about insects, *A Bug's Life,* DreamWorks released PDI's film *Antz.* When Pixar's director John Lasseter personally called up Jeffrey to express his outrage, Jeffrey shrugged, " Hey guy. Nothing personal. Just business."

FIGURE 16.1 Jeffrey Katzenberg and Steven Spielberg at the dedication of the DreamWorks Studio Glendale lot, 1997.

(collection of the author.)

By the late 1990s, the 2D Animation Renaissance was beginning to slow down. Over-saturation of product, inferior titles, and the public's new fascination for more and more CGI innovations began to shift the balance of power from pencils to pixels.

Philosopher Max Jacob (1876–1944) once wrote, "Nobody ever created a classic on demand. No one asked Beethoven to write the 5th Symphony. He was just writing the symphony after #4, and before #6." Yet the 5th is the masterpiece everyone remembers." In the modern concept of genius, a genius cannot create anything but works of genius. In the real world, this is hardly ever the case. Bram Stoker wrote a dozen novels, but Dracula was the only one that was genius. When not inventing Sherlock Holmes, Sir Arthur Conan Doyle wrote books like "The Firm of Girdlestone" that no one remembers. Charles Dickens only wrote "A Christmas Carol" because his previous novel flopped, and he needed to make some money.

Yet try to explain this to the corporate leaders of Hollywood. After the Walt Disney Feature Animation did *The Lion King*, their investors expected every subsequent film to do The Lion King profits or better. The following year's release *Pocahontas* was just as successful as *Aladdin*, but it still was not The Lion King successful. So, the powers-that-be were disappointed. When Jeffrey Katzenberg teamed up with Steven Spielberg and David Geffen to form DreamWorks, everyone expected more Lion Kings from them. Disney's filled up with executives. One animator commented bitterly, "In the 70s the ratio was one production exec to every 50 artists. Now its 50 production execs to every artist." The studio execs locked in Howard Ashman's oft-recited formula for musical structure until it became holy writ. Intro song, main character "I Want Song." Patter Song (comic), Villains Song. Love Duet. Fight song, then Finale, reprise. You could set your watch by its regularity. By 1995, studios created a glut of musicals, some good, some not. When Brad Bird did *The Iron Giant* at Warner Bros., he deliberately did not want it to be a musical. Likewise, in *Toy Story*, John Lasseter had songs from Randy Newman but did not consider it a musical. The major celebrity voices, who used to do animation for union scale or better, now demanded the kind of multi-million-dollar rates they got for their live-action work. When Joe Pesci was offered an animated role and heard the money offered, he reacted, "What? You mean I don't get my usual rate and you guys go out and make millions of bucks with this? F**k you, I'd rather spend my time playing golf." Ultimately, he did do the role in *Quest for Camelot*, and he did get paid his rate.

On top of the accelerated production schedules, the studios engaged overseas animation units to crank out sequels of lesser quality at a quarter of the budget of the original. *Belle's Magic Christmas, Aladdin the Return of Jafar,* etc. The Walt Disney Studio used to jealously guard its name-brand recognition and resisted work done outside the walls of Mousedom. Now besides the sequels, they bought up lesser efforts and released them as Disney Animation classics. Like *Valiant,* animated independently in the UK with no Disney artists at all. All of these efforts saturated the market and exhausted the public the way westerns did in the 1960s, and video arcade games did in the early 80s. Slowly, the public's taste turned away from animated features.

At first, the studios thought it was because of the interest in 3D CGI[5] films spawned by hits like *Toy Story, Ice Age* and *Shrek*. Since *Toy Story*, Pixar had been turning out one hit after another. A *Bugs Life, Toy Story 2, Monsters Inc.* In all, 14 hits before their first disappointment (*The Good Dinosaur*). An unprecedented record.

DreamWorks pushed as their maximum effort *The Prince of Egypt*. Directed by Brenda Chapman (*Lion King story supervisor, Brave*), Simon Wells (*American Tale 2 Fieval Goes West, Roger Rabbit*) and Steven Hickner (*Roger Rabbit, The Bee Movie*). Movie star voices like Val Kilmer, Sandra Bullock and Patrick Stewart. Music by Steven Schwartz, who did *Godspell, Pocahontas* and *Wicked*. Steven Spielberg even sent his family rabbi to lecture the crew about Moses. Animator Esther Barr laughed, "I never knew I'd have to return to Yeshiva class to do my job!" I worked on storyboards and spent a lot of time coming up with jokes that were not used. I pinned up on the storyboards a gag drawing of Moses giving Ramses an old-fashioned cartoon hotfoot with lit matches. It was up just as the directors were showing Val Kilmer the story. The producer came to me with the sketch and said "Very funny, Sito." Yet despite all this effort, *The Prince of Egypt* did respectfully well, but not *The Lion King* business.[6] Meanwhile, *Shrek*, a smaller all 3D effort by the studio's CGI satellite PDI, scored a big hit, four sequels, spinoffs (*Puss in Boots*) and won the first-ever Academy Award for Best Animated Feature in 2001.

Twentieth-century Fox had been bankrolling the 2D animated films of Don Bluth. After the huge successes of *An American Tail* and *Land Before Time*, Bluth films went into a popular decline: *Anastasia, Rock a Doodle, The Pebble and the Penguin, A Troll in Central Park*. Fox ordered Don Bluth and his team to step in and complete a troubled 2D project *Titan A.E. Titan A.E.* wound up running up a huge budget and became for them a major disappointment. At the same time, Fox had acquired a little CGI house on the East Coast north of New York City in the Hudson Valley. It was called Blue Sky and was headed by Chris Wedge, who had won an Oscar for his short film *Bunny*. It was the first theatrical animation studio in the New York area since Max Fleischer left in 1938. Chris Wedge and his team created the charming comedy *Ice Age*, featuring the voices of Queen Latifa and Ray Romano. When *Ice Age* debuted in late March 2001, Fox had been trying to unload Blue Sky onto another studio. *Ice Age* not only became a massive hit but it also even outdid that year's Best Picture Academy Award winner, *A Beautiful Mind*. When he received the news of their success, the Fox production chief exclaimed, "Aw shit! Now we have to stay in animation!"[7]

By 2002, the message to the Hollywood execs was clear. CG animation sells. Hand-drawn cartoons no longer did. Theatrical animation commenced a transition as radical as the 1927 transition from silent to sound films.

On Monday, March 25, 2002, Disney Feature Animation head Tom Schumacher brought the Disney animators department by department down to their theater. He explained the studio's situation. That the hand-drawn films were not performing like they used to, so the decision was to downsize and completely transition to 3D digital. There would be retraining for a few. But most of them were being laid off for good. When the artists asked why, Tom replied, "Didn't anybody see *Ice Age*?" Animators who dedicated their entire creative careers to Walt Disney, artists who were raised on the Frank & Ollie example of permanent employment, "Part of the Magic" were unceremoniously shown the door. Thank you for your loyalty and hard work. And uh, if you want you can have your animation desks, for $1,500 each. Payable to the Walt Disney Company. Career 2D effects animator Jaqueline Sanchez cried at him, "You have the London Philharmonic here, and you're turning it into a boy band!"

FIGURE 16.2   Gag drawing by John Pomeroy of the animation building deserted. (courtesy of John Pomeroy)

FIGURE 16.3   Local newspaper headline about Disney animators' layoffs. (courtesy Pasadena Weekly)

At the same time, Walt Disney California was being downsized; the studio closed its Florida and Paris units. They also closed the Secret Lab, the CGI unit that produced *Dinosaur.* About 1,300 employees in total were out on the street. DreamWorks and Warner Bros also phased out their 2D animation artists but did so quietly. DreamWorks announced the 2D animators were being retrained for digital. While in actuality, 65 animators had to compete for 16 slots. Walt Disney tried one more 2D film in 2011, *Winnie the Pooh* directed by Steve Anderson and Don Hall. But when its Box Office failed to reach blockbuster status, they abandoned the effort once more.

In Japan, Hayao Miyazaki reacted, "I think 2-D animation disappeared from Disney because they made so many uninteresting films. They became very conservative in the way they created them. It's too bad. I thought 2-D and 3-D could coexist happily."[8]

Interestingly enough, the overall output of Japanese animation studios remained stubbornly hand-drawn. There are some digital elements to augment the look but overall, most of it is still 2D.

Despite its legendary heritage as the home of Bugs and Daffy, Warner Bros in modern times has had a tepid interest in animated features. After a few years trying to get a project going based on Will Eisner's comic The Spirit, in 1998, Brad Bird directed *The Iron Giant.* A beautiful movie that experimented with its main people 2D animated and the giant himself 3D animated. The Giant was rendered by a software developed by Brian Gardner and Tad Gielow called Toonshader. It made hard 3D characters look indistinguishable from 2D cartoons. Iron Giant was a great favorite with audiences. It was one of the few movies I saw when at the climax there were more men weeping than women. Yet Warner Bros did not know how to advertise it. They put all their summer's advertising money behind Will Smiths' remake of *The Wild Wild West.* Brad left Warners and went north to Pixar to do *Ratatouille* and *the Incredibles. The Iron Giant* has since become a classic film. Warner Bros then did *Osmosis Jones* (2001) and *Looney Tunes Back in Action.* (2003)

People had been clamoring for years to see a feature film of *The Simpsons.* It had always been held up in issues of development and rights. When it was finally ironed out, *The Simpson's Movie* was issued by Twentieth-Century Fox in 2007. With all of the original cast and directed by veteran director David Silverman. Although much of the public was fixated on 3D animation, they were willing to give *the Simpsons* a pass to see it drawn and painted as they were used to. *The Simpsons* Movie made its budget back the opening weekend and went on to earn half a billion dollars worldwide.

The extraordinary thing that happened was in television animation. Before the era of *The Simpsons*, the longest running animated TV series was *The Flintstones*, at six seasons. As of this writing, *The Simpsons* has been running for 34 years steady. *South Park* for 27 years. *Family Guy* 24 years. When DreamWorks animated features seemed to falter, DreamWorks did very well with its TV streaming series. In 2013, they entered a multiyear content deal with Netflix to provide exclusive original content.

By 2017, most of the key players had retired, died or otherwise stepped away. Roy Disney, Steve Jobs, Jeffrey Katzenberg, Michael Eisner, Ed Catmull and George Lucas. As it was in the 1980s, it was time for a new generation to assume the mantle.

FIGURE 16.4 Gag drawing of the old animator's home after the success of Pixar's *The Incredibles* 2007.

(by Tom Sito, collection of the author.)

NOTES

1 COO-Chief Operating Officer, as distinct from CEO, Chief Executive Officer.
2 Quoted from *Drawing the Line: A History of the Animation Unions* by Tom Sito (University Press of Kentucky, 2006).
3 Of that time, Jeffrey says he was fired by Eisner, but most say he chose not to renew his contract option and so was forced out.
4 In 1969, Francis Ford Coppola and George Lucas announced their studio American Zoetrope. But it never grew beyond being Coppola's private production company.
5 Animators differentiated between films hand-drawn by pencil and paint as 2D films. Films animated using computer imaging as 3D. Not because you need special stereoptic glasses to watch them.
6 Since its initial run, *The Prince of Egypt* went on to become a holiday classic on cassette, DVD, and streaming.
7 Fox of course was the home of hit animated TV shows like *The Simpsons* and *Family Guy*. Studios treat their broadcast and feature divisions as completely separate entities. Separate crews, separate management.
8 IMDB.com

Epilogue

17

If [hand-drawn animation] is a dying craft, we can't do anything about it. Civilization moves on. Where are all the fresco painters now? Where are the landscape artists? What are they doing now? The world is changing. I have been very fortunate to be able to do the same job for 40 years. That's rare in any era.

—Hayao Miyazaki

FIGURE 17.1 Disney animation vets celebrating the anniversary of *Beauty and the Beast* Oscar nomination in 2024. (Seated) James Baxter, Ruben Aquino, Andreas Deja, Will Finn, Tom Sito. (Standing) Ed Ghertner, Lisa Keene, Kirk Wise, Jim Hillin, Don Hahn, Gary Trousdale and John Carnochan Brian McEntee.

(Collection of the author.)

DOI: 10.1201/b22394-18

On a warm night in the autumn of 2009, the animation crew of Walt Disney Feature Animation gathered at a theater to see the premiere of *Waking Sleeping Beauty*. A documentary about the great Disney renaissance of the 1990s, created by our old producer turned documentarian Don Hahn. By now, the artists and technicians who had created the great films like *Beauty and the Beast, Aladdin* and *The Lion King* were mostly gone from Disney. Retired, moved on to other studios or caught in the huge layoffs of hand-drawn artists in 2001–2003. But this night was not about being bitter. It was a time to remember. It was a fun evening, with lots of laughing and reminiscing. Beyond enjoying a film that seemed like home movies to us, we could see the significance of the moment. Just like at the Grim Natwick birthday celebration in 1990, we witnessed the changing of the guard from one generation to another, so now it was our turn to pass the baton. At this exact moment, many of us still were unwilling to accept that it had become our turn to leave the stage. I am sure at Grim's party, there were also many who also felt that way. Yet in retrospect, the *Waking Sleeping Beauty* documentary was a nice punctuation to our era. It put our contributions in perspective.

The funny thing about being part of an era is you are rarely aware of it until it is over. Most of the old artists I knew who worked during the original Hollywood Golden Age (1935–1945) told me that they were unaware. "Golden Age? What golden age? I worked my ass off!"[1] Now film historians were calling the 1990s The Platinum Age, the Second Golden Age, or the Great 2D Animation Renaissance. But to us, we were just trying to make a living and make good movies. We went into the era creating with pencils, kneaded erasers and Cel Vinyl paint. And we ended with Maya, Renderman and Photoshop. Calling what we created film was in of itself redundant since nobody seriously used celluloid film anymore. Our mentors were all gone, Joe Grant, Eric Larsen, Tissa David, Chuck Jones, Roy Disney and Richard Williams.

Of the crew of artists and technicians who made the original Beauty and the Beast, probably four or five remain full time at the Disney studio.

Now, today we are the cranky old-timers, complaining things will never be as good when we were young. We were now sporting their weak eyes, silver hair and stooped posture.

It is our turn to let someone else drive. We Baby-Boomers, raised on Saturday Morning TV, have the satisfaction of knowing we did not just have a turn making animation. We literally saved the animation business and passed it on to our successors much greater than when we found it. Animation has become central to the way people around the world experience modern media. All digital games, interactive programs and big comic-book-style live-action spectacles depend heavily on animation. And so it goes.

Tom Sito

2026

NOTE

1 Disney background painter Ralph Hulett, as recalled by his son Steve Hulett to the author.

Acknowledgments

Roger Allers
Beck, Jerry
David Block
Don Bluth
Nancy Cartwright
Mario Cavalli
Marc Davis
Ken Duncan
Ron Clements
Gladestone, Frank
Howard Green
Don Hahn
Dan Haskett
Steve Hulett
Kausler, Mark
Ted Kierscey
Ward Kimball
Bill Kroyer
Sue Kroyer
Glen Keane
Dorse Lanpher
Duncan Marjoribanks
Sherry McKenna
David Pruiksma
Jerry Reese
David Silverman.
Alvy Ray Smith
Dave Stefan
Tad Stones
Ben Washam
Richard Williams

Thank you also to Sean Connelly of Taylor & Francis publishers and especially my wife Pat.

Bibliography

Anderson, Ross, *Pulling a Rabbit out of a Hat, the Story of Who Framed Roger Rabbit?* (University Press of Mississippi, Jackson, 2019)

Arnold, Mark, *Frozen in Ice, the Story of Walt Disney Productions 1966–1985* (BearManor Media, Boalsburg, PA, 2013)

Barbera, Joe, *My Life in Toons* (Turner Publishing, Atlanta, 1994)

Bendazzi, Giannalberto, *Cartoons, One Hundred Years of Cinema Animation* (Indiana University Press, 1996)

Bluth, Don, *Somewhere Out There* (Smart Pop Books, Dallas, 2022)

Bossert, Dave, *Kem Weber: Mid-century Furniture Designs for the Disney Studios* (Google Books, 2018)

Brightman, Homer, *Life in the Mouse House* (Theme Park Press, 2024)

Byskind, Peter, *Easy Riders and Raging Bulls: How the Sex, Drugs and Rock & Roll Generation Saved Hollywood* (Simon & Schuster, NY, 1998)

Canemaker, John, *The Animated Raggedy Ann & Andy: An Intimate Look at the Art of Animation, Its History, Techniques and Artists* (Bobbs Merrill, NY, 1977)

Culhane, Shamus, *Talking Animals and Other Funny People* (St Martin's Press, NY, 1981)

Ghez, Didier, *The Hidden Art of Walt Disney's Early Renaissance: The 1970s and 1980s* (Chronicle Books, San Francisco, 2019)

Ghez, Didier, *Walt's People, Talking Disney with the Artists Who Knew Him*, Vol. 27 (Skyway Press, 2023)

Hanna, Bill, *A Cast of Friends* (Taylor Publishing, Dallas, 1996)

Hulett, Steve, *Mouse in Transition, an Insider's Look at Disney Feature Animation* (Theme Park Press, 2014)

Issacson, Walter, *Steve Jobs* (Simon & Schuster, New York, 2011)

Johnson, Mindy, *Ink & Paint: Girls of Walt Disney Animation* (Disney Books, 2018)

Komorowski, Thad, *Sick Little Monkeys, the Unauthorized Ren and Stimpy Story* (Bear Manor Media, Albany, GA, 2013)

Kroyer, Bill, *Mr. In-Between: My Life in the Middle of the Animation Revolution* (CRC Press, London, 2025)

Lyons, Michael, *Drawn to Greatness: Disney's Animation Renaissance* (Theme Park Press, 2021)

Mazurkevich, Karen, *Cartoon Capers: The Adventures of Canadian Animators* (MacArthur & Company, Toronto, 1999)

McCloud, Scott, *Understanding Comics* (Harper-Collins, New York, 1993)

Miyazaki, Hayao, *Starting Point 1979–1996* (Viz Media, San Francisco, 1996)

Napier, Susan, *Miyazaki World a Life in Art* (Yale University Press, 2018)

Neuwirth, Allen, *Makin' Toons* (Allworth Press, 2003)

Ortved, John, *Simpsons Confidential* (Ebury Press, UK, 2009)

Pierce, Todd James, *The Life and Times of Ward Kimball, Maverick of Disney Animation* (University Press of Mississippi, Jackson, 2019)

Schodt, Frederik L. *Manga! Manga! the World of Japanese Comics* (Kodansha International, 1983)

Scott, Keith, *The Moose That Roared* (St. Martin's Press, NY, 2000)

Sito, Tom, *Drawing the Line, the Untold Stories of the Animation Unions from Bosko to Bart Simpson* (University of Kentucky, Lexington, 2006)
Sito, Tom, *Moving Innovation, a History of Computer Animation* (MIT Press, Boston, 2013)

Articles

Lyons, Michael, *Cereal Killers, Part 1* (Animation Scoop, Sept. 12, 2021)
Peraltha, Ederlyn, *Panda and the Magic Serpent Gave Hayao Miyazaki His First Waifu* (CBR.com, 2021)
Real, James, *When You Wish upon a School* (Los Angeles Times, Sept. 23, 2001)
Sach, Mike, *John Swartzwelder, Sage of the Simpsons* (The New Yorker, May 2, 2021)
Sito, Thomas, *Walt and the Professor* (USC Trojan Magazine, 2018)
Weiss, Josh, *How Steven Spielberg and J. J. Abrams Helped Bring 1995's Casper to the Big Screen* (scyfy.com, Sept. 20, 2022)

Podcasts

Draper, Matt, *The Disney Don Bluth War* (June 1, 2022)
Harrison "Buzz" Price, CalArts Oral History (Oct. 2001)

Illustrations

Chapter 10 *The Little Mermaid*

Chapter 11 Cowabunga!: *The Simpsons*

Chapter 12 Toontown Boomtown: Television 1989–1997

Chapter 13 Toontown Boomtown Animated Movies 1989–1997

Chapter 14 The Digital Revolution

Chapter 15 The Fall and Rise of Stop Motion: 1993–2022

Chapter 16 The Retreat of Hand-Drawn Animation

Chapter 17 Epilogue

17.1   Disney animation vets celebrating the anniversary of Beauty and the Beast Oscar
        nomination in 2024. (Seated) James Baxter, Ruben Aquino, Andreas Deja, Will Finn,
        Tom Sito. (Standing) Ed Ghertner, Lisa Keene, Kirk Wise, Jim Hillin, Don Hahn,
        Gary Trousdale and John Carnochan Brian McEntee. (Collection of the author.)

Index

For Product Safety Concerns and Information please contact our EU
representative GPSR@taylorandfrancis.com
Taylor & Francis Verlag GmbH, Kaufingerstraße 24, 80331 München, Germany